PERSONALITY DEVELOPMENT
FOR
WORK
7TH ED

Harold R. Wallace
Professor of Occupational & Educational
Studies, Emeritus
Colorado State University
Ft. Collins, Colorado

L. Ann Masters
Administrator, Curriculum/Instruction
Nebraska Department of Education
Lincoln, Nebraska

South-Western
Educational Publishing

Project Manager: Laurie Wendell
Editor: Marianne Miller
Associate Director/Photo Editing: Devore M. Nixon
Photo Editor: Fred Middendorf
Cover Design: Tin Box Studio
Internal Design: Ann Small
Marketing Manager: Carolyn Love

ISBN: 0-538-63665-3
Library of Congress Cataloging-in-Publication Data

Wallace, Harold R., 1929–
    Personality development for work / Harold R. Wallace, L. Ann
  Masters. — 7th ed.
      p.   cm.
    Includes index.
    ISBN 0-538-63665-3
    1. Vocational guidance. 2. Success. 3. Personality and
occupation.   I. Masters, L. Ann. II. Title.
HF5381.R7895 1995
158.7—dc20   95-16940
                                                                   CIP

   2 3 4 5 6 MT 00 99 98 97 96

Printed in the United States of America

I(T)P
International Thomson Publishing Company
South-Western Educational Publishing is a division of International
Thomson Publishing Inc. The ITP trademark is used under license.

Table of Contents

Unit 1 • • • • • • • • • • • •

Chapter 1 **Self-Esteem And Your Personality** 3
A Theory Of Personality 3
Know Yourself 7
Do Not Hide From Reality 8
Be Sensitive To Feedback 13

Chapter 2 **Self-Improvement** 19
The Self-Improvement Process 19
Visualize The Best That You Can Be 20
Design Your Self-Improvement
  Program 21
Self-Improvement Strategies 24

Chapter 3 **Developing Positive Attitudes** 33
Your Attitudes Reflect Your Image 33
How Attitudes Develop 35
Attitudes Are Visible 36
Attitudes Are Catching 36
Improving Your Attitudes 38
Coping With Other People's Negative
  Attitudes 40

Unit 2

Chapter 4	**_Fitting In And Getting Along_**	47
	Value-Added Qualities	48
	Nonvalue-Added Qualities	53
Chapter 5	**_Working With Coworkers_**	61
	Keys To Getting Along With Others	62
	Your Position On The Team	67
	Understand And Use Group Psychology	70
Chapter 6	**_Getting Along With Your Supervisor_**	81
	Know Your Supervisor	82
	Supervisor's Expectations	87
	Relating To Your Supervisor	89
	What Do You Have The Right To Expect?	92
Chapter 7	**_Relating To Clients And Customers_**	101
	Customer Expectations	102
	Customer Communication	107
	Is The Customer Always Right?	108

Unit 3

Chapter 8	**_Communication Channels_**	115
	Communication Takes Two	116
	Communication Barriers	118
	Channel Openers	120
	Communication Styles	124
	Listening Is Part Of Communication	126
Chapter 9	**_Getting Your Message Across_**	137
	General Rules For The Sender Of Communication	138
	Conversational Skills	139
	Conversation—What Do I Say?	143
	Speaking Before Groups	146

Chapter 10   Communicating To Resolve Conflict   155
What Is Conflict?   155
Types Of Conflict   156
Stages of Conflict   159
Handling Conflict Adjustments   160

Unit 4

Chapter 11   Motivation   173
Be Self-Motivated   173
Show Initiative   175
Go Beyond What Is Expected   178

Chapter 12   Work Habits   183
Responsibilitiy   183
Self-Management   187
Organization   189

Chapter 13   Thinking Skills   199
Employers Want People Who Can Think   199
Thinking Defined   200
Higher-Order Thinking Strategies   205
Your Thinking Skills Can Be Developed   210

Chapter 14   Managing Stress   215
What Is Stress?   215
Handling Stress   221

Unit 5

Chapter 15   Standards Of Conduct   231
Integrity And Ethics   231
Loyalty   233
Honesty   234
Avoid Abusing Fringe Benefits and Privileges   239
Avoid Drug And Alcohol Abuse   240

Chapter 16 **Recognizing Discrimination**   247
              Prejudice And Sterotyping   247
              What The Law Provides   251
              The Rights of Persons With Disabilities   254
              Sexual Harassment   255
              Subtle Discrimination   257
              Avoiding, Resisting, Or Fighting Discrimination   258

Chapter 17 **Diversity**   265
              Diversity In The Workplace   266
              Appreciating Diversity   267
              Avoiding Cultural Conflict   270

Unit 6   • • • • • • • • • • •

Chapter 18 **Getting The Job**   279
              Job Campaign   280
              Job Resources   282
              Job Search Documents   285
              Job Interview   297

Chapter 19 **Keeping The Job**   307
              First-Day Events   308
              Rules Of The Job   309
              Work Environment   311
              Employment Insurance   312

Chapter 20 **Moving Ahead In Your Career**   321
              A Vision For Your Future   321
              Visualize Success In Your Career   322
              Energize Yourself   324
              Performance Appraisal   325
              Raises and Promotions   326
              Changing Jobs   328

Success in the world of work requires not only the ability to perform according to the requirements of the position, but also the ability to adjust and get along as a member of a working team. *Personality Development for Work* is designed to help the new employee recognize the important role personality plays in the work environment and to develop the personal qualities, interpersonal skills, and values that are in demand by employers.

Research For The Text

The chapters on work adjustment and interpersonal relationships are based on thorough reviews of recent research and theory development in modern psychology. This research helped to ensure that the ideas presented are valid and realistic in the work world. A comprehensive review of studies about employer expectations and causes of failure on the job provided direction for the chapters on developing work habits and thinking and self-management skills. Of special interest was *Skills and Tasks For Jobs*, a Department of Labor report prepared by the Secretary's Commission on Achieving Necessary Skills (SCANS). The SCANS skills emphasized throughout this text will allow new workers to fit in and to perform according to the expectations of employers.

The Critical Personal Qualities And Skills

A person's *personality* affects his or her performance on the job. Stress, conflict, and miscommunication in the workplace can often cause difficulties unless positive personality characteristics influence a worker to make personal adjustments and establish comfortable relationships with supervisors and coworkers. Negative personality traits can hamper or prevent individual adjustments and alienate others.

Personality traits affect *productivity* as well. The most relevant and effective technical training for the job is useless if the employee is not a good worker. To become a good worker, the employee must have a commitment to personal growth and apply that commitment to developing effective work habits, self-management skills, thinking and communication skills.

This book helps students assess their strengths and weaknesses with respect to personality and productivity. It offers direction in using that information to design a specific, focused self-improvement program—to pave the way for students to attain realistic goals and objectives in preparation for successful employment.

What The Text Offers

The purpose of this book is to offer the student a relevant, systematic program for developing self-understanding, promoting personal growth, and preparing for successful employment through a highly readable and understandable text.

Success Identity

Unit 1 is concerned with self-esteem and commitment to personal growth. Chapters 1–3 set the stage for self-understanding and self-improvement. Specific activities and suggestions help the individual develop positive attitudes and visualize his or her needs for personality development in preparation for successful employment.

Interpersonal Relationships

Unit 2, Chapters 4–7, deals with work adjustment and the interpersonal relationships that occur on the job. This unit is designed to help the student face the challenges of fitting in and becoming a member of a working team.

Ideas and strategies for developing good relationships with coworkers, supervisors, and customers are presented.

Communication

Communication is listed by many employers as the number one human relations skill needed on the job. Unit 3, Chapters 8–10, is devoted to the improvement of communication and conflict resolution skills.

Productivity

Unit 4, Chapters 11–14, concentrates on helping students become good workers. This unit includes information on self-motivation to get the job done—to develop effective and efficient work habits and self-management skills. It also includes information on managing stress and, most importantly, developing and using the ability to think.

Social Conscience

Unit 5, Chapters 15–17, addresses problems of potential conflict, misunderstanding, and unfair treatment in the workplace. The objective of this unit is to help the student develop a good social conscience and to let it guide his or her behavior as a worker and as a citizen. Chapter 15 deals with issues and problems of personal ethics, loyalty, and standards of personal conduct. Chapters 16 and 17 are concerned with discrimination and diversity in the world of work.

Career Development

Unit 6, Chapters 18–20, prepares the student to face the challenges of transition from school to work. This unit includes managing the tasks of finding, selecting, and keeping a job, realistically and aggressively. Chapter 20 prepares the student for the long road of career development. It provides a framework for building a successful, satisfying career in the world of work.

Features To Enhance Teaching And Learning

Some specific features of this new edition are:

Objectives

Each chapter begins with a brief list of expected learning outcomes and achievement expectations.

Workplace Scenarios

Expanded use is made of cases that highlight the concepts, problems and issues presented in the text.

SCANS Notes

Specific references from the SCANS report are presented to highlight relevant demands and expectations of the employers surveyed by this commission.

Critical Thinking Questions

Questions are integrated as marginal notes to challenge the reader to engage in critical thinking and creative problem solving.

Quotations

Marginal quotations are included to add interest and to reinforce learning.

Self-Assessment

Increased use is made of features and activities for student self-assessment. This provides students with more opportunities to interact with the text material and to apply the learning.

Questions and Projects

Application exercises and activities at the end of each chapter are designed to help the student more clearly understand and apply the main ideas presented in the chapter.

Case Problems

Thought-provoking exercises in decision making and analysis are also found at the end of each chapter.

Teacher's Manual

The updated Teacher's Manual provides suggested answers to questions and projects and to case problems. Also included are general guidelines for teaching and specific suggestions pertaining to each chapter.

The manual has been revised with new features, including transparency masters and a list of instructional resources. A special section has been added offering teaching strategies for the effective use of the features of the text.

Tests

A variety of questions are available to instructors for unit testing and for a comprehensive review of student achievement. The answers to the printed tests are given in the Teacher's Manual.

Student Workbook

A complete workbook is available to assist students in self-managed enrichment and reinforcement activities. Workbook features include self-testing on terms and concepts, practice tests, and creative learning experiences for application of important principles.

Acknowledgments

The authors wish to thank all of the instructors who have given valuable direction and feedback in the development of this new edition, with special thanks to the following reviewers:

Elizabeth Collins Dart, Vancouver, Washington
Jann LeCroy, Birmingham, Alabama
Ellen McGonigle, Houston, Texas
June St. Clair Atkinson, Raleigh, North Carolina
Marsha Smith, North Miami Beach, Florida

Message To The Student

We hope this book will capture your interest and be easy to understand. But we challenge you to do more than just read it. If you *apply* what you learn, this experience can change your life.

There are three important keys for your success in the workplace. First is the technical knowledge and skills to do the job. Second is the ability and motivation to work effectively. Third is a personality that will allow you to fit in as a member of a working team. This book is based on real-world demands with respect to the second and third keys to success. It is a self-improvement guide.

Self-improvement may not be easy, but it is worth the effort. If you make a personal commitment to become the best that you can be and if you are willing to be conscientious in your study and application of what this book has to offer, our desire and best wishes for your success in the world of work will be realized.

Harold R. Wallace
L. Ann Masters

Unit 1

Developing Your Success Identity

Success identity defines the image you have of yourself as a person who can fit in and get along in the work environment. To be successful you will need to develop

- good job performance skills
- good work habits
- thinking skills
- communication skills
- positive attitudes

Positive personality characteristics can help a worker adjust and fit in. Negative personality traits can hamper or prevent critical adjustments. This book helps the worker assess his or her personality to find out what changes and improvements must occur in preparation for successful employment. As you work on developing your success identity, you may need to evaluate your personality and make plans for self-improvement to become the best that you can be.

The information in this unit is designed to help you prepare to meet the demands of the workplace and the expectations of employers and coworkers and to develop the personal qualities that appear to contribute to success. Chapter 1 will help you gain a clear perspective of who you are and where you are in your personality development. Chapter 2 presents a systematic process of self-improvement that will get you started in developing your success identity. Chapter 3 offers help in the development of positive attitudes.

Contents

Chapter 1
Self-Esteem And Your Personality

Chapter 2
Self-Improvement

Chapter 3
Developing Positive Attitudes

Self-Esteem And Your Personality

G loria was assigned to help train David, a new employee, as they worked together behind the counter in a cafeteria. Gloria took her responsibility seriously. She gave David detailed instructions on how to operate the cash register, how to cut and serve pie, how to arrange vegetables and meat on a plate, and how to perform a dozen other simple tasks. Gloria also watched over David, reminding him whenever he did anything wrong or when he chose to do something his own way. Can you see any possibility of trouble developing between Gloria and David?

A Theory Of Personality

To prepare for your study of the following chapters, which deal with developing your personality, it will be helpful to understand some basic principles. These principles are shown in **transactional analysis**, a theory of personality developed by Eric Berne.[1] This theory explains how your inner self, your "ego," influences your communication with others.

Communication Transactions

Communication behavior is affected by three **ego states**, according to Berne. An ego state is the way a person feels about something that causes certain behavior. These three ego states

[1]Eric Berne, *Games People Play* (New York: Grove Press, 1964).

Objectives

After completing this chapter, you should be able to:

1.
Explain transactional analysis— a theory of personality.

2.
Explain the meaning of self-esteem.

3.
Explain the impact of conflict between real-life experiences and a person's self-image.

4.
Explain how masks and role-playing are used to create false impressions.

5.
Avoid using masks and role-playing to hide from reality.

6.
Confront the reality of mistakes or failure and, at the same time, maintain self-esteem.

7.
Be sensitive to feedback that can be used to evaluate yourself.

8.
Use a trusted friend or counselor to help with self-understanding.

are present and operating in everyone. They are the Parent ego state, the Adult ego state, and the Child ego state.

When you act as your parents did, or as some other person who took the place of your parent, you are in your Parent ego state. In that case you might make statements like these: "You look sloppy in that outfit," "You will never learn to play the piano," "You are so stupid," "Don't drive so fast," or "This room is a mess." These statements suggest that the Parent self is operating. They are what a parent might say to a child. Unfortunately, most often such statements are critical.

Being in the Parent ego state causes you to say things that a parent might say to a child.

Photo by Jim Whitmer

However, rather than being critical, the Parent self may want to take care of other people, give them advice, and see that they do the right thing. Even though the person's intentions are good, statements made while in the Parent ego state can cause resentment. The Parent in you may give others the impression that you are bossy, critical, or overbearing.

The Adult ego state allows a person to be less emotional and more realistic. When your Adult self is in control, you are able to deal objectively with facts, free from personal opinions and feelings. Your behavior reflects mature, good judgment. This creates the impression that you are not passing judgment or "talking down" to the other person.

The third ego state, the Child self, is different for everyone. While in the Child ego state, a person behaves in a childlike way. Some childlike behavior is undesirable for an adult, and some of it may be desirable at times. The Child in you is the self that feels free, that likes to discover new things, and that is able to be spontaneous. The negative aspects of the Child self are shown in behavior such as selfishness, whining, and sulking.

In theory, all three ego states must operate as the personality develops. However, the Adult self must emerge and be in control in a mature, healthy personality. The ideal type of communication is Adult to Adult; that is, when two people communicate, the Adult self is operating for both. In a communication event, which Berne refers to as a **transaction**, there is no apparent reason for conflict when it is "complementary." Following are some examples of **complementary transactions**:

- Gloria speaks Adult to Adult. David responds Adult to Adult.

- Gloria speaks Parent to Child. David responds Child to Parent.

- Gloria speaks Child to Parent. David responds Parent to Child.

Much of the stress and conflict in the workplace comes from what Berne calls **crossed transactions**. Following are some examples:

- Gloria speaks Adult to Adult. David responds Child to Parent.

- Gloria speaks Parent to Child. David responds Adult to Adult.

- Gloria speaks Child to Parent. David responds Child to Parent.

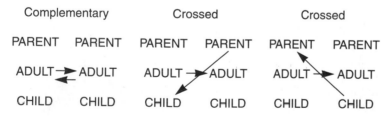

Illustration 1-1
Complementary and crossed transactions.

Learn to Apply the Theory

Here is an example of an office manager speaking Adult to Adult and a worker responding Child to Parent: "Hilda, when will you be done with the cost estimates on the Billings contract?" Hilda responds, "Why are you picking on me? I'll get to it after I prepare the invoices you needed in such a rush."

Now consider another type of crossed transaction. The office manager asks, "Hilda, when will you be done with the cost estimates on the Billings contract?" Hilda's Parent self answers: "You should know how much time it takes to do a job like this. Can't you see I'm busy preparing these invoices?" Hilda is letting the Parent self influence the transaction.

When crossed transactions happen, conflict and unpleasant reactions are likely. When complementary transactions occur, however, the communication is more effective and pleasant. For instance, the office manager says, "Hilda, when will you be done with the cost estimates on the Billings contract?" Hilda answers, "In about 20 minutes. I'm sorry about the delay, but I was interrupted by the rush job on these invoices." Hilda's Adult self answered an Adult question. The Adult is in charge of her personality.

Critical Thinking

Think about...

what your adult-to-adult response might be to a teacher who asks, "Did you carefully edit your essay for spelling errors?"

Try to be aware which of your ego states is speaking when you communicate with others. When someone speaks to you in a childlike way, answer in the same fashion. For example, a kidding statement is best answered with more kidding. If you take the kidding seriously, you are guilty of a crossed transaction. Also, if someone speaks seriously to you, you may offend that person if you answer with a "smart" remark. Just keep in mind which of your ego states is in control, and learn to communicate in a way that causes complementary and not crossed transactions.

To apply this theory of transactional analysis in your relationships with others, you need to strengthen your Adult self. This involves three steps.

1. You must understand yourself.

2. You will need to develop your self-esteem. This means that your attitudes about yourself must be positive and constructive. (This chapter is intended to help you with these important tasks.)

3. You will embark on a program of self-improvement as suggested in Chapters 2 and 3.

If you are successful in your self-improvement program, your Adult self will emerge as the most natural influence on your personality. Little by little you will find that you have built up a great deal of inner strength, and you will find it much easier to avoid crossed transactions.

Know Yourself

ackie quickly slipped the term paper under her notebook after catching a glimpse of the red 'C' on the cover page. She made sure that no one saw the grade as she browsed through the paper in class. She found comments such as "disorganized," "syntax problems," "look up uses of semicolon," and "do not use jargon." Later when Jackie and her friend Julie were comparing notes, Jackie said, "He only gave me a 'C' grade, but it really is a good term paper. I think Mr. Nelson gave me a lower grade because something I wrote offended him. He can't stand it when someone comes up with an idea that he disagrees with."

The first, most basic step in gaining the respect and esteem of others is to develop **self-esteem**. When you really like yourself—when you have a high level of self-respect—you are said to have self-esteem. Your self-esteem has many dimensions. It can include your feelings about your:

- physical appearance

- aptitude for mathematics

- athletic skills

- romantic appeal

- ethics and morals

- mechanical ability

- sense of humor

- artistic talent

Appreciate the Good in Your Personality

When you *dislike* yourself, you have low self-esteem. Of course, everyone has faults and imperfections. However, being less than perfect should not cause you to lose self-respect. Just as you can respect and like someone else who has a less-than-perfect personality, you should also be able to like yourself—just as you are. There is an important distinction between believing you are a good person who has weaknesses and believing you are a faulty person. When you can appreciate the good in your personality, even with a clear view of your faults and inadequacies, and can genuinely *like* yourself, you are ready to move ahead in developing your success identity.

Accept Responsibility for Your Actions

When there are things about yourself that you do not like or when something happens that you feel should not happen to a person like you, there are several ways that you might choose to deal with it. For example, suppose you are involved in an accident. You are driving in the right lane of a four-lane highway. As you move into the left lane, your car is sideswiped by another car that is passing on your left. What caused the accident to happen? Was the other driver talking to someone in the back seat and thus did not see your car? Were you in the wrong place at the wrong time and in no way responsible? Or is it possible that your carelessness caused the accident? Did you fail to use your turn signal or to look behind before changing lanes? In similar cases this type of accident was caused by the driver in the right-hand lane not making sure the left-hand lane was clear before moving into it.

It is important for you to realize that sometimes things happen *to you* and you are not at fault. Other times things happen that *you cause*. In the example above, assume that you see yourself as a careful driver. If you were driving carefully, you should not fall into the trap of blaming yourself. But if you *did* behave in a careless manner, that behavior would be in conflict with your self-image. To manage this conflict, you might:

- Make excuses and blame someone else.

- Try to ignore what happened or pretend to be unaware of what you do not like about yourself.

- Feel sorry for yourself.

- Label yourself as a failure.

- Accept the experience as real, face it, and tell yourself "I'm still okay."

The last choice is the best choice—the one that will preserve your self-esteem. It is the choice that shows that you are accepting responsibility for your actions.

Do Not Hide From Reality

Closing your eyes (or the eyes of your inner self) to reality can prevent you from understanding and accepting the *real* you. Trouble begins when something happens that is in conflict with an aspect of your self-image that you feel is important. Your inner self is offended. Your self-esteem is threatened. This behavior is something that you

Critical Thinking

Think about...

which of the following is the best way to manage this conflict. Why?

would not expect of a person such as yourself. As a result, a kind of tension (anxiety, distress or conflict) grows inside you. In your disappointment you may feel deep resentment. If the conflict is extremely offensive to your self-esteem, you may blame yourself for allowing it to happen.

Do Not Ignore Your Experiences

When something happens in conflict with your self-image, it is natural to try to ignore it. Here is why. If you can pretend that the event did not actually happen or convince yourself that it was not as it seemed to be, your self-image can be protected temporarily. You convince yourself that the *real* you had nothing to do with the event. However, the more you use this kind of pretense, the greater the psychological stress that you will have to endure.

A better way to preserve your self-esteem is by facing up to the fact that something has happened in conflict with your self-image (you understand and accept it as real) and you do not allow your self-respect to waver. You must learn to recognize and accept your experiences as real. Then your self-image will not be in conflict with your life experiences. You will know and like your inner self. Your tension and conflict with reality will disappear. At the same time, the barriers to building your self-esteem will also disappear.

Masks Off

lex slumped on the couch in his apartment and stared at the ceiling. "I suppose it's because I'm so stupid when math is involved," he mumbled. The papers for his statistics project were scattered on the table and chair where he had been working. "I can't let my friends in class see how confused and miserable I am when we get together to go over the assignment." Then Maria walked in and said, "Hey, Alex, how are you doing on the statistics project?" There was a pause. "Are you upset or something?" "No," Alex said as he pressed his hand to his forehead. "I just have a headache. The stats are almost done. But I don't feel like going to that boring review session. Why don't we check the TV schedule?"

Everyone occasionally puts up a false front to **mask** his or her true feelings. Or they may put on an act—playing a role to create a false impression. Their purpose may be to inflate themselves in the eyes of others—to appear to be better than they really are. Or there may be times when a person might wear a mask of being less than he or she really is to avoid the appearance of being smart or stuck-up.

> 66 Many fail in their work because they are unable to overcome personal deficiencies. Check up on yourself. Don't be afraid to put yourself under a microscope. Eliminate your negative qualities. Develop your positive ones. 99
>
> —M. Winette

*Everyone occasionally
wears an emotional
mask to cover up her or
his true feelings.*

Photo by Jim Whitmer

Sometimes wearing a mask is the right thing to do, considering the circumstances. It would be unrealistic to suggest that one should always be absolutely open and honest about everything. If people could not mask their true feelings occasionally, the world would be less civilized. For example, if a person has a headache but is required to serve customers, wearing a smile (hiding the physical discomfort) is better than complaining.

However, feeling that you always have to wear a mask or play a role can be a tiresome burden. You are not likely to relax and feel good about yourself if you constantly have to keep up false pretenses—trying to present yourself to the world as if you are somehow better than you really are. To help you visualize and understand how transparent masks can be, think about people in your life who try unsuccessfully to appear to be intelligent, ambitious, popular, open-minded, courageous, or well-informed about something when they are not. Although masks may be effective in fooling some people, in the long run, you can expect others to detect what is behind the masks. Eventually they see them as they really are no matter how they try to cover up and present false images of themselves.

As you grow in self-understanding and self-esteem, you will feel better about revealing your true personality to others. You will feel less need to cover up—to present a false image of yourself. You will be willing to take off some of the masks you have been using to hide your real self or to create false impressions.

Let Failure Lead to Success

Here is a story that illustrates how one person was able to maintain her self-esteem when she found her life experiences in conflict with her self-image. Sue was employed as a hairstylist in a salon that went out of business. In her search for a new job, she was offered a position with Beautiful Hands. The job was to include nail sculpture, manicures, tip overlays, and similar jobs requiring good eye and hand coordination. Sue accepted the job and went to work with enthusiasm. She assumed that her successful experience in hairstyling was proof of her ability to work successfully at nail sculpting.

Sue had some problems during her training period. She found that she could not keep up with the other trainees. Also, her instructor gave Sue lower grades on her work. Often she was required to do the work over again. This caused some customers to ask for another technician when they came in a second time. Sue felt crushed. She had expected to succeed in her new job, but she found herself in a struggle to maintain her composure when confronted with what appeared to be failure.

At first Sue made excuses for her inability to learn her new job. She told her supervisor that she was not feeling well and could not

Almost every job requires special talents and skills.

Tim Barnwell/Stock, Boston

concentrate. She commented that probably the other trainees were more experienced and were faster because of that. But then she learned that they were no more experienced than she was. Another excuse Sue made to herself was that she was not trying hard enough, so she worked as fast as she could. But that seemed to result in more criticism of her work—more failure.

Finally, Sue found herself at a crossroads. If she continued to make excuses and deny the reality of her failure in nail sculpting, she would only create more anxiety and distress for her inner self. It would be very difficult to ignore or hide the reality of her experiences in the training program and, at the same time, maintain her self-esteem. However, if she accepted her experience as real—as a natural thing to have happen in her life—the result would be different.

Sue made the best choice. She confronted the reality of her failure and allowed her inner self to gain insight about this conflict between what she valued and the evidence presented by this experience. She thought, "I tried my best to do the job well and to keep up the pace my supervisor expected. But I was unsuccessful. This experience tells me that my natural ability in the skills required for success in nail sculpting is less than I had thought. But that's all right. I can cope with and accept this failure because there is so much in my life that's rewarding and successful. I don't have to be the best at everything. I'm good at hairstyling. I have artistic ability and good styling skills, and it's realistic for me to have high self-esteem in this occupational area. I need to find a job where I can use my talents." Sue thought about many of her success experiences and felt good. Her experiences in hairstyling were consistent with her image of herself.

This story illustrates an important concept. Sue was able to face her failures, accept them as real, and still maintain her self-esteem. Everyone experiences failure. The only way to avoid failure in life is to refuse to try. The benefit of Sue's experience was to give her valuable information about herself—information she was able to use to redirect her career. She was able to avoid the frustration and disappointment of continuing to work in an occupation that required talent and skill that she did not have. However, Sue discovered a direction for her career that would allow her to build on what she *did* have. Her failure in one career paved the way for success in another. You can use this concept by taking a positive view when you experience failure. Realize that you are good at something else, and let the experience provide new directions so that you can let failure lead to success in your life.

Critical Thinking

Think about...

what Sue should do at this important decision point in her life. Is she a failure? How might she plan for success?

Be Sensitive To Feedback

If you try to hide from reality, you will find ways to ignore the **feedback** that comes from negative experiences. However, these experiences provide information, or feedback, that you can use to evaluate yourself—to judge how you are doing. For instance, if you want to think of yourself as an excellent student but fear that you are not, you might refuse to look at your report card. Or finding a low grade, you might accuse the teacher of being unfair or incompetent. However, if you are to grow and improve, you *need* feedback.

Be on the Alert for Praise and Criticism

If you are listening and observing, you will pick up all kinds of feedback. If you take the initiative to ask, you will learn even more. Here are some examples:

Feedback. . . "Paul, the stockroom is still in a mess."
Interpretation. . .Paul tends to delay or avoid unpleasant tasks.

Feedback. . ."I visited with Mrs. Lucero in the supermarket line. She said to tell you that her loan application was approved."
Interpretation. . .One more satisfied customer...I must be doing my job well.

Feedback. . .The supervisor says, "It appears that we need more training in projecting a positive image over the telephone."
Interpretation. . .The person who receives the calls projects a negative image over the telephone.

Feedback. . .Dan reviews the copy he has written for a newspaper advertisement. The copy editor has circled several punctuation errors and has written in the margin, "Good selling point!"
Interpretation. . .Dan's technical writing skills are weak, but he writes well from a creative standpoint.

These are examples of how you might collect and interpret evidence of praise or criticism from informal feedback. Also, there are occasions when a friend, an employer, a teacher, or anyone in a position to judge your behavior will give you evaluative feedback. You should welcome these opportunities to learn about how others perceive you. Try not to be hurt, offended, or resentful. Even when criticism is given in anger, you should try to learn from it; do not allow the anger to detract from the value of the criticism.

Always try to be open, alert, and sensitive to the feedback that is available. You should be aware that there are things we can change

Critical
Thinking

Think about...

one example of praise and one example of criticism you received recently. How do you interpret this information?

about ourselves and things we cannot. Concentrate your energy on what is possible—on what is realistic.

A Friend Can Help

One good source of feedback is your friends and close associates. Also, counselors, teachers, and possibly employment supervisors or coworkers can help. They can provide you with valuable information about what they see in your behavior. But more importantly, you may feel a sense of trust and safety in talking with them about yourself. In an environment of trust, you can feel safe to reveal your real self. As you share this information, you think about what you are saying. You reflect upon it and turn it over in your mind. This process can generate insight and understanding that would not happen without the help of someone to listen, think, and talk things over with.

Talking about yourself with a trusted friend can help you understand the real you.

Photo by Jim Whitmer

Talking with someone who can understand and accept you allows you to more clearly see yourself as others see you. It helps to talk about:

- what you wish were different about yourself

- the events in your life that conflict with your ideal self-image

- your inner feelings

- your disappointments

- your hopes and dreams

Talking with someone and reflecting on these things can allow you to more clearly visualize and reflect upon where you are in your effort to unmask your inner self.

When the masks come off, self-understanding and self-esteem are allowed to grow. When you come to understand and accept yourself as being okay, even though there are things about yourself that you want to change and improve, you are ready to engage in serious self-analysis and begin self-improvement.

Summary

When you really like yourself—when you have a high level of self-respect—you have self-esteem. There is an important distinction between believing you are a good person who has weaknesses and believing you are a faulty person. You should realize that everyone makes mistakes, and you should accept yours and learn from them.

Your self-esteem is threatened when your life experiences are in conflict with your self-image. A natural reaction is to try to ignore the inconsistent experience or to avoid responsibility for it. A way of hiding from reality is to put up a false front to mask your true feelings or to appear better than you really are. However, masks and role-playing can be burdensome. In the long run, others will see through them. You need to learn to face reality and maintain a positive self-image.

Being sensitive to the many sources of feedback (information that you can use for self-evaluation) can help you set the stage for self-improvement. Actively collecting evidence of praise and criticism is one effective method. Another is to develop a safe, trusting relationship with a friend, a counselor, or someone with whom you can share your inner feelings and reflect upon your experiences.

End of Chapter Activities

Questions and Projects

1. As a new worker, you will often find that your work takes longer and sometimes fails to meet the quality standards of work done by more experienced coworkers.

    a. How might this affect your success identity?

    b. What actions might you take to soften the effects of these experiences?

2. Think of all the people you know who might be willing and able to talk with you about your personality. Identify someone with whom you have a trusting, friendly relationship—someone with whom you would feel comfortable sharing your inner feelings. Make an outline of the topics and questions you would like to discuss with this person. The outline is for your eyes only—not to be shown to your teacher or classmates.

3. Everyone has mental pictures of themselves. Sometimes they are good likenesses, and sometimes they are not. On a grid such as the one shown below, place a check in Column 1 next to the statements that correspond to what you think you are like. In Column 2 on your grid, check the statements you believe other people think you are like. In Column 3, check the statements you would most like to be true someday. Your responses are not to be shared with your teacher or classmates.

a.
HOW I FEEL ABOUT MYSELF	1	2	3
Inferior to most of my peers			
Superior to most of my associates			
Self-confident			
Lacking self-confidence			
Proud of my achievements			
Modest about my achievements			
Conceited about my appearance			
Ashamed of my appearance			
Feel good about my appearance			

b. HOW I FEEL TOWARD OTHERS

	1	2	3
Tolerant			
Intolerant			
Friendly			
Unfriendly			
Like being with others			
Dislike being with others			
Like most people			
Dislike most people			

Case Problems

1. Feeling Down

Barbara was depressed. It seemed that her work, social life, hobbies, and recreation meant nothing to her. Other people annoyed her more often now than ever before. She found herself lashing out in anger, brooding in frustration, and feeling very "down" most of the time. It seemed she was not really interested in anything or anyone except herself. Barbara began to see her friends slipping away. She began to pick up clues that her employer was not supporting her for a promotion she had been hoping for. Finally, it was obvious to Barbara that she was her own worst enemy. She asked herself, "Is there any way I can turn my life around?"

a. What clues in this case indicate something about Barbara's self-esteem?

b. What are the important questions Barbara must answer as she considers how to "turn her life around"?

2. Career Change?

Carl was ending his day at the bakery, a family business that he would someday own. After high school he completed a two-year training program—the best in the country; he knew the bakery business very well. He did his job well and felt satisfaction in his achievement. However, the day seemed long. The routine seemed unchallenging and a bit depressing. Now in his mid-twenties, Carl felt as though he had reached the end of the road in his career; and the prospect of another 20 or 30 years in the bakery business (thousands more days like today) was depressing.

a. If Carl considers a career change, what are some factors that might influence his decision?

b. Assuming Carl asked you to help him decide what to do, what information would you want to obtain if you were going to play the role of friend and counselor to him?

c. What advantages, if any, would there be for Carl if he chose *not* to make a career change?

Self-Improvement

G eorge answered the doorbell and was surprised to see a friend from high school—Leon. They had played basketball together and were casual friends. After they exchanged greetings, Leon asked to use the telephone. "My car stalled a couple of blocks from here, and I need to call a tow truck," he explained. "Well, okay," George responded after a short pause. "I hate to have anyone see my place in this condition." Leon looked around, smiled, and quipped, "No problem; it reminds me of your locker back at school—but it doesn't smell quite so bad!" This experience inspired George to make a dramatic change. He resolved to clean up his apartment and his locker at the health club and to develop a reputation for being neat, clean, and well-organized. "So," he whispered to himself, "how can I motivate myself to get my sloppy habits under control?"

The Self-Improvement Process

The purpose of Chapter 1 was to help you understand how to develop a realistic and positive self-image—a clear and accurate concept of your personality. With this preparation, you are ready to take charge of your life—to plan for the self-improvement that is needed as you develop your success identity. The following illustration shows the steps in the self-improvement process.

Objectives

After completing this chapter, you should be able to:

1.
Visualize improvements in your personality that will allow you to reach your full potential.

2.
Identify long-term goals and specific short-term objectives for self-improvement.

3.
Develop plans for achieving your goals and objectives for self-improvement.

4.
Establish mentoring relationships with coworkers and supervisors who will support you as you plan and work toward self-improvement.

5.
Use counseling, testing, and try-out experiences for self-evaluation, setting goals, and making plans for self-improvement.

IMAGE OF YOUR FUTURE PERSONALITY

Illustration 2-1
The process of planning for self-improvement.

> *Experience shows that success is due less to ability than to zeal. The winner is he who gives himself to his work, body and soul.*
> —Charles Buxton

SCANS
Focus

A competent worker...

■ accurately assesses his or her own knowledge, skills, and abilities

■ sets well-defined, realistic goals

■ monitors progress toward goal attainment

■ is self-motivated through goal achievement

The steps in the process of planning for self-improvement are as follows:

1. Develop a realistic vision of your future self—an image of the personality that you want and need to attain as you prepare for success in your career and in life. That vision will give you something to plan for and work toward.

2. Analyze the personality that you envision and bring specific goals into focus. Then identify specific, measurable objectives for each goal.

3. Plan the accomplishment of the objectives. The vision of your future self in terms of self-improvement goals and objectives describes *what you want to happen.* The action plans describe *how you will make it happen.*

4. Work on developing your success identity. Your action plans will point the way.

As you move ahead in implementing your action plans, remember this: Self-improvement is not a goal to attain. It is a process that continues as you grow to become the best that you can be.

Visualize The Best That You Can Be

Developing a clear image of your potential starts with what was emphasized in Chapter 1. It begins as you face the reality of your experiences, take off the masks that may be used to create false impressions, and seriously consider the praise and criticism from those who know you well. As you reflect on the masks you found yourself using, think about what you were trying to accomplish with the pretense or role-playing. As you reflect on the praise and criticism, think about the changes in your personality that might eliminate the criticism and bring even more praise. It will help to take notes. As ideas for self-improvement occur to you, jot them down.

Another way of visualizing your potential is by what psychotherapists call **imaging.** This is a deliberate effort to imagine your renewed and improved personality. Find a quiet, pleasant place where you can relax. Take your time; do not try to hurry. Close your eyes and search your mind for images of yourself doing what gives you satisfaction. If there are sources of distress in your life (anxiety, depression, anger, loneliness), try to imagine what might relieve the distress.

If you follow these suggestions, you should have a list of notes about the various personal qualities and characteristics you would like to develop. Review and organize these ideas into a profile of your improved personality.

Design Your Self-Improvement Program

Psychologists use **self-actualization** to describe the process of growing to reach your greatest potential. This process does not culminate in a final achievement of your self-actualized personality. You should not assume that there will come a time to sit back and rest in your self-improvement efforts. Rather, you must expect to reassess and redefine your success identity as you move ahead in your career. You will need to keep working to maintain your self-esteem. Your success identity will evolve and be renewed as you grow to become the best that you can be.

Develop Long-Term Goals

As you analyze your future personality profile, you will probably see that it can be logically broken down into several areas for self-improvement, focusing on:

- your career

- social status and relationships

- education and training

- communication and interpersonal skills

- your physical well-being

- what you want to acquire or achieve financially

These elements of your personality profile are the basis for your long-term **goals** for change. Goals that are too broad or too vague or are built on "psychobabble" ("I want to get my head together" or "I want to be a fully actualized human being") are neither helpful for planning nor are they easily achieved. You must be specific enough in

Critical Thinking

Think about...
changes that might prepare you for a brighter, more fulfilling future. After letting your imagination soar, take out a pen and paper and write down what you imagined about being the best that you can be.

66 We don't need more strength or more ability or greater opportunity. What we need is to use what we have. 99
—Basil S. Walsh

66 Concentrate on finding your goal, then concentrate on reaching it. 99
—Col. Michael Friedsam

Your self-improvement plans may mean further education.

Richard Pasley/Stock, Boston

stating your goals to allow for evaluation of your progress and to know when you have achieved your goals.

Following are some examples of vague long-term goals and some more specific examples of measurable goals that are more useful for planning.

Critical **Thinking**

Think about...

what might be a more specific, measurable goal corresponding to *Better health and physical condition.*

VAGUE GOALS	SPECIFIC GOALS
■ A good education.	■ Earn an associate degree in retailing.
■ Leadership ability.	■ Be promoted to supervisor.
■ Handle conflict.	■ Avoid shouting matches.
■ Self-confidence.	■ Be able to answer questions in a job interview.
■ Be less of a wimp.	■ Say "no" without apology.
■ Creative expression.	■ Have poetry published.

Develop Short-Term Objectives

With a profile of specific goals in view, you are ready to develop the short-term **objectives** that will be the stepping-stones to the achievement of your goals. As you do this, it is important to make the objectives observable or measurable in some way. Here is how to do this. For each specific long-term goal, you need to ask yourself, *"What evidence will indicate progress or achievement of this goal?"* The answers to this question will be the measurable or observable objectives that will describe the short-term, specific mileposts that indicate progress along the way as you work toward accomplishing your objectives.

Here are some examples:

Long-term goal: Be promoted to office manager in four years.

Short-term objectives:

- Complete a course in office management.

- Receive "excellent" or "superior" ratings on job performance reviews.

- Gain experience in positions as receptionist, bookkeeping, and inventory control.

Long-term goal: Improve in self-confidence and assertiveness.

- Be strong enough to ask my employer for a raise.

- Read two good books on assertiveness.

- Maintain calm, candid, and firm behavior in challenging a manipulative coworker.

Long-term goal: Become computer-literate.

- Obtain a personal computer to use at home.

- Obtain and learn to use a word-processing program.

- Learn to manage personal finances using a spreadsheet.

Develop Plans of Action

After you have produced a list of specific objectives, you are ready to develop plans of action (**strategies** and **tactics**) that will ensure the achievement of your objectives. For each objective write down what you intend to do. Ask yourself, *"What can I do to make this happen?"* Here are some examples of specific actions that might lead to the accomplishment of short-term objectives and, eventually, long-term goals:

- Take an assertiveness training program.

- Join a support group.

- Practice job interviews with a coworker.

- Stop eating "junk food" snacks after dinner.

- Use a budget to control spending.

Determining what you would like to do with the rest of your life involves your personality, beliefs, dreams, ambitions, and imagination. Your success identity will depend to some extent on how determined you are to reach your goals. Too often people fail to achieve their goals simply because they get discouraged and give up.

Staying focused on your goals helps if you hold yourself accountable for your action plans. One way to do this is by keeping your goals in a journal or diary. Another is by sharing them, when appropriate, with others. Think of your goals, objectives, and plans as promises—contracts with yourself. If you share what you are doing with your family, friends, coworkers, and employment supervisors, you will have greater determination to follow your self-improvement program. Your motivation to improve will also be sustained by your vision of the benefits of success in your career and by your appreciation of your progress. Remember that you can achieve a realistic goal if it is something you sincerely want, if you carefully plan a way to reach it, and if you have the perseverance to stick to it.

Self-Improvement Strategies

There are many strategies, techniques, or plans for self-improvement. Several of these will be described in this section. You may already be using some of these strategies without realizing it. There may be others that you will want to try.

Behavior Modification

One approach to self-improvement that has been successful for many people is to use **behavior modification**. The theory behind behavior modification suggests that people act in ways that bring some kind of reward. If you want to change your behavior, you must have some payoff or benefit as motivation. Psychologists refer to the reward as **reinforcement** of the desirable behavior.

Behavior modification may be used to help you carry out your action plans for self-improvement by developing your own system of rewards. You might begin by considering what you enjoy. Take a piece of paper and list 10 to 20 things that you might use to reward yourself. Do you like to spend time relaxing with a good book? Do you look forward to going out to dinner? Do you enjoy skiing, racquetball, golf, tennis, or windsurfing? Are you thinking about buying something that you want but do not absolutely need?

Whatever you list as rewards for behavior modification, be realistic. If achievement is a step-by-step process, plan additional small rewards at each step along the way. Of course, these rewards must be possible in your present circumstances. You cannot say that you would like to buy a new sports car if you can only afford an older car.

Use your recreation as a reward for behavior modification.

H. Armstrong Roberts

With your potential rewards' list at hand, review your self-improvement action plans. Try to match up specific objectives or activities with appropriate rewards. Prepare a contract in which you promise yourself that you are going to change in some way. You may decide to use more effective study skills. You may decide to control your bad temper.

Put your "contract" in writing. One way to do this is to keep a card file with each contract or promise to yourself written on a card. The contract should include a date on which the contract takes effect, what you intend to do ("I promise to. . ."), and what benefit you expect to achieve. Include in your contract something pleasant and rewarding to look forward to when you achieve the objectives in your self-improvement plan. If appropriate, a date for fulfillment of the contract may be included.

Mentoring and Coaching

When you begin a new job, you can expect your employer to be concerned about your training. In most cases there is a period of adjustment to the new work situation. There may be a lot to learn about what the job consists of and how it is to be done. There are procedures, policies, rules, and expectations understood by those who have been on the job for a while. All this becomes the focus of training and adjustment for the new person.

Usually someone will be assigned to assist the new person with on-the-job training. Also, without a specific assignment to do so, coworkers may voluntarily help with the orientation and training. You can expect support as you learn to fit in, get along, and become productive in a new work situation. The person who takes a personal interest in helping someone with training and development on the job is called a **mentor**.

You could consider a coworker or supervisor who is responsible for your on-the-job training as a resource person, helping you achieve your plans for self-improvement. However, for this person to assume the role of mentor and assist you with your personal self-improvement program, he or she should take a personal interest in helping

A mentor can help you with self-improvement.

Photo by Jim Whitmer

you reach your potential at work and in life. You may need to put forth an effort to cultivate a friendship with someone, or possibly with several people, who will want to fulfill the role of mentor and coach as you work on your self-improvement program.

Aptitude and Interest Tests

Your local Job Service Office or career counseling center can provide testing services and help with interpretation and assessment of your strengths and weaknesses. Vocational interest and aptitude tests can help you better understand your potential for success in various career fields. These tests can also help in determining what you need to learn to prepare for success in an appropriate career. Some of the tests measure characteristics that relate to the demands of various work situations. For instance:

- Do you like detail?

- Are you naturally an orderly person?

- Do you like to solve problems?

- Would you do well working with mechanical things?

- Do you enjoy teamwork and cooperative relationships?

- Do you enjoy the challenge of variety and change in your work?

- Do you have an aptitude for selling?

- Do you have an aptitude for work involving mathematics?

Answers to these types of questions will help you focus on your interests, aptitudes, and preferences and can give you clues about what to do as you strive for self-improvement. Also, the information obtained from standardized scholastic aptitude and achievement tests (used by most educational institutions) can provide detailed information about where you are in your preparation for success in your chosen career. Usually an employment or school counselor will help you with interpretation of your tests and with plans for future career preparation.

Counseling

psychologist tells about a client, Barbara, as an example of how the self-improvement process works. "She had come through her divorce successfully, had moved to a new apartment, and was thinking of changing her job. After several sessions we were sorting out the kind of future she wanted. It was the first time in her life, Barbara told me, that she felt truly responsible for her future. The experience was a bit frightening. 'It seems someone else has always made my decisions,' she explained. 'I guess I just came to rely on others for direction in my life.' My job as her counselor is to help Barbara grow. I don't tell her where or how. As we became seriously engaged in the self-improvement process, Barbara was doing the hard work—setting goals for herself, her future. 'It's scary,' she admitted, 'this taking charge of my life. But then again, it feels pretty good.' "

A professional counselor or therapist can help with the process of developing an understanding and appreciation of who you are and where you are in your personal and career development. Sometimes it helps just to talk to someone about yourself. A mental health professional, school or college counselor, or even a relative or personal friend whom you feel comfortable talking with can consult with you about your concerns as well as about your self-assessment and plans for self-improvement. Often just the process of talking with someone allows you to explore your feelings about yourself. Talking with a counselor can help you appreciate the many positive aspects of your personality, your educational and employment experiences, and your natural abilities.

Critical Thinking

Think about...

why talking with someone—having someone listen and reflect what they hear—helps more with self–improvement than simply "talking to yourself" and thinking.

Try-Out Experiences

A very good way to evaluate your potential for success in an occupation is by trying out actual experiences. For the musician, the athlete, the cook, the taxi driver, the health care worker, or the salesperson, experience provides clear and obvious signs of success and failure. If you have the opportunity in a work environment to test the

Taking music lessons would be a way to try out your natural musical abilities.

©Ulrike Welsch/Photo Researchers

validity of your new image of yourself as a potential auto mechanic, for example, successful performance is bound to have a positive impact on your self-esteem—to strengthen and reinforce it.

Another kind of **try-out experience** that can help you find and confirm your natural abilities and preparation for a career is to enroll in a course related to the field you want to explore. You can find these courses through adult education programs, community college or high school classes, apprentice training programs, and instruction sponsored by employers in business and industry. If you do not want to enroll in the class formally, you can talk to the instructor and students. You may be allowed to sit in on a few sessions and look at the course outline or text materials. However, you should be aware that what happens in class represents only part of what actually happens at work. This is especially true in classes that serve as preparation for advanced study. For example, an introductory marketing course does not cover what the work is like for an advertising copywriter or a merchandising manager.

Another possibility for testing your interest and ability and building your self-confidence before you fully commit yourself to a career is cooperative education. In these programs classroom and laboratory training is coordinated with on-the-job training in the work environment.

Summary

Developing a clear vision of your success identity (the personality that represents the best that you can be) sets the stage for your self-improvement program. It emerges as you review the feedback you get from those who are close to you and as you imagine your renewed and improved personality. With this image in view, long-term goals for self-improvement are formed. For each goal, short-term, measurable objectives are written. For each objective, you design a plan of action that will result in the achievement of the objectives and, eventually, the long-term goals.

Strategies for self-improvement include:

- Behavior modification—using rewards to motivate you in the achievement of your objectives.

- Mentoring and coaching—having someone in your workplace assist you with your personal self-improvement program.

- Aptitude and interest tests—providing clues about what to do as you strive for self-improvement.

- Counseling—talking with someone about your self-improvement goals, objectives, and plans.

■ Try-out experiences—exploring different careers in a work environment and taking courses related to the field you want to explore.

End of Chapter Activities

Questions and Projects

1. Carefully consider what you know about yourself (your talents, your hopes and dreams, your past successes and failures, the kind of person you are and want to become) and prepare a list of goals, objectives, and action plans.

   a. List two or three long-term goals. The goals should present a profile of the kind of person you want to be in five years.

   b. For each goal list several specific short-term objectives that will lead to its achievement. State the objectives in measurable terms.

   c. For each specific short-term objective, work out a plan for its accomplishment. Be specific about what, when, and how.

2. Identify someone you admire.

   a. Arrange for an interview, and ask for "keys to success" that you might use in your self-improvement action plan. You might invite this person to lunch and, if possible, spend some time observing him or her at work.

   b. Share your information about "keys to success" with other class members in small group discussions.

3. If you are employed, identify someone in your workplace who might act as your mentor for on-the-job training and supervision. Select one of your personal objectives that, when it is achieved, will improve your job performance. Share your objective with your mentor. Explain the concept of behavior modification as described in this chapter, and have your mentor help you with specific rewards for evidence of progress or appropriate behavior.

4. Go to a public library or a school counseling center and gather information about vocational interest and aptitude tests. Prepare a written report on what tests are available and what they measure. Select several tests that you might use to better understand yourself and your potential for success in your career.

Case Problems

1. Try-Out as a Temporary Worker

Shari's high school program included several courses in business education. These experiences gave her some understanding of the business world and the variety of job possibilities open to her. For a few months, she worked as a receptionist but found the job to be somewhat frustrating. There were many interruptions, so she could not concentrate on the task at hand. Also, Shari felt pressured because of having to deal with complaints of dissatisfied clients of the insurance agency where she worked. She shared her feelings with a coworker, Sylvia, who temporarily took over for someone who was absent from work because of illness. Sylvia explained that she was employed by a firm that provided temporary short-term workers in secretarial, accounting, data processing, and administrative fields. She told Shari about the many different job experiences she had enjoyed over the past several months. She said that the manager was always looking for good workers, and Shari began to consider the possibility of a job change.

a. What are the possible advantages or opportunities for Shari if she obtains temporary positions? What are some risks and disadvantages?

b. What might Shari do to use her employment to provide try-out experiences in the world of work?

2. A New Direction

Ben has been working as a meat cutter for seven years. He earns a good salary and likes his work, his coworkers, and his employer. He got the job just before his marriage to Bev, and now they have three children. The youngest is two years old and stays with Bev's mother during the day. Bev recently resumed working as a bank teller. Bev and Ben had a serious discussion about their future. They concluded that Bev is content in her banking career, but Ben wants more than meat cutting in his future.

a. Describe what Ben might do to assess his potential to prepare for a new career in business management.

b. Discuss what Bev might do to support and encourage Ben.

Developing Positive Attitudes

P hil was assigned to sit between two people on a flight to Anchorage. As a flight attendant walked by, he caught her attention and said, "Could I have a pillow, please?"

"Pillows are all gone; here's a blanket," she quipped as she tossed it on Phil's lap and walked away. Making the best of his situation, Phil struck up a conversation with the person next to the window. "Are you enjoying the view?" he asked. "I hadn't noticed," the woman responded, "I guess I'm paying too much attention to that red-headed flight attendant." "Oh, what's going on?" She looked up and rolled her eyes. "Well, that woman has an attitude problem. I've been watching her, and it irritates me to see how she's acting. I think she could have found a pillow for you." Phil continued, "How does her attitude reflect her image as a representative of this airline?" "Well, it's so obvious—her tone of voice. She was short and snappy when you asked for a pillow. And her body language—hands on her hips, slamming things around in the galley, stomping off and hiding in the cockpit when passengers need her. And she never smiles. What a grouch! I work for another airline, and I know we would never tolerate that kind of attitude problem in a flight attendant."

Your Attitudes Reflect Your Image

Psychologists and educators tell us that human beings are learning constantly. The

Objectives

After completing this chapter, you should be able to:

1.
Define attitudes and explain how they develop.

2.
Explain how attitudes are visible and how one person's attitudes can influence others.

3.
Avoid negative influences and benefit from positive attitudes of others.

4.
Take positive steps to improve your attitudes.

three general types of learning that take place are knowledge, skills, and attitudes. It would be easy to identify the first two types, but have you given much thought to the third type of learning: attitude? An **attitude** is how a person feels about something based on a type of learning. By this definition a major portion of your personality consists of the many different feelings you have. You may or may not be attracted to different people. You may or may not enjoy doing certain things. At a more intense level, you may fear or despise someone or something.

Avoid negative attitudes that leave bad impressions and turn people away.

   In another sense your attitude is the general feeling you communicate to others. You will hear someone say "He has a bad attitude," or "Her attitude about the project was very positive."   You are constantly sending signals that others pick up. It is almost as if those around you can "tune in" to your attitudes. Your attitudes can cause people to be drawn to you and have positive feelings (or attitudes) toward you. Or your attitudes can have the opposite effect, signaling others to avoid you. Your attitudes can cause others to see you as attractive or repulsive in varying degrees. Therefore, the image your friends, coworkers, and even casual associates have of you is what you project by your attitudes.

How Attitudes Develop

Each kind of learning requires a different method or strategy, and what works for one kind of learning may not work for another. A method that might help you memorize the anatomy of an insect may not work to help you learn to swim. You gain knowledge by studying and by using your logical and critical thinking abilities. You develop skills by practice and careful repetition of behavior with demonstration and coaching to help you improve.

You cannot develop attitudes in the same ways that you develop knowledge or skills. Educators and psychologists who have studied human learning say that **emotion** is the critical factor in the development of attitudes. Emotions such as fear, joy, anxiety, or compassion seem to shape our feelings about the events in our lives. When emotion accompanies an event time after time, it creates an attitude or feeling that may be very intense and difficult to change.

Here is an example of how emotion and a stressful experience were used to develop an attitude of safety consciousness. A company that was involved in heavy construction found that the frequency of accidental injuries was very high. The training program had stressed safety procedures, and the workers were thoroughly acquainted with what they *should* do to protect themselves from injury. However, simply knowing the safety rules in this case did not cause the workers to behave in a safe manner. The supervisors concluded that while the workers knew what was expected, they simply were not doing it. Some were found to be welding without safety glasses. Equipment was being serviced without being turned off (as safety codes required). Power tools were being operated without shields, and workers were not wearing gloves when they should have been. The workers *knew* the rules, but they had not developed the proper attitudes toward them. What was needed was a learning experience that would create a change in how the workers *felt* about the rules.

One of the supervisors hit upon the idea of having a "debriefing" after each accident. As soon as an accident happened, all work would stop. The accident victim was required to tell other workers what happened, why, and how it might have been prevented. There was a dramatic reduction in accidents under that particular supervisor. When these spur-of-the-moment meetings were held in other construction units, the results were the same—a reduction in the frequency of accidents. Where lectures on safety practices in training sessions had failed, the emotionally charged learning that occurred in the "debriefing" sessions had a powerful effect on the attitudes of the workers.

This example shows that highly emotional experiences can shape attitudes, and those attitudes can effectively influence behavior. These workers had all the *knowledge* they needed to behave appropriately. What they lacked was the motivation to do what they knew they should. A change in attitudes provided that motivation.

Attitudes Are Visible

Attitudes are hard to hide. Of course, they are not directly visible. No one can see your inner feelings. But those feelings have such a profound effect on your behavior that you are unable to hide them. They give those around you a clear view of your attitudes because of your behavior. Of course, you would not want to hide a positive attitude. It shines through to create a favorable impression. However, we tend to reject and express negative feelings toward those we perceive as having negative attitudes.

The fact that you see and judge people by their attitudes can be illustrated with this exercise. Think of someone you admire. If you share your ideas about this person with others and have them tell about their favorite people, the illustration will be even more effective. Now respond to this question about the person you have chosen: What are his or her outstanding qualities? Write these qualities on a sheet of paper. As you review your list, consider how many of the items are attitudes that tell something about how the person feels, as compared with other qualities such as physical features, what the person owns, or the person's accomplishments. Your list is likely to show two things. First, most of what you consider important in describing someone comes under the attitude classification. Second, most of the attitudes are positive. Your most admired person's attitudes are visible to you, and it is those attitudes that cause you to admire him or her.

Attitudes Are Catching

It was a busy Friday afternoon in the tire shop. Arnold, Kimberly, and Mark had been installing snow tires for hours; and because of the early snowstorm, customers' cars were lined up in the parking lot. There was not much conversation. Ray, the shop supervisor, opened the door to the customer waiting area and said, "Hey, we're behind schedule and it's only an hour until we close shop. Can we handle the six cars lined up out there?" No one said a word. After listening to the clanking of tire irons and the muffled sound of the air compressor for a few seconds, Ray shouted, "Hey, is anyone alive in this disaster area?" Kimberly quickly shouted back, "I am, chief! And I think Mark is showing signs of life.

We can handle it!" "Great! After work the sodas are on me, " Ray said as he closed the door. Mark looked up, wiped his forehead, and smiled at Kimberly. "Sure, I'm alive—and thirsty." Finally, Arnold said, "What a bunch of eager beavers!" Then he smiled and quickened his pace. By closing time the three were tired but pleased.

One person's attitude can have a powerful influence on the others who may be around him or her. This is especially evident when people are involved in a team effort. You have probably experienced the feeling you get when someone causes a positive change in the attitudes of a group. Also, you may recall times when someone had a negative effect by allowing his or her negative attitude to infect others.

A group of people having similar positive feelings and emotions are said to have "high morale" or "team spirit." Even in the face of adversity, a group working together for a common goal and having success can have high morale. As you might expect, when a working team experiences failure, the effect can be depressing on the attitudes of everyone.

Critical Thinking

Think about...

an occasion when someone caused a positive change in the attitudes of a group. Also, think about an occasion when someone created a negative effect by allowing his or her negative attitude to infect others.

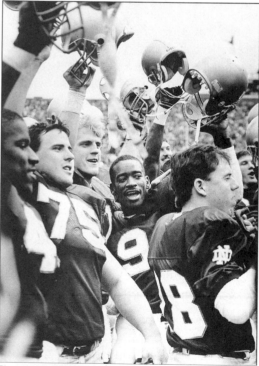

The attitudes of just one person showing positive, energetic leadership can motivate a group.

Photo by Jim Whitmer

Usually when a group attitude changes, it is because just one individual takes the initiative to spark the change. Because attitudes are catching, when the leaders of the group let their attitudes show, the effect on the group can be almost electric. You see this when a member of an athletic team with positive energy ignites a winning spirit in his or her teammates. Everyone seems to respond and performance improves. This principle was operating when, after being lost in a blizzard, one mountain climber literally saved the lives of her companions because her positive attitude inspired the others to make the effort required for their survival. This principle also applies in the world of work. A positive team spirit and high morale contribute to effective job performance.

Improving Your Attitudes

It may not be easy, but there is one person you can "get tough with" without fear of reprisal. There is, in fact, one person whom you can change. That person is you! Changing your own attitudes can be very satisfying. It can also be enlightening. If you have been having trouble with your supervisor or if you feel you have been criticized too much and too often, you (being human) have probably tried to get even. Perhaps you were sullen. You may have answered abruptly, or you may have threatened to quit. Consider what might have happened if, instead, you said sincerely, "I know I made an error. You're right to tell me about it, and I appreciate it. Is there anything you can suggest or do to help me correct it? I want to improve." No matter how stern and demanding your supervisor may have been, your remarks would probably have created a positive response. Chances are your supervisor would have said, "That's all right. I'm sure you can improve. Here is a suggestion about how to handle it next time."

Developing positive attitudes and eliminating negative ones is the best kind of reforming you can do. But how should you start? There are no rules for self-improvement that will work for everyone. However, these ideas and suggestions can be helpful if you have the inner strength to put them to the test. Remember, because attitudes are shaped under the stress of emotions, it may take courage for you to try these suggestions. The reward can be a more positive attitude. Here are three steps in the process of attitude improvement:

1. Identify the attitudes you want to improve. It may help to write a brief description of the image you have of yourself after you have achieved your attitude improvement goals. Keep in mind the image of the kind of person you wish to become. Your mental picture must be so clear and so constantly present that it can create a pattern for your behavior.

> " A pessimist is one who makes difficulties of his opportunities; an optimist is one who makes opportunities of his difficulties. "
> —Reginald B. Mansell

2. Resolve to develop within yourself those attitudes that are reflected in your ideal personality and cultivate those qualities that are needed for self-renewal.

3. Use the image of your ideal personality as a model for your behavior. By practice and effort, you can make the desirable behavior come naturally, and the improved attitudes will transform your personality.

You may feel that you have no need to improve your attitudes—that you already have a positive outlook on life. Perhaps you do; but you are unique, indeed, if you do not occasionally say something uncomplimentary about a coworker or grumble and complain about something.

Everyone is negative some of the time. Negative feelings, negative attitudes, negative words—all are depressors of the spirit. They all take everyone down instead of up. You can get up in the morning feeling great. Yet if you meet four or five friends during the day who tell you of depressing happenings, who complain, or (worst of all) who criticize you and call attention to your mistakes, your happy mood will soon disappear. Fortunately, this works both ways. If you are tired and discouraged, your mood can change when you meet someone who gives you a sincere compliment or greets you with a smile.

Negative attitudes can creep up on us because it is so easy to be negative. It takes no effort to let a feeling of self-pity steal over you. There are disappointments in every day. The easy way is to let them engulf us. It does take effort to replace negative thoughts with positive ones, but the effort is well spent. Here are some suggestions that may help.

Smile. You can create a smile, even though it may not at the time feel natural. Simply raise your eyebrows and turn the corners of your mouth up instead of down. Make a real effort to look pleasant and interested in what is going on around you. Under the stimulation of your own interest, those around you may become interesting!

Say something pleasant. Think of something positive, good-natured, or complimentary to say to someone else at every opportunity. This will do wonders for those around you. It will also keep you busy thinking of positive things to say and you will not have time to be negative.

Take a positive approach. Another way to survive in a negative atmosphere is to view the negative situation as a challenge. Is there a coworker you dislike? Is there a friend who rubs you the wrong way? Whatever it is, try the positive approach. Try to change the situation

A smile shows that a person has a positive attitude.

by being positive. You may become a positive influence, as Kimberly was in the tire shop incident.

Here is another example. Let's say you have a friend, Jeff, who gets on your nerves. He talks about himself all the time. He boasts about everything—his car, his job, his school. Ask yourself, "What can I say that is positive?" Suppose he begins to tell you about a test on which he knew all the answers. Why not say, "Jeff, I wish I had your confidence." If you keep out the sarcasm and say it sincerely, this may cause Jeff to stop and think a minute. He may not have too much confidence, and his bragging helps boost his self-confidence. He may say, "To tell you the truth, I've always thought you were the confident one." If something like this should happen, the hostility on both sides will begin to evaporate. Your campaign to become more positive will get you over a big hurdle. When you learn to look at problems with a positive attitude, you can begin to solve them more easily.

Coping With Other People's Negative Attitudes

Audrey was in good spirits as she began her new job in the produce department of a supermarket. But soon her positive attitude was threatened. At coffee break she joined a group of coworkers. No one smiled or welcomed her. An older man wearing a dirty gray sweatshirt seemed to be leading the conversation. He talked about how "management is greedy and the union representatives are their puppets." He complained that "the only way to get a fair share of overtime work (for time-and-a-half pay) is to be one of the favored few." Then the conversation turned to gossip about how an absent member of the meat department crew was taking frozen shrimp home in her lunch box. After her coffee break, Audrey began to feel a bit depressed. "How am I going to cope with this?" she whispered to herself.

Critical Thinking

Think about... ·

how Audrey might cope with this situation. What should she do?

You may recall a time in your life when the emotions and attitudes of those around you were negative. You felt yourself being dragged down. Just by being aware of them you can resist and avoid negative influences on your attitudes. For example, when your coworkers get together to complain, gossip, or create dissension at work, you can refuse to participate. You can walk away or simply ignore what you hear and see.

Of all the many factors that influence a person's success, one of the most important is a positive attitude. You can improve your attitude and help others to improve by following the suggestions outlined in this chapter. Your improvement campaign will pay off in greater satisfaction and in greater ability to fit in and get along on the job and in daily life. As your positive attitude develops, the people around you begin to respond accordingly. They think of you as being enthusiastic, willing to learn, cheerful, and easy to get along with. Their favorable image of you causes them to expect positive, productive behavior. As you sense these positive expectations, your motivation to live up to your image is increased. The result is a cycle of reinforcement and improvement, greater appreciation of your positive attitude, and even higher levels of self-esteem.

In addition to the beneficial effect of your positive attitude on your own behavior, you find yourself in a new position of power. The influence of your positive attitude on other people allows you to influence them—to help them improve their self-esteem and develop positive attitudes.

Summary

Attitudes are a reflection of a person's inner feelings. The image they project to your associates can cause them to be drawn to you, or they can signal others to avoid you. Attitudes cannot be effectively developed by the methods used for teaching knowledge and skills. Emotion is the critical factor in their development.

Attitudes can be infectious. A person's attitudes can have a powerful influence on others. Usually when the attitudes of a group change, it is because of the inspiration created by the positive or negative attitudes of an individual. When the emotions and attitudes of those around you are negative, you can resist their influence by ignoring or avoiding what is negative in their behavior.

Developing positive attitudes and eliminating negative ones are important in the process of fitting in and getting along in the world of work. One way to improve your attitudes is to make an effort to smile and show an interest in what is going on around you. Also, your attitudes can improve when you say something pleasant to compliment or encourage others and when you take a positive approach in a negative situation. As your negative attitudes disappear and positive ones are developed, your self-image will improve and the image you project to others will be more positive. This will motivate you to greater productivity and success.

End of Chapter Activities

Questions and Projects

1. Reflect on your past experiences in school or at work. Prepare written responses and share your ideas in a group discussion of the following.

  a. Describe a situation in which you found yourself with a negative attitude. How was your attitude reflected in your behavior?

  b. Describe an occasion when you demonstrated a positive attitude.

  c. Identify a teacher or an employment supervisor who demonstrated an obviously negative attitude. What behavior gave you clues about this person's attitude?

  d. Identify someone whom you felt demonstrated "the power of positive thinking" with a motivational effect on others.

2. Is there someone who really bothers you—a friend, relative, or coworker? For a change be positive in your relationship with this person. Do not nag or complain. Instead, try to use a positive reinforcement approach and compliment him or her for appropriate behavior. While doing this, you must ignore the behavior that annoys you. Share the results of this project in group discussion. What were some of the positive reinforcements that seemed to work? What were some examples of successfully ignoring negative behavior?

3. Write down five negative statements you have made recently. Can you think of more positive language you might have used? Do you think a more positive approach would have improved the situation? Share your ideas in group discussion.

Case Problems

1. To Sell or Not to Sell

Teru worked in his family business in Japan during his teen years. There he learned the value of "suggestion selling." He applied these lessons as a salesperson in a large U.S. department store. Soon after he began his new job selling fine china and silverware, Teru became the top salesperson in his department. The merchandising manager was pleased, but Teru's coworkers were not. Sally and Fred took him aside and expressed their feelings. "Hey, squirt, you're overdoing it. If you don't slack off, the rest of us will look bad," Sally said. Fred continued, "Management doesn't appreciate all this customer harassment, and they'll just assume you're sucking up to them." At that moment Teru almost caved in to the emotional pressure. He clenched his fists, looked down, turned away, and said, "I'm only doing what they pay me for." Then he walked away. As the weeks passed, Teru continued selling as before, and his coworkers continued trying to discourage him. They spoke to him only when necessary—never with a smile or pleasant tone of voice. Occasionally Teru found his sales invoices missing or tampered with. Once someone put trash in his locker along with a note suggesting that he needed an "attitude adjustment."

a. What are some clues about the attitudes of Sally and Fred, and how do you interpret those clues?

b. What do you think Teru did wrong? What did he do right? Give reasons for your answers.

c. Write a continuation of this story, giving specific actions and responses by the various characters, with a development of improved attitudes for Sally and Fred.

2. The Grouch

B.J. was in charge of the copy room where college faculty and staff took work to be done. The work included production of tests, teaching materials, brochures, text materials, and instructional aids. Following are some bits and pieces of B.J.'s conversations in a one-hour period. "No, I'm *not* having a good day." "You forgot to sign for the transparency masters. You can't just take what you want without recording it, you know." "Who messed up the cover of this brochure?" "No, I can't afford to go to lunch at the student center. I'll just eat my peanut butter sandwich by myself." "Tell Professor Nelson not to send students in here. He should know the rule about student use of the copy machine." "How does she expect me to read these instructions? You would think someone with a Ph.D. could write so a person could read it."

a. Can you recognize some specific attitudes demonstrated by B.J.'s conversation? For each of her comments, list an attitude that is apparent from it.

b. What attitude changes would you recommend for B.J.? Explain.

3. Body Language

"Who does she think she is, Queen of the Universe?" Carl tossed the sweater he had just tried on back on the display table. His friend Bill smiled and said, "Don't let the attitude of that salesperson keep you from buying that sweater. You look good in it." Carl stuffed his hands into his pockets and looked at the floor. Then he slowly began to move toward the door of the sporting goods store. "I don't need the sweater, " he said. "When she said that a short guy with a full figure shouldn't wear horizontal stripes and looked down her nose at me that way, I got her message." "Oh, really?" Bill said. "What was her message?" Carl looked at the floor and said, "That tall, good-looking women think short, chunky guys are dirt."

a. What are some examples of behavior that might have caused Carl to interpret the salesperson's attitude as he did?

b. What suggestions do you have to help Carl cope with the influence of the salesperson's negative attitude?

c. How would the salesperson's attitude affect sales? Should her supervisor be made aware of this attitude? Why or why not?

Unit 2

Developing Your Interpersonal Relationships

Your success in the workplace will be determined by your ability to get along with your coworkers, supervisor, clients, and customers. This unit will discuss techniques for you to utilize in this effort. Each day in the workplace you will need to work to show a cooperative spirit; exercise politeness in dealings with others; demonstrate patience, dependability, and loyalty; and build the self–esteem of others.

Chapter 4 focuses on developing your ability to fit in and get along with people on the job. As you read through Chapter 5, you will mentally list your value–added qualities—the qualities you possess, those you need to improve upon, and those which you need to develop in order to fit in and get along in the workplace. Chapter 6 reminds you that your future in the work world may hinge on your ability to establish a good working relationship with your supervisor. The final chapter of the unit reviews the keys to getting along with the clients and customers.

Contents

Chapter 4
Fitting In And Getting Along

Chapter 5
Working With Coworkers

Chapter 6
Getting Along With Your Supervisor

Chapter 7
Relating To Clients And Customers

Fitting In And Getting Along

4

*After completing this chapter, you
should be able to:*

*1.
Describe the qualities and traits to
strive for to be a success in the workplace.*

*2.
List those negative qualities and traits
to be avoided in the workplace.*

*3.
Eliminate personal habits that may
detract from your effectiveness in the
workplace.*

Oki graduated with honors from an excellent community college in a health occupations program. During her first few weeks on the job at the community hospital, Oki frequently received compliments from her supervisor on the quality of her clinical skills and her attention to detail. At the end of her new employee probationary period, her supervisor called her into the office and informed her that she was being dismissed. Her supervisor told her that her coworkers found her unpleasant and difficult to work with. The supervisor stated that several times she had been observed as being in less than a cheerful mood. According to the floor nurses, she had been rude and uncaring to patients. This information was documented in Oki's personnel file. Oki snapped at the supervisor and said, "I do quality work. I am not here to be cheerful!" Oki stomped out of the session muttering something about being unfairly judged. How can Oki avoid this type of crisis in her next position?

Think about the last person you know who was dismissed from a job. What was the reason? Chances are the person was unable to fit in and get along with others. Surveys in many industries indicate that the most common reasons for failure on the job involve difficulties in working with others. You may spend several years studying to become technically competent for a position, and you may have special talents that enhance your abilities; but if you cannot get along with others, job success may escape you.

Value-Added Qualities

Critical Thinking

Think about...

the characteristics of a quality employee that you possess. How do you know these are qualities you possess?

There are specific personal traits and qualities that are considered to be valuable in the workplace. Think of these as **value-added qualities** because they *add value* to the assets you already possess, such as your technical skills, expertise, and work experience. You do not have to be the most popular, interesting, or entertaining person to be successful on the job. You simply need some positive characteristics that others expect and appreciate. These characteristics will not only help you get along with others, but they will also increase your chances for promotion. Your employer will expect you to get along with your coworkers so as not to reduce the productivity of your work area. Employers cannot afford to keep employees who interfere with the company's ability to get the job done. Consider these value-added qualities:

- Cheerfulness
- Empathy and sympathy
- Sense of humor
- Willingness to particpate
- Tactfulness

Cheerfulness

Cheerfulness is contagious. If one employee is cheerful, the mood will be "caught" by others. You can test this theory: Get into an elevator with several people and say something such as, "Isn't this weather wonderful!" Say this with a smile on your face, and look directly at several of the elevator occupants. Did you get some smiles? Did you get some agreement? Did you get someone else to make a cheerful remark?

Cheerfulness is contagious.

James Carroll/Stock, Boston

A cheerful atmosphere is a productive one. This is why employers try to hire, retain, and promote people who have a cheerful personality.

The single trait of cheerfulness will make your coworkers want to work with you. Think about the people whom you enjoy being around; chances are they are cheerful. A cheerful worker makes things less difficult, dispels gloom, makes others happy, and looks at the bright side.

Remind yourself each day to be cheerful. Cheerfulness will keep you in a positive frame of mind, and you will be happier with yourself and more pleasant to others. Try it. It is "catching." Cheerfulness is a quality you can *add* to make yourself a more valuable employee.

> 66 Those who bring sunshine to the lives of others cannot keep themselves from it. 99

Sense of Humor

Most people enjoy a good sense of humor. Yes, there is a place for humor in the workplace. How is your sense of humor? Is this a value-added characteristic you will take to the workplace? Do you appreciate humor? Do you appreciate the humor of others? Can you laugh at yourself?

A sense of humor is something you can cultivate if you feel it is a quality you lack. Typically, there are two reasons why people have little or no sense of humor. One, they may not appreciate humor most of the time. What appears to be funny to others is not funny to them. Two, they may not react when something appears to be funny to everyone else. When others are laughing, this person barely cracks a smile. Such a person may actually enjoy a funny joke or situation but does not show this enjoyment. If you think either or both of these situations describe you, work on them. If you do not see humor where others do, you will need to sharpen your sense of humor. This does not mean that you should begin laughing loudly every time someone else does. Don't act like you "get it" when you do not. Pretending will just make you feel foolish.

> 66 The sense of humor is the oil of life's engine. Without it, the machinery creaks and groans. 99
> —G.S. Merriam

Try these suggestions to develop your sense of humor:

1. Make every effort to look for humorous elements in mishaps and problems you may encounter. For example, if you trip on a sidewalk, think about how funny you must have looked when you tried to keep from falling. If you embarrass yourself by misspeaking, make every effort to laugh at your error after it is corrected. Realize that everyone sometimes says something that comes out differently than planned.

2. Ask a friend to explain a joke when you "don't get it." There is nothing wrong with admitting that you missed the punch line or failed to see the humor. For example, you may read a Gary

Larson FAR SIDE cartoon and miss the point because you do not have the scientific background to understand it.

3. Make a habit of watching comedies on television and seeing funny movies and plays. Discuss funny parts with others. This will help you become more sensitive to humor.

If you do not laugh when everyone else does, work at reacting to humor. Simply allow yourself to be more expressive. At first, it may make you feel uncomfortable to laugh aloud when you normally only smile or giggle. Keep in mind that laughing aloud is a good emotional release. With a little practice, you should be able to relax and bring your reactions up to a level that shows others you really do have a sense of humor. Think about the famous quote of Sir Max Beerbohm . . .

> 66 *Strange, when you come to think of it, that of all the countless folk who have lived before our time on this planet, not one is known in history or in legend as having died of laughter.* 99

As you work on your sense of humor, remember that jokes which are crude, poke fun at others, or put others down as individuals or groups are not in good taste anywhere—especially in the workplace.

Tactfulness

Tact is a sense of what to do or say in an effort to maintain good relations with others without offending them. It is knowing what to do or say at any given moment. Tact has been defined as the ability to change a porcupine into a possum, the ability to hammer home a point without hitting the other person on the head, or the ability to make your guests feel at home when you wish they were.

Tact involves understanding the other person's needs and wishes. You can make your life much easier for yourself and those around you by using tact as a value-added quality. You may be a tactful person by nature, or you may need to practice being more tactful. Wanting and intending to be tactful is not good enough. It takes good judgment and careful wording of your remarks. Take a look at a situation where tact is used and not used:

Situation: Myra, Clarise, and Katy are coworkers in a factory where being on time is important. Myra is late because she was involved in a traffic accident on the way to work. Myra is visibly upset by the incident.

Tactless: Clarise says: "Hi, Myra. It's about time you got here. I'm tired of covering for both of us. You look stressed out. What happened? Did you stay out too late last night?"

Tactful: Katy says: "Hi, Myra. Glad you're here. You look upset. Is everything okay? Here, have my coffee; I just poured it."

Who was more tactful? Clarise or Katy?

Think about the following situations, and describe how you might address them tactfully:

- finding out a caller's business before disturbing your supervisor

- asking a coworker about a close relative who has been ill

- telling a customer that your store policy does not allow sales merchandise to be returned

- asking for a promotion or raise

- asking the name of someone whose name you have forgotten

- asking a customer to pay a past due account

- helping to settle differences between two fellow workers without appearing to take sides

- telling your supervisor that you have found a better paying position

- making visitors feel at ease if they are kept waiting

Empathy and Sympathy

Another quality closely related to tact is empathy. **Empathy** is the ability to understand and feel another person's emotions or feelings—"to walk in another's shoes." For example, if you have a friend who has suffered the loss of a parent, you can understand his or her feelings of sadness if you have experienced the same loss. You have empathy. If you are sensitive to the feelings of others, you will try to make them feel at ease. The ability to make others feel at ease is important in getting along with others.

Everyone has problems of one kind or another that may influence the way they act in the workplace. The display of emotions or feelings by others may annoy or disturb you, but you must realize that there are reasons for their actions. Be empathetic: Try to understand their feelings.

There is a distinction between the words *empathy* and *sympathy*. Both terms have to do with how you respond to another person's

Empathy shows caring without becoming too emotionally involved.

emotions. Many people use the terms interchangeably, but the *difference* is real and important. **Sympathy** involves identifying with, and even taking on, another person's emotions. A sympathetic response is, "I'm furious about the new policy too." An empathetic response is, "I can understand how that policy makes you angry."

Responding to coworkers with sympathy can put you on an emotional roller coaster and leave you exhausted at the end of the day. It is appropriate to be emotionally aware and sensitive to the needs of others without becoming too emotionally involved. When you stay in control, you respond with empathy. This allows you to be ready, willing, and able to assist your coworker. Empathy permits you to be professional and caring at the same time.

S ilvia knew that Arthur, her coworker, was having a difficult time with his youngest daughter. At one point Arthur raised his voice at Silvia for not answering her phone immediately. Silvia recognized that Arthur was really shouting because of frustration about his personal life. This enabled Silvia to understand Arthur's outburst. Later Silvia asked Arthur to have a cup of coffee with her and gave him the opportunity to talk. Arthur appreciated Silvia's empathy.

Treat others as you would like to be treated. Take time to be kind to those with problems or troubles. Be sensitive to others' moods without intruding on their privacy. You may think that there is no room in the workplace for empathy, but this is not true. There is always time for an expression of empathy.

Willingness to Participate

As you grow in your ability to get along with your fellow workers, you may want to spend some time with them away from the job. Many employers have programs for just this purpose—bowling leagues, softball teams, company picnics, or tennis tournaments.

Participation can help you fit in and get along.

Michael Dwyer/Stock, Boston

In some companies employees can volunteer to participate in civic improvement activities. For example, companies may sponsor park cleanup days, transportation of senior citizens to the polls, or walk-a-thons for charitable organizations. As your schedule will allow, participate in as many of these activities as you can. You will make friends and work for public good. Working side-by-side with coworkers in community improvement activities will enhance your ability to fit in and get along. When you are called upon to contribute to charitable organizations, donate your time or money cheerfully. Your employer will recognize your willingness to help others.

Nonvalue-Added Qualities

Some positive value-added qualities have been discussed in the first part of this chapter. Now let's take a look at some of the negative traits you will want to *avoid* in order to achieve success on the job. These are

- Resentment
- Irritating habits
- Envy and jealousy
- Self-pity

Resentment

Nothing consumes a person more quickly than the harboring of resentment. **Resentment** is a feeling of displeasure over something that you consider wrong. Resentment, expressed openly, comes out as grumbling and complaining. Eventually the grumbler finds himself or herself alone and excluded by coworkers. Those who complain and grumble because they resent others, the workplace, or a specific situation are not pleasant people to be around. Eliminating this trait may require extra effort. You already know that cheerfulness is contagious; unfortunately, complaining is also contagious. If you constantly complain, you may be creating a very unhealthy work environment. Perhaps you resent a coworker who was promoted. Thinking about your resentment—dwelling on these feelings—will not help. When you find yourself complaining and grumbling on a continuous basis, do something about it! The best cure for this type of behavior is to take some positive action. Do something you enjoy. Do a part of your job that you find interesting, take a walk during your break or lunch period, go for a ride, or do anything that is fun for you. Combining action with enjoyment will overcome resentment and put the original cause for resentment in a better perspective.

Action + Enjoyment – Resentment = Proper Perspective

Illustration 4-1
Winning formula.

Another way to break the grumbling habit is to surround yourself with cheerful and positive people. This is another way to cure the "grumbling" disease.

Irritating Habits

Like it or not, you may have an irritating habit or two that you need to eliminate in order to fit in and get along. You may not always recognize your own unwelcome, annoying habits. Check the following list to see if you have any habits that could be offensive to others:

- Clearing your throat continually

- Popping or snapping gum

- Fiddling with your hair

- Sniffing

- Playing with jewelry

- Constantly adjusting your clothing

- Whispering when others are talking

Critical Thinking

Think about...

other irritating habits you have observed and add them to the list. Ask a close friend to check you against the list. Do the same for your friend.

- Jiggling change or keys in your pocket

- Tapping your fingers or a pen/pencil

- (Add others) _____

_____

Mario and Kari shared a small office. Mario was continually irritated because every time a customer called with an unusual or seemingly unreasonable request, Kari would slam the phone down at the end of the conversation. Mario finally lost his cool and said, "Kari, I wish you would quit slamming the phone down at the end of conversations. I find that very annoying!" Kari looked at Mario and said, "I wish you would stop popping your gum. I find that very annoying." Kari and Mario both smiled. They realized at the same moment that everyone has a habit or two that others may find unpleasant.

When you discover you have irritating or objectionable habits, work to eliminate them. To drop an undesirable habit, be aware that you practice it. Desire to get rid of it; then stop it.

Envy and Jealousy

The closely related feelings of envy and jealousy are two of life's most destructive emotions. If you want to fit in and get along, these traits need to be controlled. Each time you feel these emotions in the workplace, think about the old adage, "Every time you turn green with envy, you're ripe for trouble." **Envy** is wanting something some-

Expressing happiness for accomplishments of coworkers will give you positive feelings.

Critical Thinking

Think about...

a situation where you observed envy or jealousy to be a destructive emotion. What were the effects?

❝ Don't just envy another's good fortune; duplicate the work that helped earn it. ❞

one else has. **Jealousy** is feeling a rivalry toward one whom you believe has an advantage over you. In our highly competitive world, these feelings often occur. You may never eliminate these emotions completely, but you can continually accept the advantages enjoyed by others and express happiness over the accomplishments of coworkers. The key is to be glad for others and hope for the same or similar rewards for yourself, but not at the expense of others. If you can become the kind of person who is pleased when you hear words of praise for someone else, you will have taken a giant step toward your own emotional health. If this step is not taken, you can become consumed with envy and jealousy that could destroy any happiness or pleasure you might experience with your coworkers.

Often you may find yourself having to share honors you feel rightfully belong to you. You must realize that your superior or coworkers may be praised for your work, ideas, contributions, or plans. Developing an unselfish attitude is not easy. Try to eliminate feelings of envy and jealousy by helping another person accomplish a goal and then praising that person. This is the way to begin. You can receive great pleasure from the success of someone you have helped.

Self-Pity

If you wish to fit in and get along, dump your feelings of self-pity. **Self-pity** is feeling sorry for yourself and your situation without looking at the good things in your life. If you talk continually about your problems and dwell on them, others will get tired of hearing about them, and you will be dragged down by them also. If you have a habit of the "poor little me" syndrome, get rid of it. "Pity parties" can result when this trait takes over. The bad thing about a pity party is that no one else wants to attend. Every now and then you will naturally feel sorry for yourself. Recognize your self-pity, and put a time limit on how long you are going to let these feelings last. Then turn your thoughts to the things in your life that are working well for you, and focus on your successes.

How much of this dialogue would you like to listen to?

> I'm so tired. I work here all day and then go home and work evenings. Then I get up and start all over again. My neighbor stays home all day and has time to play cards and golf. I'll never have that kind of luxury. I wish I made more money so that I could buy some new clothes. I get tired of wearing the same old things day after day. My old car is about to give out. It's developed a clanking noise; I'm sure it's going to need expensive repairs. Everything costs so much to repair these days.

66 What poison is to food, self-pity is to life. 99
—Oliver C. Wilson

This kind of self-pity talk can be exhausting to those around you and to you. If others seem to be avoiding you, think about what you have said in the past few days. Does your conversation sound like the previous paragraph?

Summary

As you read through this chapter, you probably mentally listed your value-added qualities—the qualities you possess, those you will need to improve upon, and those you will need to develop. This is the first step in fitting in and getting along in the workplace. Each day analyze how you did.

1. Was I cheerful today?

2. Did I display a sense of humor?

3. Did I use tact with others?

4. Was I empathetic?

5. Was I willing to participate?

The negative traits to avoid need daily analysis also.

1. Do I have any irritating habits?

2. Did I have feelings of envy or jealousy?

3. Did I indulge in self-pity?

If your goal is to be successful in the workplace, fitting in and getting along is essential.

End of Chapter Activities

Questions and Projects

1. What qualities or characteristics do you like or look for when you choose friends? List these qualities.

2. Measure your cheerfulness ability. For two weeks keep a log of cheerful statements or actions that you say or do. At the end of each day during the first week, log any cheerful remarks or actions that you delivered to others. During the second week, make an extra effort to be cheerful; think cheerful thoughts, look for ways to cheer up others, and go out of your way to brighten another's day. Does your log have more entries in Week 2? List what you can do to assure that being cheerful will soon become a fixed part of your personality.

3. Read the comics section of a Sunday newspaper. Share the humor of two of your favorite cartoons or comic strips with a friend or coworker. This will help you get in the habit of sharing humor.

4. Have you ever had a "pity party?" How long did it last? What brought about the self-pitying mood? How could you have avoided these feelings of self-pity?

5. Write a paragraph on why envy and jealousy are often called the destructive emotions. You may want to refer to your own life experiences or the experiences of others.

6. As a result of reading this chapter, have you set any new goals for yourself? If so, list them and describe how you plan to reach them.

Case Problems

1. Irritation in the Library

Marty works in the reference section of the city library. His senior coworker, Melissa, is very sensitive to noise and is easily irritated by it. Marty has a habit of chewing gum loudly and popping it. This annoys Melissa and she discusses the situation with Sergio, her supervisor. Melissa tells Sergio that Marty must be reprimanded or dismissed for this behavior because she simply "cannot stand working near him" with his annoying habit.

a. Should Melissa have reported this situation to Sergio? If not, what else should she do?

b. Would your answer to question (a) be different if the workplace were a factory rather than a library?

c. Can Marty correct this habit? How?

d. What should Sergio say to Marty if he chooses to discuss this with him?

e. If you were Sergio, what would you say to Melissa after she had explained her problem to you?

2. Participation

Angela Graham is a new checker at the Hi-Low Supermarket. She is good at her job. She enjoys helping customers. She is described as efficient, prompt, and skilled. She has an excellent understanding of the computerized inventory system used by the market. Mark McKenzie, the store manager, asks Angela to join the market's bowling team. Angela's reply is, "I don't bowl!" A few days later Katy, a fellow checker, asks Angela to join the other checkers in cleaning up a neighborhood park. Angela's reply is, "I have my own cleaning to do."

a. How would you interpret Angela's responses?

b. What additional information about Angela would help you decide if there are other reasons why she is choosing not to participate?

c. Should Mark insist that Angela be a "participating" employee?

d. Who should make the final decision on whether or not to participate in activities sponsored by a company?

3. Contagious Attittude

Edward has been a productive worker in an automobile assembly plant for seven years. He enjoys his work and his coworkers. Edith, his newest coworker, seems to have many problems. She is a single parent with two children, who are having difficulty in school. She is responsible for an elderly mother, and she feels that her salary is not adequate. Each day she finds fault with the weather, the government, the plant, and life in general.

Edward listens empathetically to Edith during break periods and hears her negative muttering while they are on the job. He begins to notice that her attitude is affecting his. He thinks of the negative aspects of life and starts to feel a general dissatisfaction with the workplace.

Edward recognizes the change and decides he must do something about it.

a. What would you suggest that Edward do?

b. Based on what you know about Edith, do you believe that her feelings about life are justified?

c. How could Edith help herself enjoy life more?

d. Should Edith's attitude be of concern to plant management?

Working With Coworkers

D anielle had been employed as a receiving clerk for a large department store for five years.

Her immediate supervisor frequently complimented her efficiency. Danielle did not join her coworkers for breaks or lunch. She chose to take a walk, balance her checkbook, or catch up on family correspondence. Her coworkers, after asking her numerous times to join them, decided that she was antisocial and perhaps a little "stuck up." A new position was created in the shipping-receiving department, and Danielle felt she was qualified for this promotion. She was interviewed for the position but was not offered the job. When she asked her supervisor, Thomas, why she was not selected, he explained tactfully that she was perceived as not being a team player.

You are aware from what you have already read in this text that your ability to succeed and be promoted often depends upon how well you get along with your coworkers. On the job, getting the work done is a team effort. You will enjoy your work more if you have a good relationship with your fellow employees, and the productivity of the work team will be improved. The supervisor, of course, is also an important member of this working team. The importance of establishing an appropriate relationship with your supervisor is discussed in Chapter 6.

Objectives

After completing this chapter, you should be able to:

1.
Describe the personality traits conducive to working with others.

2.
Describe the importance of being a team player.

3.
Recognize the traits of the nonteam player.

4.
Describe the techniques used to get along with difficult coworkers.

To better understand how important it is to get along with coworkers, imagine that you are a member of the bucket brigade engaged in putting out a fire. A long line of people pass the buckets of water from a stream at one end to the fire at the other. Each person in the brigade is an important element in putting the fire out. So it is in the workplace. Everyone has an important role in getting a job done.

Keys To Getting Along With Others

Wouldn't it be terrific if you could choose the persons with whom you work each day? Unfortunately people are not hired because they have similar interests, personalities, and backgrounds. Rather, they are hired because they have the specific skills and knowledge to get a job done. Therefore, establishing a harmonious working team is not always an easy task. No two people are alike. Those with whom you work may perceive things very differently from the way you do. They may have values, habits, traits, and beliefs that are different or in conflict with yours.

Your behavior as a worker impacts, directly or indirectly, on everyone else in the workplace. Whatever you do matters: the way you perform your job, the way you speak, the way you feel, and even the way you look. All of these things influence, in one way or another, the general effectiveness of your work group. It is necessary that you carry out your job tasks properly and work to develop desirable traits that will help produce "team spirit." Coworkers are counting on you— just as you are counting on them. There are some personality traits or characteristics that are vital to helping you get along well with your coworkers.

Cooperation

One key to working with others is to be cooperative. **Cooperation** is the ability to work smoothly with others. It is also going out of your way to help others and helping when you have a few free moments. Cooperation is like a savings account. It may not pay immediate dividends; yet if deposits are made regularly, the dividends will eventually pay off. As with a savings account, cooperation may demand that you give up short-term conveniences for the sake of future rewards.

Cooperation may be a simple act of sharing your materials or equipment with a coworker. It may mean

■ helping to cover the territory of another salesperson

■ going out of your way to help a customer or coworker

- holding back when you want to disagree

- being a good sport when you have lost a sale

- showing tolerance in listening to the ideas of others when your own ideas seem superior

In all careers you will be expected to cooperate often and in varied circumstances. For example, you may be asked to

- work overtime willingly

- offer services even when you are not obligated to do so

- surrender your own ideas if someone else's are better for the welfare of the work team

- inform others of devices or ideas that may make their work easier

- pass on ideas or results of your experiences to others

- listen to others when they try to help you as a result of their experience

- work harmoniously with others to advance the interests of the work team

Politeness

Positive body language and pleasant words are very powerful in developing a good work environment. Expressions of **politeness** are signals to others that you care about them and appreciate them. And, more importantly, they indicate to others that you think they are important.

 yle's morning was not off to a good start. His uniform was missing a button, his boots were scuffed, and the breakfast food box was empty. He got caught in the rain between home and the bus stop without an umbrella. He tripped on a crack in the sidewalk, ripped his trousers, and scraped his knee. As he entered the work area, he was greeted with a big smile and a cheerful "good morning" by his coworker, Bella. Kyle couldn't help responding to this warm greeting in the same manner, and he began to feel better immediately.

Politeness contributes to a pleasant, cooperative working environment.

Patience

Not everyone "catches on" to tasks and routines at the same rate. Try to remain calm as you help a coworker with a new process even when you must explain the process more than once. Be patient when coworkers ask questions that you believe are unnecessary. A less-than-patient attitude may lead to conflict and a negative work environment. Lack of patience will also guarantee you a high level of frustration.

When your patience is running thin, take a deep breath and do some self-talk: "Take it easy." "Don't lose your patience." "I can do this." "Let's try it one more time."

Sheila was explaining the fringe benefits package available from the company to Paul, a new employee. The package was somewhat complex because it included information about health and life insurance, the retirement plan, and profit sharing. Because this was Paul's first job, he was not familiar with the terms used to describe fringe benefits programs. After Sheila had completed her explanation, she asked Paul if he had any questions. Paul had many questions that Sheila felt she had already answered. Although Sheila answered Paul's questions, her body language let Paul know she didn't like the questions. Paul said, "If you didn't want to answer my questions, why did you ask if I had any?" Sheila replied, "If you had been paying attention, you wouldn't have needed to ask any questions."

Sheila and Paul each lost their patience. Much repair work will need to be done on the relationship before Sheila and Paul will be comfortable working together.

As you prepare for the workplace, keep in mind, "An ounce of patience is worth a pound of brains."

Enthusiasm

Enthusiasm is a very contagious feeling. If you are enthusiastic, it seems to spread to others. **Enthusiasm** means to inject energy into your work. People who are enthusiastic are inspired to do their work. They enjoy what they are doing, and it shows. If you are enthusiastic and eager about your work, this will often cause others to get work done more quickly and easily.

Emma said, "This is an impossible task. How can we separate all of these charts and graphs and make any sense of them? I just don't want to do this; it's impossible." Murray enthusiastically replied, "I think if we work together, we can make some sense of this information in short order. Let's get to it, get it done, and move on to more pleasant tasks."

Murray's enthusiasm and spirit of cooperativeness will spread and inspire Emma, and the task will be completed.

If you do not look forward to going to your workplace and cannot express genuine enthusiasm about your job, it is time to look for other employment. You will be doing yourself and others a great favor.

Dependability

Another key to getting along with coworkers is the ability to be dependable. Teamwork is based on the ability of one worker to depend upon another. Think of mountain climbing teams. The life of one climber may depend upon the actions of another. Their teamwork is built upon dependability. The same is true in the workplace.

Teamwork is based on the ability of one worker to depend upon another.

Peter Menzel/Stock, Boston

A dependable coworker should be able to answer the following questions with a "yes."

- Can your coworkers count on you to be punctual?

- Do you have a good attendance record?

- Do you complete tasks on time?

- Do you follow through on requests?

- Can coworkers depend upon you to assist them if they get overloaded with work?

Loyalty

Demaris works for McDuff Tool Manufacturing. She frequently tells members of the community that quality-control measures are nonexistent at McDuff. She tells anyone who will listen that McDuff products are overpriced. Demaris has announced publicly that she wouldn't buy anything produced in that place.

Loyalty is believing in your place of employment and having a commitment to it. Obviously Demaris is not a loyal employee. She does not respect McDuff Tool Manufacturing. Demaris believes that McDuff pays for her time and effort to work in the plant. She does not think she is paid for loyalty to the company. If you have questions about the quality of products or services of your employer, discuss your concerns with the employer.

Loyalty goes beyond a respect for your employer. Loyalty is key to getting along with your coworkers. Your coworkers count on you for support and commitment just as your employer does. This means supporting your coworkers by helping them. Ignore or correct gossip about coworkers. Support their efforts whenever appropriate. Would you remain friends with a person who always tells others about your faults and secrets? You probably would not. You want and expect your friends to be loyal. The same expectations hold true for coworkers. Loyalty and faithfulness to your workplace are important to your success on the job. If you are not loyal to your coworkers and do not promote the place where you work, you may be in the wrong job.

Building the Self-Esteem of Others

Another key to working with coworkers is to do whatever you can to bolster the self-esteem of others. Positive remarks, simple gestures, or the demonstration of an interest in others can do a lot to enhance how others feel. Think about how you feel when someone pays you an honest compliment. Wouldn't you like to share that feeling with others? Positive people will provide a great work environment. Review the following list of tips for some ideas for building the self-esteem of others.

Critical Thinking

Think about...

someone who has helped to build your self-esteem. How could you bolster the self-esteem of a friend in need?

- Give the "okay" sign when you agree with others.

- Give the "thumbs up" signal to show support to others.

- Use their names when talking to them.

- Pay deserved compliments.

- Pass on compliments from third parties.

- Inquire about their interests.

- Say "hello," "goodbye," "please," and "thank you."

- Ask them for help.

- Write down their ideas.

- Ask their opinions.

An effort to be cooperative, polite, patient, enthusiastic, dependable, loyal, and supportive of others will go a long way as you work to get along with coworkers. As you develop these characteristics, you will set an example for others. Remember, it is not fair to expect others to demonstrate these traits unless you are willing to exhibit them also.

Your Position On The Team

Teamwork is based on the key traits of getting along with others. Think of yourself as playing a certain position on your organization's team. No single employee, no matter how good he or she may be, can make a company successful. As an employee, make it your business to be a team player. Do not focus on what great work *you* can do. Focus on what great work your company can do because you are part of the team.

For example, your job may be keeping records. If it is, make sure that these records are accurate and thoroughly checked. If you are a shipping clerk, see that each order is filled perfectly; see that there is no slip-up in your part of the team play. If you write the first draft of a report, check the information that goes into the report. Do your very best to see that the report is written as well as you can do it. Remember, like the player in a football game who throws a forward pass, you pass your part of the report to the person who will write or

Everyone in the workplace is important, no matter what the job entails.

Gale Zucker/Stock, Boston

dictate the final draft. That person will make the touchdown, but you will be the team member who made it possible for someone else to catch the ball and carry it over the line. You can see why, as a worker, you must understand why people behave as they do. Computers may supply facts and figures, but people still make the business enterprise go—or break down. Being a good team player every day is a tough job. Some days you will not feel well, or you will be worried about something that happened at home. Do your best everyday; others are counting on you.

As you think of yourself as a team player, keep in mind that there are some "don'ts." These are some pitfalls that you should carefully avoid.

Don't Take Advantage of Coworkers

It will be necessary at times to ask a coworker to assist you in some way or to take care of some of your assigned responsibilities. However, you should never take advantage of another or shirk your own work.

E velyn was a new administrative assistant in a large insurance company. After several days on the job, she was feeling very comfortable with her work and the relationships she was developing with coworkers. Jeanette was especially helpful to her during those first rough days. During Evelyn's third week, Jeanette explained to her that she needed to be away from the office for a few minutes to take care of a personal business matter. She asked Evelyn to skip her break and cover her phone while she was out for a few minutes. Evelyn was happy to help out. Evelyn was somewhat concerned, however, that whenever she had an opportunity for a break, Jeanette always seemed to need help at her desk and left Evelyn to handle both jobs.

It was obvious that Jeanette was taking advantage of a new employee. This type of arrangement is not conducive to teamwork. When someone does assist you with your work, be sure to thank them and return the favor whenever possible. It is not necessary, however, to allow someone to take advantage of you. Nor do you want to take advantage of others.

Don't Speak Before You Think

You should feel comfortable about expressing your ideas when you think they are appropriate. It is important to use good judgment in deciding when you should speak up and when it is better to keep silent. There may be some situations that you should protest, but you should also listen to the ideas of your coworkers, supervisors, or customers. Many times others will see a perspective that you may have overlooked. If a decision is made and your ideas are overruled or rejected, you must abide by the decision of the majority in a cheerful manner.

A good working environment depends on speaking—when to speak, when not to speak, what to say, and what not to say—when working for advancement. But it is true that sometimes silence is golden. Consider the following tips for speaking in the workplace:

1. A beginning worker should be slow to suggest changes in working procedures. Before you make such suggestions, study the reasons for the present processes. You might learn why your changes would not be practical at the moment. Suggesting changes just to prove you are alert and aware of current practices can be detrimental to you.

2. When you do speak up, come directly to the point. If explanations are essential, organize them in a logical fashion. State your case, and answer the questions that result from your comments. It may be that your employer will welcome your suggestions.

3. If you find that your supervisors have different ideas on the subject, respect and abide by their decisions. It will not be in your best interest to argue or refuse to cooperate.

Remember, be sure to set your mind in gear before engaging your tongue.

Don't Let Your Emotions Get Ahead of You

Thinking first is important when you are preparing to speak. No one can hope to be 100 percent objective—even part of the time.

Critical Thinking

Think about...

a situation in which your attitudes and emotions affected negatively your communication with a friend or family member. How were you feeling at the time? Can positive self-talk help you in the future?

Your feelings, emotions, and attitudes can interfere. Also, people sometimes do things and say things for unconscious reasons. Be on guard for this possibility. If you are promoted to a new and difficult job, for example, you may find yourself in a state of panic. If this should happen, consider the real source of your fears. They may be caused by an excessive desire to be perfect. In others words, you may be afraid of failure and not afraid of the job. You can then address your panic with some positive reinforcement and self-talk. Reassure yourself that mistakes will almost surely occur at first. The expected, you see, is not so frightening as the unexpected, and you may find your fears disappearing.

Don't Make Hasty Judgments about Others

Understanding the possible reasons for others' behavior will keep you from making unfair or hasty judgments about coworkers. If Mo's desk is next to yours and he challenges everything you say, it may be tempting to stop speaking to him altogether. But this will not solve your problem, and it will not help build team spirit. Attempt to figure out why Mo feels the need to contradict and challenge your comments and decisions. He may feel inferior to you. He may feel extremely insecure in his position. He may have no idea how to seek help for real or imagined inadequacies. You can help by providing reassurance now and then. Your help may stop the challenges he tosses at you.

Your coworkers are struggling along in life just as you are. Sometimes unattractive personality traits cover up a reality that is the exact opposite. The clown may be unhappy; the braggart may be insecure; the person who laughs too much may be shy; the aggressive person may not feel well; the excessively sweet person may be covering up a true dislike of people. Give others a chance before passing judgment.

Understand And Use Group Psychology

Now let's talk about how you can understand, get along with, and even help others to fit in as members of a working team. Most workplaces are made up of groups of people. If you work now or plan to work someday, you should learn as much as you can about group psychology or, as it is sometimes called, group dynamics. What makes groups tick? How does group behavior differ from individual behavior? Why is the study of group behavior important?

The study of group behavior is important because whatever you do affects the way someone else in your group feels. When your actions make others feel positively toward you and toward the group, you help others do a more effective job. When your actions cause friction and bad feelings in the group, you hold others back from doing their best work. Thus, your actions will diminish the effectiveness of your group. You then need to work on yourself. Be the kind of person who brings out the best in people in the group, not one who contributes to the problems that may exist when people work closely together.

Helping the Problem Coworker

Even if you personally do not create problems in your group, what do you do to help others?

Many groups have members with personal insecurities, negative attitudes, or closed minds. Consider the following two suggestions to help the problem person in your group.

1. Share with the worker who has a problem some problem you had when you first joined the group. Most of us go through an adjustment period when first joining any kind of work or social group. Perhaps you had a hard time adjusting to so many different personalities or felt inferior when everyone else seemed to be so much more competent than you. If you can encourage the troubled group member to open up to you, his or her troubles become less troublesome.

2. Comment favorably on something someone else did to make the work go more smoothly or to help get things done.

Shaping is the theory behind changing a group so that it works better. Shaping means that you pay no attention to irritating things the group member does, but you give reward or praise for the things said and done that are helpful and correct. Most of the difficulties people have when they become part of a group are caused by lack of confidence. Praise is a good confidence builder.

Shaping = Rewarding + Praising – Acknowledging Irritating Things

Shaping = More Confident Person

Illustration 5-1
Shaping formula.

Shirley wears clothing that is too showy for the work environment. Her dresses are sequined, her jewelry is more appropriate for evening wear, and her heels are too high for comfort. Shirley has become the talk of the work group. She doesn't understand why her coworkers avoid her. What sort of shaping activities could you engage in to help Shirley?

When you want to help make a change in your coworkers, you may decide to proceed indirectly. People do not like to be forced to do things—even if it is for their own good. Shaping works best when the technique begins with you. When you are more truthful in dealing with your coworkers, that truthfulness becomes catching. In an organization where everyone is truthful and considerate of others' feelings, bad relationships that can hurt a group's effectiveness are minimized. Work no longer seems like work in such an organization. It becomes a very pleasant activity.

How to Talk with Complainers

Most groups have one or more complainers. The complainer can be a very dangerous member of the working team because complaining can be highly contagious. It is important to feed the complainer positive and cheerful statements whenever possible. Whatever you do, do not let the complainer influence your thinking so that you become a complainer too. Consider the following strategies for dealing with the complainers you know:

1. Attempt to minimize the other person's troubles. You might say, "Now is your problem really that serious?" or "Don't take everything so hard." This technique may not be effective with some complainers who may feel that you are not willing to listen.

2. Repeat the complaint but in different words. Suppose the complaining coworker says to you, "I'd like to take the day off. I'm tired of working on this stupid project. Byron has been on my case all day." You might respond, "I can tell Byron has made you unhappy and that this day is not going well for you." This technique is an attempt to put the person's feeling into words. By doing this, you are not saying that you agree with the feelings or that you condone the outburst, but you do let the complainer know that you understand the feelings behind the complaints. Counselors use this technique, commonly called a **nondirective approach**, to reflect back what the person has said. This approach eliminates your natural tendency to give advice, to agree with, to preach, to take sides, or to defend the complainer. The nondirective approach also has positive benefits for the complainer. It draws out negative feelings and provides an opportunity for the complainer to pause, take stock of the situation, and think it through.

How to Talk with Angry Coworkers

Anger is an unpleasant but common behavior in the workplace. If you talk with someone who is angry, use the nondirective approach. Take responsibility for your actions when a coworker yells or expresses anger at you. For example, in response to "Why did you leave that file drawer open for me to trip over! How can you be so careless?" answer calmly, "I did leave the file drawer open. I'm sorry I was careless." Admitting your own faults is almost guaranteed to defuse some of the anger of your coworker. You must keep all traces of sarcasm from your voice as you give your calm reply. Any other response or increase in the tone of your voice may escalate the anger. Bad feelings and conflict between people do not just happen. There is usually a cause. Without knowing it, you may be part of the cause. If you can take the giant step of admitting your part in causing the trouble, you will help the other person take the equally hard step of admitting to a share of the blame.

❝Anger is the wind that blows out the light of reason.❞

The nondirective approach toward talking with angry coworkers helps diffuse emotion so conflict can be discussed calmly.

Other Character Types in the Work Group

Most working groups have several types of characters. These characters may be recognizable at once, or they may be hiding behind a false front. This is one reason why you should take your time in joining one of the many groups you will encounter in the workplace.

Along with the problem coworker, the complainer, and the angry coworker, you will encounter other characters in the work group. The following paragraphs describe some of the typical characters and give suggestions on how you may interact with them.

The Grouch. Generally every group has a grouch. Remember that the grouch is not mad at you. Usually the causes for the grouch's behavior and feelings are unrelated to the workplace. Physical problems, family conflicts, or financial troubles may cause the grouch's behavior. Also, some people have little or no reason for their grouchy moods and seem never to have an interest in changing their behavior. If you are pleasant and caring and refuse to take the grouch's complaining personally, you may help such a person become less of a grouch.

The Tattletale. You can recognize a tattletale by the stories told about other employees. Do not tell your own stories about other employees, no matter what the provocation. Gossip is unwise at any time, but gossip with a tattletale can be disastrous. When the tattletale starts telling you some tale about another person, be polite but firm. You might say, "I don't want you to share that information with me," or "Why are you telling me this?" Or say you have work to do and do not have time to talk. The tattletale will leave you alone if he or she does not find you to be a receptive audience.

The Bossy Nonboss. This person criticizes everything you do (and everything others do too). The nonboss has suggestions and recommendations for everyone in the workplace. These bossy coworkers are primarily dissatisfied with themselves. Calling attention to the faults of others is just a way of trying to feel satisfied with themselves. Pay little or no attention to the suggestions of the bossy person who is your coworker. Do your work to the best of your ability. You are responsible only to complete your tasks to the satisfaction of your assigned supervisor (boss).

The Favorite. The employee labeled "the favorite" is the one who seems to have the "inside track" with the supervisor. Avoid labeling a coworker as a favorite. Your coworker may have a good rapport with the supervisor because he or she is a quality worker. Recognize the good qualities of the coworker and emulate them. Avoid the name calling. If you find yourself as "the favorite," it is important not to capitalize on such favoritism. Continue to treat your supervisor with respect and a formality that indicates respect.

The Arguer. You may have coworkers who actually enjoy an argument. When you meet the arguer, arm yourself with two ingredients— relaxation and patience. If someone makes a controversial statement or attempts to get you to argue, RELAX. Consciously let your muscles

Critical Thinking

Think about...

a gossip or tattletale you know at school or work. How could you discourage that person from sharing information with you in the future?

go limp. Then patiently wait and listen until you have heard the whole story. Many arguments are merely the result of not letting the other person finish. Decide to say nothing until your "opponent" has finished talking. By that time, particularly if you are relaxed, you will find yourself much less likely to say something rash, something that might hurt the other person's feelings, or something that will increase the level of the conflict. Perhaps you can help "the arguer" realize that arguing is not conducive to a good work environment.

Garth says, "I don't understand why you won't support our efforts requesting management to allow us to change our summer work hours from 7 a.m. to 4 p.m. rather than the usual 8 to 5. What's wrong with you? Don't you want to support your coworkers? Are you trying to become the favored employee? What are you doing, bucking for a promotion?" Abigail is tempted to defend herself several times. However, she takes a deep breath and tells herself to relax and let Garth finish. Then she replies as calmly as possible, "I understand that you would like to change the work hours this summer. This time adjustment would not work for me as my child-care arrangements are not available at 7 a.m. I hope you respect my point of view."

After Abigail expressed her thoughts, she removed herself from the area and went back to work. She did not escalate the argument by raising her voice or by becoming defensive. She simply stated her position and feeling. It may be difficult for Abigail to overlook Garth's harsh words, but based on the way she handled the situation, she may even get an apology from him.

Summary

This chapter has pointed out to you the importance of getting along with your coworkers. Each day in the workplace, you will need to work to show a cooperative spirit; exercise politeness in dealings with others; demonstrate patience, dependability, and loyalty; and build the self-esteem of others.

You will recognize that to be happy in your job, you will need to be a team player. If you are a team player, you will not

1. Take advantage of coworkers.

2. Speak before you think.

3. Let your emotions get ahead of you.

4. Make hasty judgments about others.

5. Make hasty decisions about the actions of others.

You will recognize the problem coworkers and deal with them using such techniques as shaping and the nondirective approach.

End of Chapter Activities

Questions and Projects

1. Use the nondirective approach with someone you know when they complain to you. Record the situation, your nondirective comment, and the reaction of the complainer.

2. List the five characteristics you would like the person working most closely to you to have. Compare your list with others. Rate yourself on each characteristic on a scale of 1 to 10 with 10 being the highest rating. List the qualities you have that would make you a good coworker.

3. Find or develop cartoons that depict "the grouch," "the complain-er," "the arguer," and "the nonboss."

4. This chapter emphasized that making incorrect perceptions about people can be dangerous and lead to conflict. What perceptions have you made about others that turned out not to be true? Did your perceptions lead to conflict? How did you discover that your perceptions were not accurate?

5. Luke works in a furniture store. He is so enthusiastic about his responsibilities that he steps all over his coworkers in an attempt to get to the customers first. He does not notice the negative reactions of his coworkers. Luke and his coworkers are paid on commission. If you were one of Luke's coworkers, how would you handle this problem? Whose problem is this? What changes does Luke or his coworkers need to make in their behavior?

6. The way to avoid an argument is to relax and wait for the whole story. The next time you are tempted to argue with someone, say nothing. Just be patient and listen. Write down the results of your experience. Did you accomplish anything? Do you feel this is a helpful solution for you?

7. As a coworker concerned about getting along, what action would you take in the following situation? Mimi has worked at Jessons Sporting Equipment for the past week. Mimi notices that several of her coworkers make a big deal of going to lunch on Friday. They do not ask Mimi to join them. Mimi should:

____ run after the group and ask to be included.

____ send them a memo and ask why she was not included.

____ be patient and give people a chance to get to know her better before taking any action.

What additional information about this situation would be helpful to you in determining what Mimi should do?

8. A birthday party for the supervisor is being planned. A sheet with all the employees' names on it is being passed around. People mark whether or not they plan to attend. Donovan is a new employee. The sheet is passed to him, but his name is not on it. Donovan should:

____ tell the person who made up the sheet that his name was forgotten.

____ add his name to the list and mark whether or not he plans to attend.

____ assume that he is not wanted at the birthday celebration.

9. Few of us could live happily without friends. Try the following steps in winning new friends:

a. All day Monday smile at those you meet at school or work. Praise at least one person you greet.

b. On Tuesday relay a kind or an encouraging word to every close associate you talk to during the day.

c. On Wednesday seek out someone in need of a friend and invite that person to do something with you.

d. On Thursday choose a stranger to talk with, discussing only that person's interests—not yours.

e. On Friday write a friendly letter to someone.

Evaluate the experiences of the week. Do you feel more friendly with someone? Has anyone made friendly overtures to you? Would a similar approach to gaining acceptance by your coworkers work?

Case Problems

1. Gregg, the Grouch

Your coworker, Gregg, begins the morning by telling you that you should not have parking lot privileges as you have been with the company only a short time. A few minutes later Gregg growls that you spend too much time away from your desk. At midmorning Gregg comes by and says that he thinks the room temperature is set too high, and he is going to complain to management. He asks you in early afternoon who you are trying to impress by keeping your suit coat on all day. You note that you are not the only victim of Gregg's comments. He makes similar remarks to others.

a. Is Gregg angry or unhappy with you?

b. How can you help Gregg be a comfortable member of the working team?

c. What can you say in response to Gregg's comments to you?

d. Is Gregg dangerous to the success of the work team?

2. To Cover or Not to Cover

Arnie Baum, one of your coworkers, has been asking you to "cover" for him while he takes extended lunch breaks. In addition, he leaves his desk for 30 to 45 minutes during peak telephone hours. You make every attempt to answer his calls, but sometimes it is difficult. Today he called in before the office opened. He asked to speak to you. Arnie said that his car broke down and that he would be late for work. He asked you to "punch in" for him so that he would not lose any pay.

a. Will you punch in for Arnie? Why or why not?

b. Is Arnie violating any of the basic rules of working with others? If so, what are they?

c. Should you discuss this situation with Arnie? With your supervisor? If so, what would you say to Arnie? What would you say to your supervisor?

3. Gaining Acceptance

Lydia is a new salesperson at Gold's Department Store. She is working in the men's clothing department with five other employees. Lydia was informed that all price tags were to be saved and then sorted at the end of the day. It took approximately 20 minutes to sort the tags. Lydia felt this was a stupid process. She designed a box with punched holes that made it easy to sort the tags after each sale. She presented the process to the other employees and encouraged them to begin using it immediately. The other employees did not accept the idea since they liked getting in the extra time after work. They also felt that it slowed down the selling process and took time from the customers. Lydia and her ideas were ignored. Lydia did not like this type of treatment and quit.

a. Did Lydia (who needed a job) do the right thing?

b. Was the new method of sorting a good idea? Why or why not?

c. How could Lydia have gained acceptance of the new idea?

d. What steps could Lydia have taken to be accepted again as a part of the sales team?

Getting Along With Your Supervisor

R aymond and Alfred are coworkers at Awards Magnified, a company that designs, produces, and sells trophies, plaques, and other recognition items. Raymond is the manager in charge of design and production. Alfred is responsible for the salesroom and catalog orders. Larry Hilligas, owner and general manager, is away from the company a good deal. Hilligas feels that the company is in good hands with his two managers. He spends his days recruiting customers and searching for new markets.

Raymond enjoys his work very much. He likes the freedom given to him by the general manager. He selects the design equipment and raw materials. As long as he can justify his decisions to Hilligas, no questions are asked. Alfred does not like working at Awards Magnified. He works long hours. He feels that Hilligas gives him too much responsibility. Alfred frequently says, "I don't get paid enough for the type of decisions I have to make! Hilligas should hang around here once in awhile and find out how tough this business really is!" Mr. Hilligas is very complimentary about the work of his managers. How can two people working for the same person feel so differently about their employment?

Your future in the work world may hinge on your ability to establish a good working relationship with your supervisor. Your supervisor will determine whether you are retained, promoted, or terminated. A good working relation-

Objectives

After completing this chapter, you should be able to:

1.
Describe the basic management styles.

2.
Understand the importance of relating to your supervisor.

3.
Demonstrate how to take a problem to your supervisor.

4.
Demonstrate how to seek, accept, and handle deserved and undeserved criticism.

Critical Thinking

Think about...

what you would do if you were Raymond and you wanted to help Alfred change his attitude about working at Awards Magnified.

" Basically the problem of management is to produce more goods and services for satisfying people's wants at prices more people can afford to pay. "

—Paul Garrett

ship with your supervisor does not mean apple-polishing, conniving, or manipulating to assure that you are in good standing with him or her. A good relationship between you and your supervisor means making a conscious effort to manage your relationship so that it achieves the best possible results for you, your supervisor, and the organization that pays both your salaries. Your relationship with the supervisor should be one of mutual respect.

Know Your Supervisor

A **supervisor**, for discussion purposes in this chapter, is a person who is in charge of a group of workers. A supervisor is a human being. He or she has the same feelings as you. Your supervisor has strengths and weaknesses. Like everyone else, supervisors have good days and bad days, hopes and fears, and personality quirks. They are skilled at some things and not as skilled at others. They may be football fans, tennis players, bowlers, golfers, songwriters, gourmet cooks, or distance runners. Supervisors are unique in that they are assigned the task of leading a group of people toward the development of a quality product, the sale of merchandise, or service to customers. Keep this information in mind as you seek to understand, respect, and respond to your supervisor. He or she is a *real* person with special responsibilities.

Management Styles

The way a supervisor gets the work done is called a **management style**. This style is how he or she manages people to help accomplish the goals and objectives of the organization. One of your first tasks in a new position will be to become acquainted not only with your supervisor as a person but also with his or her management style.

The three basic management styles are

1. *laissez-faire* (a French phrase meaning "to let someone do something alone")

2. democratic

3. autocratic

Each management style has its own set of characteristics.

The *Laissez-Faire* Supervisor. The *laissez-faire* **supervisor** is portrayed in the opening story of this chapter on page 81. Mr. Hilligas gives his managers responsibilities and expects them to carry them out without a great deal of direction or close supervision. The *laissez-faire* supervisor exercises a "hands-off" policy in dealing with employees.

Illustration 6-1
Characteristics of laissez-faire management.

This management style works well in businesses requiring creativity from employees. These businesses need to allow employees to work in a free and open environment. This management style could create chaos in some businesses, but is ideal for others. Advertising agencies, research companies, and fashion design firms are examples of businesses that thrive under a *laissez-faire* style of management.

 Monica has a flair for interior decorating. She is attending classes in design and preparing for a career in this field. She is offered a job as a salesperson in a furniture store. She is thrilled because she thinks she will have a chance to work with customers and do some design work. The position will be beneficial to the customer and provide job satisfaction for Monica. After a few days on the job, Mr. Davidson, her supervisor, tells her to stop spending her time sketching and looking for special fabrics and furniture pieces for customers. He tells her to sell what is on the floor and not to waste time doing anything other than selling products.

Laissez-faire management is not demonstrated in the preceding scenario. Monica was expecting to use her design ability, creativity, and initiative in this position. Obviously being creative was not an option when working for Mr. Davidson.

If you are a creative, self-confident, assertive person and you have the ability to set your own goals, seek a position where you will work for a *laissez-faire* style manager. You can ask questions during the job interview to see if your potential supervisor is a *laissez-faire* manager. Try asking:

"Will I be able to set goals for myself in this position?"

"Will I be given the opportunity to be creative in designing products for customers?"

"Will I need to seek approval before I produce a design?

Critical Thinking

Think about...

whether Mr. Davidson is exercising *laissez-faire* style management. Why or why not?

Occupations that require laissez-faire management often involve creative people.

Zefa—U.K./H. Armstrong Roberts

   Tailor your questions based on the job that you are seeking. Keep in mind that even in the *laissez-faire* atmosphere, you will want to check with your supervisor periodically to make sure that you are meeting expectations.

   The Democratic Supervisor. The **democratic supervisor** will encourage you to participate in the management process. This type of supervisor will seek your ideas, thoughts, and solutions. The democratic supervisor recognizes that everyone has good ideas, and he or she seeks the input of all workers. The democratic supervisor exercises only a moderate degree of control over employees. He or she has confidence in the employees. Employees have confidence in their employer. This type of supervision is often called participatory management.

   Under democratic supervision, committees and meetings are a part of the working atmosphere. These activities will encourage you to share your thoughts and ideas, participate in the decision-making process, and express your opinions.

   If you believe your thoughts are worthy of consideration and you like the idea of contributing to the success of an organization, you will enjoy working for a democratic supervisor. The democratic supervisor will not allow you to work in isolation. He or she will insist that you become involved and offer ideas, help solve problems, and be an important part of the work team. Workers in this atmosphere are expected to be enthusiastic, cooperative, empathetic, and participatory.

Rich is an entrepreneur who likes to work with his 15 employees in a democratic style. Each week they have sales meetings, production meetings, and marketing meetings in which ideas are shared and discussed and decisions are made. Rich seeks ideas about pricing, advertising, and production. He recognizes the value of his employees' suggestions as they interact with each other and customers each day. Alan is a new employee who works in the production area. He attends the production meetings but does not contribute anything, even when he is prompted several times by his coworkers and Rich. Rich talks with Alan after the meeting and asks why he did not participate. Alan says, "I get paid to work in production, not give you ideas on how to run this place. You make the big bucks for thinking." Rich plans to assist Alan in finding another job because he believes Alan will not be happy working under his style of supervision.

> *Democratic supervision gives every employee the opportunity to be a part of management.*

If you believe your only commitment to an organization is to do a specific job and you prefer not being responsible for decision making, democratic supervision is not a management style for you.

Democratic supervisors like to capture the best thoughts from all employees.

The Autocratic Supervisor. The **autocratic supervisor** is an "in-charge" person. He or she develops procedures and policies, defines and assigns tasks, and, in general, dictates how work is to be done. If you are working for an autocratic supervisor, there is no question that this person will be the leader and the employees will be the followers. You will be told what to do, when to do it, and how it will be done. You will not be asked for your opinions or ideas.

The autocratic supervisor does not **delegate authority**. In other words, he or she does not totally entrust an activity, a decision, or a responsibility to an employee. This type of supervisor will be the authority.

You may prefer working for an autocratic supervisor because you will not be responsible for the difficult tasks of planning and making decisions. On the other hand, you will need to be patient, cooperative, accepting, and reliable in order to function in this management setting. It is also very important that you follow directions carefully and always adhere strictly to the rules, regulations, and policies of the organization. An advantage to working for this type of supervisor is that you always know where your job begins and ends. If you are the type of individual who feels comfortable taking directions and prefers being given specific job instructions, you will enjoy working for a supervisor who exercises an autocratic management style.

The following scenario may give you a better idea of the autocratic supervisor.

 yla Andrews, the manager of 31 quality-control technicians in a circuit breaker manufacturing plant, is an autocratic supervisor. Lyla is very proud of the quality product produced by the company. She refers to the technicians as *her* technicians. She assumes responsibility for the job that each of *her* technicians completes. She is very specific in her instructions to the technicians about the specifications for each circuit breaker sent from the plant. She has strict rules about the number of minutes allowed for lunch and breaks, the order in which the circuit breaker stations are to be checked, the specifics to be checked for each product, and the procedures to be used in approving a completed product.

Rosie Delgado, a quality-control technician, says that she enjoys working for Ms. Andrews. She likes knowing what is expected of her. She likes just doing a quality job and does not want to be involved in the decision-making activities of the plant.

Management Style Selection

Unfortunately you will seldom have the opportunity to select the management style of your supervisor. Instead you will need to adjust your work style to the management style in your workplace. Each management style has its advantages and disadvantages. You should recognize that a supervisor may, at times, use a mixture of styles in order to accomplish a goal of the organization; however, there will continue to be a primary underlying style.

When you become angry or displeased with your supervisor, ask yourself: “Is it the supervisor who angers me, or is it his or her management style?” Focusing on the supervisor's style keeps you from being angry or unhappy with the supervisor personally. If you find there is one management style under which you work best, work toward getting yourself in a position where the supervisory style suits you and your skills, needs, and work habits. The supervisor's style will probably not change. It is your job to adapt to the style of the supervisor or to find a new workplace.

Supervisor's Expectations

As you concentrate on knowing your supervisor and his or her management style, you might want to review the chapter on "Self-Improvement." Check yourself against the list of qualities supervisors are looking for described in this section.

Are You Present and on Time?

Know that your supervisor will expect you to be on the job regularly and on time.

Your absence can cause work inefficiency, disruption of the work of others, and a general frustration for those who are called upon to fill in for you. If you have an emergency, illness, or another unavoidable problem, let your supervisor know as soon as possible. Offer to help out in any way you can to make up for absence; come in early when you get back to work, or stay late to make up for lost time. Continual absenteeism from the job will not be allowed by your supervisor and will result in termination.

SCANS
Focus

A competent worker...

■ exhibits responsibility

■ exerts a high level of effort and perseverance toward goal attainment

■ works hard to become excellent at doing tasks by setting high standards, paying attention to details, working well even when assigned an unpleasant task, and displaying a high level of concentration

■ displays high standards of attendance, punctuality, enthusiasm, vitality, and optimism in approaching and completing tasks

Your supervisor will expect you to arrive at work promptly.

Are You Diligent and Do You Show Initiative?

A **diligent worker** is one who does his or her work carefully and completely. Supervisors notice workers who do more than just what is expected. When bonuses, promotions, and pay raises are considered, big dividends may be in store for the diligent employee.

Personal initiative is also valued by supervisors. When you have finished your assigned task, do not just sit and wait for your supervisor to tell you what to do next. Look for something to do on your own or assist someone else. Work for your best possible performance. Do your best; do not accept "second best" from yourself. Be aware of your own strengths, and make efforts to improve in areas of weakness.

Critical Thinking

Think about...

how Peter is showing initiative. Discuss ways to show initiative in your school or workplace.

Peter has been working for Boyer's Construction Company for a few weeks. He likes his work. He enjoys being a part of the home building business. Peter's primary responsibility is to assist with the framing. Occasionally he has spare time because materials have not yet arrived on the site. Whenever this happens, Peter volunteers to help others with their tasks or spends time cleaning his work area. Mert Boyer, general manager, notices that Peter is busy all the time. He makes a mental note to consider him the next time a site framing supervisor is selected.

Do You Show Allegiance?

Allegiance is the demonstration of loyalty and commitment to your supervisor. Make an effort to speak well of your supervisor to your coworkers and those outside the organization. Avoid the temptation to "bad-mouth" your supervisor, even if it seems to be acceptable behavior in your workplace. It is not acceptable for *you*. If you find you are dissatisfied with your supervisor and you have nothing good to say about him or her, be a professional and say nothing. This may be a signal that you need to look for another job.

Are You Enthusiastic?

In Chapters 4 and 5, you read that enthusiasm was essential for success in the workplace. Your supervisor will also expect you to be enthusiastic about your work. Many supervisors believe that the best employees are those who like their work and show enthusiasm for it. All jobs have some unpleasant parts. Do not dwell on the tasks you dislike; instead, focus your thoughts on the parts of the job that you enjoy. When someone asks you about your position, tell them about the things you enjoy. By focusing on and sharing the positive parts of your job, you will be a more productive and successful employee. Supervisors like to sense enthusiasm within the workplace.

66 We act as though comfort and luxury were the chief requirements of life, when all we need to make us really happy is something to be enthusiastic about. 99
—Charles Kingsley

Can You Accept Change?

You are living in a fast-paced age; therefore, your supervisor will expect you to be flexible and adaptable to the changing workplace. A piece of equipment you are working with today may be obsolete tomorrow. You need to be ready to accept this kind of change and be willing to adapt to new challenges and tasks as they come to you. Keep an open mind toward change. Fear of change is natural; the fear comes when you do not understand why the change is taking place. Keep asking questions and seeking answers until you are comfortable with the change. Do not allow yourself to become obsolete by being stubborn and resistant to change. Change will keep you fresh, challenged, and enthusiastic about your work.

> 66 Fear of change is always a brake on progress. 99

Relating To Your Supervisor

To establish a good working relationship with your supervisor, you must have an open line of communication so that you will know how to respond to a supervisor's directives. The following tips will help you establish good rapport with your supervisor.

Allow No Surprises

Any time there is a problem, crisis, or new development in your work area, make sure that your supervisor hears about it from you first. Supervisors *do not* like surprises. They need to be kept aware about what is going on in order to make quality decisions.

arianne works in the shipping department of a large aircraft production company. She receives a call from a major supplier about the possibility of a steel shipment being held up because of a rail strike. Marianne decides not to mention this possible delay to her supervisor, Carmela. She does not want Carmela to worry unnecessarily about the shipment. Marianne decides that she will check on it later. Carmela hears from another worker about the possible late shipment. She is surprised and alarmed that she has not been kept informed.

Keep your supervisor apprised of all situations and possible situations. Your supervisor cannot be everywhere at once; therefore, communication from you is essential.

Know Your Supervisor's Communication Style

People have favorite styles of communicating, so it is important for you to become familiar with how your supervisor prefers to communicate. Some supervisors like information in writing backed with facts, statistical data, and other supporting documents. If your supervisor prefers this style of communication, *use it*. Prepare memos and reports when sharing information. Some supervisors prefer to receive verbal information. They like to listen and then react. If your supervisor prefers oral communication, *use it*.

Also find out if your supervisor likes to hear from you once an hour, once a day, or once a week. This, of course, will depend on the type of work you are doing and the amount of experience you have in doing it. If your supervisor prefers that you check in with him or her frequently, *do it*. Perhaps your supervisor only wants to hear summary statements from you at the end of the workday. If your workplace uses electronic messaging and your supervisor likes it, *use it*. Early in your employment, be sure to check with your supervisor to find out his or her preferred communication style.

Be a Good Listener

To understand what your supervisor expects from you, you must be a careful listener. When you are discussing a topic, listen carefully. Listen not just for what the supervisor is saying, but also for what he or she means and what implications there might be. If you are not getting the supervisor's "drift," state what you *think* has been said. After the discussion, summarize what you have learned to make sure you understood. You will gain further information about the importance of good listening when you study Chapters 8 and 9.

Quality employees are active listeners.

Take Problems to Your Supervisor

Your supervisor wants to be aware of all problems. However, you need to exercise some judgment about taking problems to your supervisor that may not be worthy of his or her attention. It is important that you approach your supervisor with problems correctly.

The following steps will help you organize your thoughts and information so that you will do a quality job in presenting a problem to your supervisor.

66 Problems are just challenging opportunities. 99

1. *Establish a suitable setting.* You are sharing a problem with your supervisor, not the entire workforce. Step into a private office, canteen area, or quiet hallway. This will help ensure that you have the supervisor's full attention.

2. *Explain the problem in your own words.* Use terms that accurately describe your concerns and feelings. Do not try to toss in a $5 word when a 50 cent word will do just as well in conveying your feelings.

3. *Present facts that support the problem.* These facts should be carefully gathered prior to the presentation of your problem. Do your homework! Your facts should be specific, documented, and accurate. You will lose credibility by stating generalizations, half truths, and innuendoes. Avoid using phrases such as "I hear that . . .," "I assume . . .," and "Rumor has it. . ." If you do not have the facts in order, you are not ready to talk with your supervisor.

4. *Ask for understanding.* Pause . . . and ask your supervisor whether or not he or she understands the problem. (Notice that you have been assuming a leadership role in this process.) This step will allow your supervisor the chance to ask questions or clarify points that you have made.

5. *Present several alternative solutions.* Be prepared with some suggestions as to how the problem might be solved. If you do not have any solutions in mind, you are not ready to talk with the supervisor. Do your homework! Be prepared with alternative suggestions.

6. *State your recommended solution.* Indicate the solution that you think is best after you have presented several; however, you should not insist that your recommendation is the one that must be followed.

7. *Thank your supervisor.* Thank your supervisor for his or her time and attention. If appropriate, request a follow-up to the conversation at a later date.

After you have completed this seven-step process with your supervisor, return to your workstation and resist the temptation to share your conversation with coworkers. They will be curious, but the employee who is skillful in communicating with a supervisor and who

SCANS Focus

A competent worker...

■ recognizes that a problem exists

■ identifies possible reasons for the discrepancy

■ devises and implements a plan of action to resolve it

■ evaluates and monitors progress, revising the plan as indicated by findings can keep those conversations confidential has an edge over coworkers who do *not* realize the importance of this skill.

What Do You Have The Right To Expect?

Relationships between supervisors and employees are better when each helps to meet the other's needs. If you provide productive service, enthusiasm, and allegiance to your supervisor, you have a right to expect to be trusted with your work, a safe working environment, and personal recognition. You also have the right to expect explanations for decisions, clarification of policies, and fair evaluations of your work. If your expectations are reasonable but not met, you should employ the seven steps of taking a problem to your supervisor and discussing the situation with him or her. Take your concerns to the attention of your supervisor, not your coworkers.

Your Right to Criticism

66 A just criticism is a commendation, rather than a detraction. 99
—Henry Jacob

The right to receive criticism from your employer is a fair expectation. You may be thinking: "What do you mean? Why should I want to seek or expect criticism?" The truth is that you *need* criticism. Criticism should not be viewed as a negative word. **Criticism** is the route to self-improvement and should be regarded as such. Without criticism and suggestions from your supervisor, you will be unaware of how to improve. No matter how skilled you become on the job, improvement is always possible. Improved skills lead to additional self-confidence, promotions, and income.

Many supervisors may try to avoid providing you with adequate criticism. When constructive criticism is not given, your employer is denying you a right. Many supervisors find offering criticism to be a very difficult and unpleasant task. Think of yourself as a future supervisor. It is doubtful that administering criticism will be one of your favorite duties. Other reasons supervisors avoid giving criticism are as follows:

1. Many supervisors hope that if you work at a job long enough, you will figure out what you are doing wrong and correct the problem.

2. Some supervisors dislike upsetting the "status quo" in any way. If things are going reasonably well, they take the position, "Why bother to upset anybody?"

3. Supervisors may fear confrontation in any form and dislike any show of emotions from employees. Some people do not take criti-

cism well and respond in an emotional way—pouting, crying, or
even emotional outbursts.

Thus, some supervisors may not want to risk the consequences of
giving criticism. When this happens, you are the loser and you will
fail to receive information that will help you become a more productive employee.

It is important for you to let your supervisor know that you appreciate and can accept suggestions. This can be done by asking your
supervisor about your job performance. Speak up during performance
evaluations, and ask for suggestions on how to improve. Whenever
suggestions are shared about your work, accept them graciously with
a sincere vow to make improvements. Thank the supervisor for his or
her interest in your success.

Reactions to Criticism

Giving Excuses. People react differently to criticism. Consider your
reactions to criticisms from others as you review the negative methods
discussed here. If the criticism you receive is deserved, do not give
flimsy excuses, provide alibis, or become defensive. There is a natural
tendency to make excuses. If a friend says, "You're in a sour mood
today," the typical human response is, "Well, you'd be sour too, if you
had the hassles I have." Excuses can carry over to your work life too.
"There are errors in this report because my work area is so noisy."
Responses such as this are not an appropriate way to indicate to your
supervisor that you can handle criticism. A better response about
errors in a report would be "Thanks for pointing those out. I'll correct
them right away."

Verbally Attacking. You may have a desire to "verbally attack" in
response to criticism. "Attackers" focus the spotlight away from themselves and blame someone else for the error(s). "I did a lousy job on
proofing that copy because I had to answer Melinda's phone and
couldn't concentrate."

The attacker does not handle criticism well and may be creating an
unnecessary conflict with a coworker. A better response in this situation may be "I do need to go over that copy again. Thanks for giving
me the opportunity."

Withdrawing. You may react to criticism by withdrawing or feeling
guilty and inadequate. Those who react in this manner ask no questions on how to improve but rather give up and take the "what's-the-
use" attitude. This type of behavior is inappropriate and obvious to
your supervisor. Again, you will be the loser because the supervisor
may not want to deal with this attitude in the future.

If you react to criticism by attacking, blaming others, or withdrawing, you are experiencing a lot of emotional pain without much healing. When you fail to use criticism to your advantage, you suffer the loss of self-esteem and the opportunity to improve your work. Begin to take a more healthy attitude about criticism; recognize it as a form of self-improvement.

Handling Criticism

Work hard to accept criticism with professionalism and maturity. Step 1 in this process is to evaluate the criticism. Is it deserved or undeserved?

Deserved Criticism. Handling deserved criticism is not difficult. Use the steps listed below to handle deserved criticism.

1. Listen very carefully to the suggestions being made.

2. Ask questions, if necessary, to clarify the error that you made or the suggestions being offered.

3. Offer to correct the error if possible.

4. Pledge an effort to try suggestions.

5. Thank the supervisor giving the criticism.

After you have completed these steps, leave the situation with your self-esteem in place and go back to work. Do not share with your coworkers any remarks made about you or your response. The comments made were between you and your supervisor. Your supervisor will recognize that you can accept criticism and will be willing to communicate recommendations to you in the future.

Undeserved Criticism. Coping with undeserved criticism requires more self-control and courage. At some point in your career, you will be unfairly criticized or blamed for something that is not your fault; it happens to everyone. The following series of steps should be followed carefully to deal with this unfortunate circumstance:

1. Listen carefully to your accuser. Do not interrupt. Do not try to deny. Do not say "but," "wait a minute," or "you're wrong." Just keep quiet and listen.

2. After your accuser is finished, take a deep breath and ask a series of calm questions. Your questions should be polite, reasonable, responsible, and related to what you have just heard. Do not become rude or raise your voice. Stay calm!

3. Through your questions, lead your accuser to the conclusion that you are being unfairly criticized.

4. Accept the apology of the accuser if one is offered. Keep in mind that apologies are difficult for some people and none may be forthcoming.

5. Say "Thank you for your time." (This might be tough, but say it!)

6. Return to your workplace and do not discuss the incident with anyone.

Above all, do not keep a "chip" on your shoulder and do not take on the attitude of "Well, I guess I got that straightened out!" This strategy may become clearer to you as you see it played out in the following scenario.

L aurie has worked part time for Doctor Goodwin for several months. The job is important to her, and she enjoys the work. Doctor Goodwin is the Anthropology Department Chairperson at the university. Laurie seldom sees her because she gets her work assignments from her secretary, Gloria Christensen. One day Doctor Goodwin calls Laurie into her office and says, "Young woman, sit down!" Shaking her finger at Laurie, she says, "You just cost the university $2,000." She tosses a letter at her. It misses Laurie's lap, and she leans over to pick it up. Because of this treatment, she now has a lump in her throat and tears are brimming in her eyes. She tries to say, "I don't understand. What has happened?" Her words are unclear because of her emotional state. Doctor Goodwin says to her, "This letter you typed offers a part-time assistantship to a graduate student; you typed in the figure $6,000 rather than $4,000. This guy is a smart cookie, and he has sent a telegram stating that he'll accept the offer of $6,000 as stated in our letter." Laurie has now recovered somewhat and looks at the letter. She realizes that she did not work on the day the letter was typed and does not recognize the name of the recipient. Most importantly, the reference initials at the bottom of the page (GC) are not hers. She states, "I didn't type this letter." Doctor Goodwin replies, "Well, how do you know that?" She tells her. She pauses, looks at her, and says, "Oh, I see. Well, I'd better talk to Gloria about this." Laurie is upset for the remainder of the day, and she is concerned about the wrath that is about to come down on Gloria.

Critical Thinking

Think about...

what Laurie should have done to handle the undeserved criticism.

Handling undeserved criticism is tough and takes practice. The rewards, however, are great. It is important to your relationship with a supervisor that you are able to demonstrate an ability to handle either type of criticism.

If you approach criticism positively, you will find that it can be as valuable as praise. You are probably aware of your strong points. Criticism allows others to help you improve your weaknesses.

Summary

It is important to know your supervisor and understand his or her management style in order to succeed in the workplace. Your supervisor has expectations of you, and you have expectations of your supervisor. Remind yourself frequently of the expectations the employer has of you in addition to doing quality work.

1. Be present and on time.

2. Be diligent in your work.

3. Be enthusiastic.

In your effort to please your supervisor, you also must be sure that he or she is aware of what is happening at your work site. Supervisors do not like surprises. Listen to your employer, and know when and how to share problems with your supervisor.

Criticism is a form of self-improvement. Seek criticism from your supervisor in order to improve your performance. Supervisors enjoy working with employees who can accept suggestions and criticism.

End of Chapter Activities

Questions and Projects

1. The following phrases describe characteristics of *laissez-faire*, democratic, and autocratic management styles. Identify the style that is being described. Be prepared to defend your answer.

_____ Frequent work team meetings are held.

_____ Authority is not delegated.

_____ Decisions are made by the work team.

_____ The supervisor makes the decisions.

_____ Workers are encouraged to use creativity and initiative.

_____ Original work is encouraged.

_____ Everyone's input is valued.

2. List five careers in which you think *laissez-faire* management would work to the best advantage of the workplace. Explain why.

3. Under what management style do you think you would prefer to work? Explain your answer.

4. Attendance is very important in any position. Missing work requires a good reason. Place a check mark by the statements that you believe are acceptable reasons to miss work. Be prepared to defend your choices.

a. _____ You are ill with a cold and cough and have a temperature of 101 degrees.

b. _____ A friend is in town just for the day and you want to show her a good time.

c. _____ A close friend dies in a nearby town and you want to attend the funeral.

d. _____ You have a slight headache and decide you would like to take a "mental health day."

e. _____ You have had a fun-filled long weekend. You feel you are too tired to go to work.

5. What questions would you ask a supervisor in an effort to get to know his or her management style? Arrange to interview someone who works in a supervisory capacity. Determine his or her management style by asking your questions.

6. Role play with classmates the scenario on page 95 involving Laurie, Gloria, and Doctor Goodwin. First, role play the situation in which Laurie did not know how to respond to the undeserved criticism of her supervisor. Then role play the situation with classmates as Laurie should have handled the criticism.

7. Write a paragraph about a change that has occurred in your workplace (or home) that required you to adapt to the change. What was the change? How well did you accept the change? How did you adjust to the change? How are you handling the change now?

8. Step 3 in explaining a problem to your supervisor, page 91, is to present facts that support the problem. Choose from the following statements those that would be appropriate in communicating to your supervisor that you need to adjust your work hours from 8 a.m. – 4:30 p.m. to 7:30 a.m. – 4 p.m. The company does offer flex hours.

	YES	NO	
a.	_____	_____	My youngest child gets out of school at 3:45 p.m., and I would like to be there when she gets home.
b.	_____	_____	I hear that people in accounting can work whatever hours they choose.
c.	_____	_____	Maybe I could get Carey to cover my phone from 4 – 4:30 p.m.
d.	_____	_____	Rumor has it that everyone will be working 7:30 a.m. – 4 p.m. after June 1.
e.	_____	_____	My spouse works in Hallam (30 minutes away) and cannot adjust his work hours to be home when our daughter gets there.

9. Using the information you have checked in item 8, write down what you would say to your supervisor if making the above request.

10. Have you ever received criticism that was helpful to you? Explain the criticism and how it helped you.

11. Have you ever received undeserved criticism? What were your feelings? How did you handle the situation? Write out the situation and what you should have said using the steps for handling undeserved criticism on pages 94-95.

12. Why is it important for you *not* to make a point of discussing with coworkers conversations you have had with supervisors?

Case Problems

1. Change of Style

Adelaine is a creative employee in a restaurant known for fine food and excellent service. The food is always exquisitely presented. Adelaine's specialty is preparing special desserts. She has an ability for decorating cakes and presenting desserts. Jacque is the owner and manager of the restaurant. He appreciates Adelaine's ability and gives her a free rein in presenting desserts. Jacque sells the restaurant and the new owner, Henriette. retains the services of Adelaine. However, Henriette closely supervises Adelaine's work and is constantly telling her to hurry up and get the desserts out. She sets maximums on the time

Adelaine can spend preparing desserts. Each dessert requires her approval before it is taken to the table. Adelaine is very unhappy with Henriette and is thinking about finding new employment.

a. What is the main source of Adelaine's frustration? Explain your answer.

b. Would you encourage Adelaine to find employment elsewhere? Why or why not?

c. What may Henriette be losing if Adelaine leaves?

2. No Surprises

Kevin has the responsibility of preparing checks for the 44 employees of the Campbell Nursery. The checks are to be ready for employees on the last working day of each month. Kevin is ill for several days, and Teresita covers his duties. When Kevin returns he finds that Teresita has not entered overtime pay and has somehow lost data in the computer. Kevin does not panic because he has several days to get everything straightened out in order to meet the payroll. He calls a computer technician in to try and locate the missing data. The day before checks are to be given out, he realizes that they are going to be delayed. At this point he informs his supervisor, Mr. Webb. Mr. Webb is furious and demands, "Why didn't you tell me there were problems?"

a. Who is to blame for the problem?

b. What should Kevin have done upon returning to work and encountering the problem? Explain your answer.

c. Why is Mr. Webb upset? What other workplace problems will result because of this mix-up?

3. To Take or Not to Take to the Supervisor

Armani is an office worker in a large publishing company. He keeps a very messy desk. Heather's workstation is about six feet from Armani's. The way Armani keeps his desk is very irritating to Heather. She frequently makes remarks about his "mess" to coworkers. She gives him looks of disgust at every opportunity. She finally gets so annoyed that she rushes into the supervisor's office and blurts out, "You have got to do something about Armani. I just can't stand looking at that messy desk." The supervisor is a little stunned from the outburst and replies, "Armani does quality work. I have more important things to worry about than someone's housekeeping."

a. Should Heather have taken this problem to the supervisor? Was the problem worthy of supervisory attention?

b. What would you suggest to Heather to help her solve this problem?

c. What damage may Heather have done to her relationship with the supervisor and Armani?

d. If you were Heather's friend or coworker, what advice would you have given her prior to her outburst to the supervisor? Now that she has taken the problem to the supervisor, what advice would you give her?

4. Allegiance?

Michael works in a government office responsible for services to senior citizens. His supervisor, Jenny, has worked in government for about 30 years. Jenny is considered competent and has been recognized publicly many times for her service to the clientele of the office. Michael does not like Jenny. He believes she expects too much of employees and coddles the senior citizens coming into the office. Michael tells workers from other offices that it is time for Jenny to retire. He frequently makes unkind comments about her decisions and seems to enjoy doing imitations of her. Michael's comments get back to Jenny, and she must decide what to do with Michael.

a. Was Michael's behavior acceptable?

b. What do you think of his behavior? Explain.

c. What information would you like to have about Michael and Jenny that might help you give advice to Jenny about what she should do?

d. Should Jenny fire Michael? Would you fire Michael?

Relating To Clients And Customers

Nancy enjoys her work in a home furnishings store. Her customers are people who, for a reasonable price, want their homes to be well decorated and comfortable. Nancy has no formal training in home decorating, but she does have a knack for helping people select furnishings to fit their lifestyle. Nancy works long hours to better serve customers. She visits their homes, searches through periodicals for decorating ideas, and spends hours looking through fabric books to find just the right touch for a client. Nancy sold more merchandise than any other worker in the store. She outsold the trained decorators by more than 35 percent. There are three reasons for Nancy's success—service, service, and service.

All businesses have someone whom they serve. Those who are served may be called clients, customers, patrons, or patients depending upon the type of business. For example, if you are working in a doctor's office, your customers are called patients. If you work in retail, those you serve are usually called customers. Regardless of how you refer to those you serve, remember that they want to be understood, listened to, cared for, and treated fairly and individually. Those whom you serve expect you to treat them as "special."

In order to treat a customer as "special," you must make the customer perceive that he or she is valuable. To the customer, *you* are the business.

Objectives

After completing this chapter, you should be able to:

1.
List the reasons why customers are important.

2.
Identify the expectations of customers and how those expectations can be met.

3.
Communicate verbally and with body language that you are there to serve the customer.

4.
Communicate the attitude that the customer is right.

As a part of your study on this topic, review Chapters 5 and 6. Many of the guidelines to getting along with coworkers and supervisors also hold true for relating well to your customers. Getting along with customers is a skill that may be challenging at times, but it does not need to be difficult. Treating each customer as you would like to be treated, trying to learn their needs, and making every attempt to satisfy those needs will be good steps toward relating well to clients and customers.

Without customers there is no business. Without business there are no profits. Without profits there are no salaries for employees. Nothing happens in a business until somebody buys something. Customers are your business. It will be your job to see that customers are served. If you do, your customers will return time and again to your business and continue to buy your products or use your services.

Customer Expectations

Customers will keep coming back if you supply them with quality products and services that are delivered in a timely manner with a sense of empathy and a focus on reliability.

Quality Products and Services

Every customer expects quality products or services. If the customer does not receive this quality, the customer is gone. No retail or wholesale store or manufacturer will stay in business long if the products sold are not of good quality. Customers expect merchandise that is of high and lasting quality, clean, and safe.

Some businesses do not sell products or tangible items. These businesses deal in services that you cannot actually keep in your possession as you would, for example, a shirt, a pair of jeans, a bottle of cologne, or a compact disc. Businesses such as beauty salons, plumbers, and hospitals sell **intangibles**, things that you cannot actually touch or possess.

The companies that sell intangible services have customers who must be served at the same level as those selling products. The customer who buys an auto insurance policy expects that the policy will cover any damage to his or her car. The customer who uses the services of a beauty salon for a permanent expects his or her hair to be curly when he or she leaves the shop.

Reliability

Any business that stays in business must be reliable. **Reliability** is the ability to supply what was promised, dependably and accurately.

Businesses sell products and services.

Location courtesy of Discovery, Hyde Park Square, Cincinnati

Photo by Jim Whitmer

If you tell a customer, "This custom-crafted chair is solid wood. No veneer was used in its construction. I'll see that the chair is delivered to you tomorrow," you had better deliver a chair tomorrow that is solid wood. A promise not kept could cost you a customer.

❝ Undertake not what you cannot perform, but be careful to keep your promises. **❞**

—George Washington

Contact the customer immediately if you cannot deliver a promise. Do not blame the computer, the delivery service, or the weather or use any other common excuse. Tell the customer what happened and why your promise has been broken. For example, you might say to the customer when you determine that the chair is not solid wood, "This is Jim at the Merchandise Mart. I sold you the solid wood chair yesterday. As I was loading it on the truck today, I realized this is not a solid wood chair. The leg supports are veneer. This was my error. I want to apologize for the misinformation, and I regret any inconvenience this may cause. Do you still want me to send the chair over to you today?" Your reliability and honesty will be remembered the next time this customer is in the market for your product. Customers usually respond well when they understand the reason you are unable to fulfill a promise or request. Provide them with *reasons*, not *excuses*.

Never make a promise or commitment about a product just to get a sale. Service begins with the sale. Making promises that you can keep is what reliability is all about.

Critical Thinking

Think about...

what Gabrielle could do to save Albert McManus as a customer.

Gabrielle has worked for Donley Medical Supply for several months. She feels competent about the information that she gives customers—so confident, in fact, that she no longer refers to product manuals. Albert McManus came to the supply house to purchase a wheelchair for his wife. Gabrielle showed him several floor models and others in their catalog. Albert emphasized to her that it was necessary for the back of the chair to be adjustable because of his wife's condition. Albert liked Model No. 212. Gabrielle did not have this model on the floor, but she did have several in the warehouse. Albert said, "Fine. Send one to my home address." When the chair arrived at the McManus home, Albert discovered that the back was not adjustable. Albert was not pleased and called the store to announce that they should pick the chair up and that he would shop elsewhere where he could get reliable service.

Empathy and Understanding

Customers want to be treated as individuals. Each customer has wants, needs, desires, expectations, and emotions. Recognize your customer's wants, needs, and emotional state so that you can better serve him or her. Each customer is different. Consider the different needs of Matthew and Melissa.

❝ Each customer is like a tree that branches out everywhere— you never lose just *one* customer. **❞**

Matthew is purchasing a sweater as a gift for his wife. He may be nervous about being in a woman's department, and he may be unsure of exactly what type of sweater he wants to purchase; in general, he is looking to you for guidance. You could help Matthew by asking him questions to determine what would be a most suitable gift. "What color do you have in mind? Does your wife like bright or pastel colors? Are you looking for a sweater for evening wear or casual wear?" You could show him a variety of sweater styles.

On the other hand, Melissa is shopping for a sweater for herself and is comfortable in the department; she knows her size; she knows exactly what she is looking for; and she really does not want to be bothered with your help. Melissa would require a different approach. You would direct her to where the sweaters are stocked and offer to answer any questions, step back, and be available to assist her with questions or requests. In other words, you would be empathetic to the feelings of your customers based on their wants and needs.

Empathy is acknowledging and affirming the emotional state and wishes of the customers. Customers want to know that you appreciate them and their business. If customers have problems with your products or services, make an effort to assure them that you understand and plan to take action. For example, if a customer brings back a small appliance that does not work, he or she is probably going to be angry or, at the very least, unhappy. Understand these feelings. Use a phrase such as, "I can understand why this makes you unhappy. Let's get this situation corrected to your satisfaction."

J oseph works in the appliance center of a major department store. A customer storms into the department and says, "What's wrong with this company? It used to be that I could depend on all of your appliances. Seems like I can't count on you or anyone else these days. I bought a dehumidifier from you last week. It's not working and I'm angry!" Joseph replied, "I can understand why you're angry. Let me get some information from you, and we'll get you a working dehumidifier."

Timeliness

Customers insist on timeliness. It seems that Americans are always in a hurry and demand immediate satisfaction. You may use a mail service that promises overnight delivery, you may drop your clothing at a dry cleaner that promises one-hour service, or you may order from a menu that promises 10-minute service or you eat free. These services remind you that customers are often unhappy with anything less than "immediately."

Here are some specific techniques you can use to show your customers that you respect their desire for immediate and timely attention.

- If you are working in retail, be sure that every customer is acknowledged as he or she arrives.

- Establish eye contact with customers so that they know you are interested in serving them.

- If you are working in a mail-order house and your business is conducted by phone, answer quickly.

- If you must be away from the phone, let the customer know why and how long you will be gone.

- Do not use comments that create deadlines you cannot meet. If you say to a customer, "That will be in the morning mail," you have created an expectation. You may create unnecessary customer dissatisfaction with promises made without much thought.

Other organizations are aware of the time-consciousness of their customers. If you cannot serve them in a timely fashion, someone else will. Keep your customers by being timely.

©Wendt WorldWide

Time is important in our society. Customers expect quick service.

Recognition and Acknowledgment

Recognize your customers, and whenever possible, call them by name. Everyone likes to be acknowledged and recognized. People also like to have you indicate the reason that you remember them—something they bought, a mutual friend, a hobby, or something about one of their children. Customers like to hear comments such as, "Hi, Ms. Applebee, glad to see you back in the store. How is your new dryer working?" or "Thanks for shopping with us, Angie. I'll look forward to helping you again."

You can pick up name clues from customers' checks, business cards, credit cards, desk signs, or office doors. Remembering names requires work. Try to associate a person's name with some unique characteristic he or she may have. This can help you recall names.

Customer Communication

You are now aware that customers have many expectations. You must live up to these expectations in order to retain customers. There are some phrases you need to avoid saying that researchers tell us customers *do not like to hear.*

I Can't Be Bothered

You would probably never say this phrase aloud to a customer, but your comments or body language may communicate the message, *"I can't be bothered."* If you commit all of your attention to one customer and fail to acknowledge a new customer walking into your area, you have delivered this message. If you are in a conversation with a coworker and do not give your immediate attention to a customer, you have communicated "I can't be bothered."

I Know Everything

When you try to have every answer and try to find immediate solutions to any problem a customer may pose, you may be saying, "I know everything." Customers do not like this. They like you to be informed about your product or service, but they do not appreciate power selling or trying to force them into a decision that they are not yet ready to make. It is important that you know your merchandise, but do not beat the customer over the head with your knowledge.

I Don't Know

Customers arrive at your place of business because they expect you to be able to serve them. They have a right to expect that salespeople are knowledgeable about their products. Replace the three words, *"I don't know,"* with *"I'll find out."*

J osie walked into a mall shoe store. She wandered around looking for a dressy shoe style. She asked the salesperson, "Are these shoes on sale?" The salesperson said, "I don't know." Josie walked a little farther and picked up a shoe she liked and asked, "Do you carry these in black?" The salesperson replied, "I don't know." After the second "I don't know," Josie moved on to another shoe store.

I Don't Want Your Business

Be sure that you treat all customers with the same quality service. Would you serve a young teenager wearing cutoffs and an oversized T-shirt the same way you would serve a person in a business suit?

Every customer is an individual and deserves your attention. The teenager you may have avoided because you think he or she cannot afford the product and is only looking may well turn out to be a good customer today and in the future. Do you avoid older people because you assume they are going to take too much of your time? They are individuals who deserve your attention. You must forget any prejudices about certain customers because of the way they dress or their ages, races, or sizes. You are in business to serve *all* customers.

You Don't Know Anything

Whenever a customer comes to you for help, you must provide that help by being sensitive to his or her needs. Never put a customer down or demean them in any way for misinformation that they may share with you. Customers are sometimes confused. Recognize the customer has misinformation and give him or her the correct information without putting the customer down. If you do not handle the situation with care, the next time the customer is in need of your services, it will not be at your place of business.

Don't Take It Personally

As you relate to clients and customers, remember that this is business/work. Do not take the remarks of the customer personally. There may be some situations where the customer may be very verbally abusive. The customer may threaten, accuse, or make critical statements about you and the business.

If this happens, understand that the customer is upset about some phase of the business, not at you personally even though some remarks may have been directed at you. Focus your attention on determining and satisfying the customer's need. Most often you will need to make some type of adjustment to satisfy the customer.

Never argue with the customer. Do not try to defend yourself with comments such as, "It's not my fault." This type of remark will only escalate the temper of the customer. Allow the customer to vent his or her frustration rather than trying to shut it off with an argumentative statement. Try saying, "I understand your anger; let's find a solution to the situation." Usually once the customer feels that you understand the problem and plan to make an adjustment, he or she will calm down and deal with the solution in a reasonable manner.

Is The Customer Always Right?

The popular phrase, "The customer is always right," is tossed around a great deal in business. You know that it is not possible for

> 66 A few words of regret is a way of saying you care, a show of sensitivity to the ragged edges of another's emotion. 99
> —Robert Conklin

anyone to be right all of the time. Customers may not always be right; however, they are always customers. If the customer is not right, your job is to manage the experience so the customer eventually is right and remains your customer.

Listen to and Believe Your Customers

Sometimes you may think a customer is totally wrong about a complaint. However, after all the information is heard, the customer turns out to be right. Listen to the customer's entire story before you respond. Always give your customer the benefit of a doubt.

 lecia is a clerk in a dry cleaners. An annoyed customer came in and said, "I specifically pointed out the grease spots on this suit when I brought it in, and when it was delivered to me, the spots were still there. Don't you know how to remove grease spots?" Alecia replied, "If you indeed did point out the grease spots, they would have been noted and removed." The customer replied, "I did note them." He then pulled out his claim check and showed Alecia that the accepting clerk had written down that there were grease spots on the left lapel of the suit. The customer picked up the suit and said, "I'll take this suit elsewhere to be cleaned. I don't appreciate being called a liar."

Critical
Thinking

Think about...

how Alecia should have handled this customer's complaint. What would your response have been?

Educate Your Customers

Many times customers will experience a problem because they do not follow or find the directions carried with the merchandise. If a customer mistakenly washes and shrinks a new blouse, you can tactfully show the customer the label sewn in the collar that says the gar-

Educating the customer is part of expected service.

Location courtesy of Northland Volkswagen

ment should be dry cleaned only. This educates the customer about the importance of reading clothing direction labels.

Here's another example. A customer returns a motion-sensor light. The light will go on when any motion occurs within 30 feet of the light. The customer returns the light saying it does not work. You say, "I'm sorry. Let's see if we can figure out what went wrong." You open the box and pull out the directions. Step-by-step you go through the directions and check with your customer to see what step may have been omitted. Eventually, this process will lead to the problem. If not, you can do an exchange or a refund and not offend the customer.

Attitude

The idea that the customer is always right is clearly not a true statement. However, the *attitude* demonstrated to the customer is a good and positive feeling. The attitude expressed is that the customer is right. You should never argue or dispute the word of a customer, but make a genuine attempt to see the customer's point of view.

Summary

Clients and customers are your business. Customers expect service. Customers expect quality products and services, reliability, empathy, and timeliness. Never communicate the following messages verbally or through your body language:

- I can't be bothered.

- I know everything.

- I don't know.

- I don't want your business.

- You don't know anything.

Do not take negative remarks made by a customer personally. Do not argue with the customer because this will only disturb him or her further. Listen to your customer and then attempt to satisfy his or her needs as soon as possible.

Customers are not always right. However, you want to communicate through your words, actions, and attitude that the customer is always right. Be sure that you listen to your customers and educate them about your products or services whenever possible.

End of Chapter Activities

Questions and Projects

1. What can happen as a result of having a customer left unserved?

2. Who benefits when you relate well with clients and customers?

3. What would you have said if you were on the receiving end of the call by Mr. McManus (see scenario on page 104) regarding the wheelchair that was not what he had requested and his statement that he was taking his business elsewhere.

4. How might you communicate the message "I don't want your business" to one of your clients or customers? As a customer, has a salesperson ever communicated the "I don't want your business" message to you? When? How?

5. How could you respond more empathetically to a customer and communicate the following messages?

"We don't carry those jeans in your size."

"Your flight has been canceled."

"The table you ordered is out of stock."

"We don't deliver packages weighing less than 20 pounds."

6. What did George Washington mean when he said, "Undertake not what you cannot perform, but be careful to keep your promises"?

Case Problems

1. Video Dilemma
Jack is a clerk in a video store. He helps customers find selections and operates the checkout register. A regular customer, Travis Obermier, comes barging into the store and slams down a videotape of the movie *Mrs. Doubtfire*. He says in a very loud voice, "I checked this tape out an hour ago for some houseguests who wanted to watch *Mrs. Doubtfire*, but it doesn't work. There's something wrong with this copy. Why don't you check these movies before they leave the store? This bet-

ter not have messed up my VCR player. I want a good copy of this film." Jack replies, "This is Saturday night. Do you expect popular movies like *Mrs. Doubtfire* to be on the shelves? Look for something else."

a. What did Travis want, need, and/or expect?

b. Did Jack handle the situation correctly? Why or why not?

c. Write down what the reply from Jack should have been. Keep in mind that there are no copies of *Mrs. Doubtfire* available.

2. Tough Exchange

Emi works in the small appliances section of a department store. Cedric brings in a hand mixer and tells Emi that he wants to return it for cash. Emi asks for the receipt. Cedric tells her that the mixer was a gift. He doesn't want it as he already has a mixer. Emi says, "Our story policy is no cash returns without a receipt." Cedric replies, "I don't care whose policy it is. I don't need two mixers. What do you expect me to do with two mixers? I want to see the store manager." Emi says, "I don't care what you do with two mixers. I'm just telling you that without a receipt, you're not going to return this mixer for cash. The manager will just tell you the same thing."

a. Did Emi do the right thing in explaining the company policy to Cedric?

b. Did Emi do anything to irritate the customer or increase the problem?

c. Was Cedric's desire to return the mixer for cash reasonable?

d. What will likely be the result of this conversation?

e. How would you have handled Cedric's request if you were in Emi's place?

Unit 3

Developing Your Communication Skills

This unit emphasizes how essential and vital good communication is in the workplace.

Chapter 8 will familiarize you with the two-way communication process. You will study the barriers of communication and how to overcome them. In the modern workplace, you will be expected to keep the channels of communication open by keeping a friendly attitude, using positive persuasion, helping others feel important, rewarding the positive and ignoring the negative, and being aware of the pitfalls of gossip. The opening chapter of the unit will prepare you to meet these expectations.

As your thoughts and ideas are worthwhile, getting your message across in the workplace is important. Chapter 9 will help you become comfortable in transferring your ideas to others through conversations as well as formal presentations. A factor related to communication that can lead to problems in the workplace is conflict. Chapter 10 will reveal the different types of conflict, the phases of conflict, and how to resolve conflict.

Contents

Chapter 8
Communication Channels

Chapter 9
Getting Your Message Across

Chapter 10
Communicating To Resolve Conflict

Communication Channels

Good morning, Glen. Happy Monday to you."

"Thanks, Sam. How was your weekend?"

"It was great. I spent some time with the staff from 4 West. I got caught up on the hospital gossip. Did you know the staff are going to be charged $50 per month for parking beginning next month? Also, are you aware that the employee cafeteria is going to be raising prices by 25 percent?"

"That's news to me, Sam. I'm glad you filled me in on the latest. I'll see you later."

"Hi, Glen. How's it going?"

"Fine, Rhonda. Have you heard the latest? Sam spent time with people from 4 East this weekend. Rumor has it that we are going to be paying $60 a month for parking beginning next week. Also, did you hear that the cafeteria is going to be raising prices by 30 percent? I guess they want us to stop eating there."

"Thanks for the information, Glen."

"Howdy, Rhonda. What's new?"

"Hi, Wally. Have you heard that the employee cafeteria is going to close? They finally priced themselves out of business. Also, starting tomorrow parking fees are going up to $70 per month."

Communication comes in many forms in the workplace. You may receive communication in written form. You can expect to receive letters, memos, bulletins, newsletters, bulletin board messages, electronic messages, or maybe even

Objectives

After completing this chapter, you should be able to:

1.
Describe what takes place in the communication process.

2.
Identify the barriers to communication.

3.
Demonstrate the use of open communication.

4.
Demonstrate the effectiveness of assertive communication.

5.
List the components of good listening.

a note scratched on the back of a used envelope. You will also receive verbal communication that may be face-to-face or through an intercom, by voice mail, or in telephone conversations. Verbal information may come from coworkers, customers, supervisors, government regulators, and suppliers. You will also receive communication through the body language of others. Even the clothing of others can communicate a message to you. If a friend shows up at your door in tennis clothes, you know at a glance that he or she probably wants you to play tennis.

The rumor mill, or "the office grapevine," will also provide you with information. Gossip is alive and well in the scenario you read in the opening. (The truth is that parking rates are to go up to $35 at the end of the year. The employee cafeteria is going to raise the price of salads by 25 percent.) The rumor mill does not always pass along accurate information because it becomes escalated each time it is passed along. In spite of all the practice we have in communicating, we still do not seem to be very effective at it. Why not?

Communication Takes Two

Communication is a two-way process. The **sender** of information produces the thought or idea that is to be sent to another. The **receiver** is the individual who is to receive the thought or idea. The thought or idea is called the **message**. The message may take more than one form. The word *hello* spoken to another is an example of a verbal message. Nonverbal messages are sent without words, such as when you nod your head or glance at the clock to indicate your acknowledgment of another or an awareness of time. Beware! If your words convey one message and your nonverbal message gives another, the nonverbal message will be stronger.

What nonverbal messages are sent by these actions?

1. Tapping a foot.

2. Pointing a finger.

3. Raising a fist above the head.

4. Crossing the arms across the chest.

5. Scratching the head.

Communication does not take place until the message moves from the sender to the receiver and the receiver understands the message intended. In other words, both the sender and the receiver share the same meaning of what is being communicated.

66 Gossip is the most deadly microbe.
It has neither legs nor wings,
It is composed entirely of tales
And most of them have stings. 99
——E. E. Opdyke

Critical Thinking

Think about...

why you feel people get involved in the rumor mill and pass along inaccurate information.

In order to know if the receiver has received your message, you watch his or her actions. The actions of the receiver generally tell you how accurately the message has been received. If you tell a coworker a joke and his or her reaction is laughter, you can assume the receiver "got the joke." The actions of the receiver are called **feedback**. Feedback is the listener's response that tells the sender if the message is understood. Feedback may come in the form of a verbal or nonverbal response.

The use of the senses can also help you to send a message. The route that a message takes to get to the receiver is called the **channel**. The sense of hearing is used to send verbal messages. The sense of sight is involved with the channel through which visual (sight) messages are sent. If the sense of touch is used, the channel is the skin. You may choose to use more than one channel to get your message across. You comfort a coworker by saying, "I'm sorry you didn't get the promotion." You can further strengthen your message by using the sense of touch—touching the coworker's shoulder.

66 That which we are capable of feeling, we are capable of sending. 99
—Cervantes

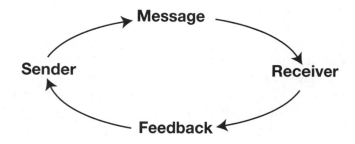

Illustration 8-1
Diagram of the communication model.

Poor communication is said to be one of the biggest problems in the workplace. Often senders and receivers do not share the same understanding of the message, and communication does not take place. There are many barriers to the communication process. The barriers block the communication process.

C arlos and Tomas were talking as they were stocking shelves. Willy, a new employee, was in the next aisle struggling with a loaded pallet of vegetable cans. Tomas said to Willy, "Come on over when you're finished!" Willy smiled and went on stocking. Willy thought that Tomas was saying to him in a joking manner, "You're working hard. We could use your kind of help." Willy went on about his business and didn't think anymore about the incident. Tomas had not communicated to

Willy what he wanted. Tomas wanted Willy to come over to their aisle where he and Carlos were working and get acquainted. Tomas has now made the assumption that Willy is not interested in making friends.

Communication Barriers

The first step to removing barriers to communication is to identify them. The following paragraphs will assist you in this identification process.

Poor Choice of Words

Word choice is the most common communication barrier. Words have different meanings to different people. Take the word *mean* for example. You may use this word to describe someone who is unkind, rough, dangerous, or intends to do you harm. Another person may use the word *mean* to describe something very special, "cool," great. You have heard the expression "mean machine." Smooth running, great operating!

Strive to use words that have a universal meaning. A word like *slippery* probably has the same meaning to everyone. But other words, such as *liberal*, may have a negative or positive tone depending upon your background and experience. If you are in doubt about how someone is interpreting your words or thoughts, ask! When you recognize a word as having possibly confusing meanings, do not use it. It is a good idea to filter your words.

As you work with people of ethnic groups who do not share your background and experiences, be aware that their definition of words and phrases may be different from yours. You may offend a coworker through ignorance by using a word that has a different connotation to

Different personal backgrounds and experiences require sensitivity and openness to eliminate communication barriers.

him or her. For example, if you refer to Asian-Americans as Orientals, you may find that they are offended by this reference. Some Asian-Americans find this term inappropriate. When you use a term that is offensive, you can unknowingly build up a communication barrier. Ask your coworkers who are from a different ethnic origin to let you know if you say something that is considered offensive, derogatory, or unkind. Also, share with them that you will do the same.

If a person lets you know that something you have said is inappropriate to them, apologize. Ask for further clarification of what you said and how it was interpreted, and eliminate the phrase or term from your vocabulary. Do *not* use words referring to minority groups that are blatantly meant to be racial slurs. Refer to your coworkers by their given names.

Avoid the use of slang terms that are used to refer to men, women, senior citizens, people with disabilities, or any minority group. Work toward using gender-free references. Do not use any words to offend others or perpetuate stereotypes. Communication may break down completely between you and a coworker because you used a word out of ignorance that was highly offensive to someone. You may want to make a list of words *not* to use.

Selective Communication

Are you guilty of **selective communication?** This means hearing or reading only what you want to hear or read. It is a common human characteristic to skip over the uncomfortable or unpleasant things in life. This may happen when you hear or read something that is in conflict with your personal thoughts, convictions, or beliefs. Or you may be selective when you receive information that you do not want to hear. Selective communication is not an option in the workplace. You need to pay careful attention to what is said and follow through.

Don's supervisor tells him to provide the accounting department with the latest income figures and the shipping department with the freight costs for the last 30 days. He also tells Don to call the state sales tax revenue department to see if they found any problems with the last revenue report filed by the company. Don heard the first two directives. However, the last directive he didn't want to hear. He dislikes calling the revenue department because if they have found a problem, it is always difficult to get it solved. Also, Don has the attitude that if the revenue department finds something incorrect, they will call. Don exercised selective hearing.

Jargon

All workplaces have a common language that is related to the work environment. The language is often referred to as **jargon**. Jargon is a simplified language used by people in the workplace to communicate in an abbreviated style. For example, you might hear a coworker say, "Bring me a copy of the PAF so I can get the info I need for the PDs." Would you know what to do? You would need to ask for a translation. Your coworker asked you to get a copy of the personal application folder (PAF) so that he or she could obtain the information (info) needed to determine the payroll deductions (PDs). The language of the workplace can be a barrier to a new employee.

When you hear an abbreviation, a technical term, or a slang term that you do not understand that is a part of normal conversation in the workplace, ask for an interpretation. You may be very frustrated in a new position if you cannot understand directions given to you because of the jargon involved. Be patient. You will soon catch on to the jargon and begin using it yourself.

Physical or Distance Barriers

Sometimes communication does not take place because the receiver is simply unable to hear what has been said or he or she only partially hears the message. This barrier is common in the workplace because background noise may interfere with the communication process. This is an easy barrier to overcome. When you are communicating, speak up. Use the volume necessary to be heard in that environment. If you are the receiver, step closer or ask the sender to speak louder. If you are working with equipment or machinery that creates noise, you may want to turn it off or down (if possible) to better hear what is being transmitted.

Channel Openers

The sharing and understanding that are essential in good communication will more likely occur if a comfortable atmosphere exists in the workplace. This type of atmosphere can be created with a friendly smile, a good attitude, and an attempt to understand others. If people are comfortable with you and feel that you care, they will be more likely to communicate freely with you.

 amon was hired as a night nurse at the Sunnyhill Care Home. This was his first job after training, and he was eager to put his skills into practice. On his first night on duty, he followed several veteran employees. He suddenly became very anxious. His thoughts were, "I'm new. Will I understand their procedures? Will the coworkers and patients accept me?"

Ramon paused at the entrance door, took a deep breath, and said to himself, "They'll like me; I can do a good job. Now get to work." Ramon entered the room where the night supervisor was preparing to update the new shift of workers. Ramon looked at each of his coworkers, smiled, introduced himself, and said to each of them, "I'm ready to get to work. I hope you'll help me learn the procedures." Ramon had no problems in establishing himself as a part of the care team at Sunnyhill.

Friendly Attitude

A friendly attitude aids effective communication. If your work brings you into contact with many people, a friendly attitude is essential. Be warm and kind to all of your coworkers, customers, and supervisors. At first you may have to work at it. Take every opportunity to say "thank you" with a smile. Look for something positive in everyone you meet. Each new acquaintance will bring a new dimension to your life.

A friendly attitude is particularly important when dealing with customers and clients.

❝One of the best ways to persuade others is to use your ears—by listening to them.❞

Using Positive Persuasion

In the workplace there are times you will want to persuade others. The art of **persuasion** is attempting to get others to adopt or agree with an idea that you have. Persuasion will be a channel opener for you. You should sharpen up some techniques you now use and perhaps become familiar with some new ones.

Questioning Technique. When you use questions to persuade others, use nonchallenging and positive thoughts with the person you are trying to persuade.

> Suzy says, "Matt, did you know that 33 percent of the people in our community are overweight and that 40 percent exercise fewer than 30 minutes per week? Doesn't that get your attention?"

> Matt replies, "Wow! Those do appear to be significant statistics!" Suzy says, "I thought you might be surprised at those facts. Would you like to be a part of the mayor's new wellness team?"

In the above scenario, Suzy most likely persuaded Matt to be a part of the wellness team before he even realized he was being asked.

Sharing a Story. The sharing of an anecdote or a story is also a good persuasion technique. Almost everyone likes to hear a story. Have you noticed that when listening to a lecture, a sermon, or a serious discussion that you really perk up when someone uses a phrase such as, "I'd like to share a story with you." The story does not necessarily need to be funny.

R ock got the attention of his coworker by saying, "I want to share with you a story about my friend JoAnne. JoAnne didn't participate in any of the neighborhood garage sales, picnics, or Christmas parties. She would just sit on her patio or look on and watch others enjoying the fun. During last year's picnic, one of the kids missed the volleyball, and it landed on JoAnne's porch. JoAnne threw it back. The kid smiled and said thanks, and JoAnne moved from her protected patio to the back of the volleyball court and began retrieving the ball for the kids. Before she knew it, she was having a good time." Rock then said, "I'll bet if you gave our company bowling team a try, you'd enjoy the experience with your coworkers."

Perhaps a similar story could help you convince a coworker to join you in an activity. Other stories might be used to get a supervisor to listen to your ideas or a customer to try a new product or service.

Help the Other Person Feel Important

You will not succeed if you make other people feel unimportant. If you boast about how well you are doing, you will make others doubt their own success. If you treat others as if they are inferior to you, you will cause them to doubt their own value. For example, if you begin with "You may not understand this, but ...," you will cause your listeners to feel stupid and incapable of understanding what you are

> "Unless the man who works in an office is able to 'sell' himself and his ideas, unless he has the power to convince others of the soundness of his convictions, he may never achieve his goal. He may have the best ideas in the world, he may have plans which would revolutionize entire industries. But unless he can persuade others that his ideas are good, he will never get the chance to put them into effect. Stripped of non-essentials, all business activity is a persuasion battle. . . "
> —Robert E. M. Cowie

about to say. This is not the way to open up the channels of communication.

The way to make others feel important is by asking for their opinions, seeking their advice, getting their points of view, and making them a part of decisions. Seek opportunities to give recognition, to build others up, and to make others feel important.

Reward the Positive; Ignore the Negative

When someone says something positive about you or your work habits, respond warmly. You need to respond this way so that the sender of the message will feel free to communicate with you in the future. Most of us have difficulty in accepting compliments or kind words. Practice saying something warm, something "giving," back to the person who compliments you. Instead of saying, "Oh, it was nothing," show the other person respect and how the compliment made you feel. Try saying, "It makes me feel good to hear you say that. I appreciate your kind words." Accepting compliments takes practice, but it is never too late to start practicing.

When someone (other than your supervisor) complains about your actions or job performance, let him or her talk. Just listen. As you listen, ignore the part of the conversation that is directed wrongly at you personally. Listening may also give you a clue or two about improving your job performance. Mean, negative statements are best forgotten. Just concentrate on what you can learn from the complainer.

Gossip

In your effort to keep channels of communication open, keep in mind that a very powerful channel of information in any organization is gossip. Gossip surfaces when people are curious about a situation and the facts are not available. When this happens, speculation begins and the grapevine goes into action. Check out the accuracy of gossip you hear before you communicate it to others or apply it yourself. Information can change when it moves from person to person for many reasons, including these:

> ❝Gossip starts where information stops.❞

1. One person may not hear part of the message and only pass along the parts heard.

2. A word may be added in place of a word that has been forgotten.

3. A part of the message may have been forgotten before it is passed along.

4. A person may misinterpret what was said.

When you hear a message that is gossip or has the potential of being gossip, listen carefully. Repeat the message to the sender to be sure you have accurately heard the message. Then check with someone who would know the accuracy of the information. Let the rumor mill stop at your workstation.

Gossip that is damaging to someone's character should be forgotten. Do not even bother to check out the accuracy of the message. Avoid hurting a coworker. If malicious gossip about a coworker is being spread, you can attempt to stop it by not furthering the information or by turning over the information to others who can put a stop to it.

Communication Styles

Standing up for your rights in the workplace is important. Your ideas and feelings need to be expressed in an open manner. Consider your personal communication style. Are you a passive, an aggressive, or an assertive communicator?

Passive Communication

Passive communication happens when you give into others without expressing your feelings or rights. If you communicate and behave in a passive manner, you serve as a "doormat" for others, never standing up for yourself. For example, if someone steps in front of you in the grocery checkout line and you do not indicate that you were in line, you exercise passive behavior. The danger of being passive is that you will fail to describe or to express anger and other feelings; the result may be resentment, depression, and a loss of self-esteem.

 haron and Lloyd are standing in line at the theater. It is a cold evening, and they have waited about 30 minutes. As they are approaching the ticket booth, two young men step in front of them and crowd in line. Lloyd looks at Sharon and shrugs his shoulders. He says nothing about the "crowders" and lets them buy their tickets and go on into the theater. Later Lloyd feels embarrassed about his inability to express his feelings. Sharon was surprised that he did not speak his mind. She also wishes that she had spoken up and not allowed her rights to be violated.

Aggressive Communication

Aggressive communication is the opposite of passive communication. If you use this style of communication, you communicate your feelings in a forceful manner without regard to the rights or feelings of others. For example, upon ordering a rare steak and receiving one that is well done, the aggressive communicator might say loudly, "Get this piece of meat off of my plate. I ordered a rare steak, not a piece of shoe leather. For the prices you charge in this place, you should be able to get an order correct." The aggressive communicator is very defensive, fault-finding, and judgmental. This type of behavior definitely communicates your feelings, but you step on the rights and feelings of others in the process. Aggressive communication can even result in physical contact—pushing, nudging, shoving. You may embarrass yourself and those around you.

S haron and Lloyd are standing in line to attend a popular movie. They are just about to the ticket booth, when two young men crowd into the line because they appear to know the two people stepping up to the ticket window. Lloyd steps in front of them, gets in their "space," and says in a very loud voice, "Who do you think you are? Get to the back of the line. You can stand in line just like the rest of us." Then Lloyd gives them a shove. Sharon is embarrassed as a shoving match develops and the management comes out of the theater to settle the matter.

Assertive Communication

Assertive communication is a more positive communication style than either passive or aggressive. Assertive communication occurs when you stand up for your rights but do not impinge on the rights of others. Being assertive allows you to express your feelings and ideas in a positive manner. Some people avoid being assertive because they think they are not important enough to have their rights respected. Or they feel guilty about their emotions. Everyone is important. It does not matter whether someone is an administrative assistant, a clerk, a supervisor, an attorney, a housekeeper, or a race car driver—all are important. Your feelings are yours, and they deserve to be expressed without any guilt. As you work to use assertive language, you should identify what you are thinking or feeling and state it in the most caring way possible.

Assertive communication is not only what you say, but also how you say it. In addition to stating your feelings and saying the right words, you will need to

1. Establish eye contact with the receiver of your message. Eye contact is important. It indicates that you are serious, you mean business, and you want to command the receiver's attention. Do not try to hold a stare. Just comfortably look into their eyes. Some peo-

ple have a difficult time looking others in the eye; begin working on this skill now. Without this skill you will have difficulty in communicating assertively.

2. Do not use gestures that are threatening or that could be interpreted as aggressive. No finger pointing or shaking.

3. Your body position is also important. Stand erect, but not stiff. Position yourself so that your eye level is about the same as the receiver. If the receiver of your message is seated, you sit. If the receiver is standing, you stand. Stand just a little bit closer than you normally would if you were talking to a person, but be careful not to get too close. You will know you are too close if the recipient steps back. If you get too close, you are approaching aggressive communication. Most of us are comfortable talking to someone 18 inches or more from us.

4. Speak in a normal voice tone. Speak loudly enough to be heard and speak clearly. Again, if you raise your voice, you will seem too aggressive. If you speak too softly, it will be difficult for your recipient to take you seriously.

Sharon and Lloyd are standing in line waiting to get tickets for a popular movie. Just as they are nearing the ticket booth, two young men crowd in line in front of them. Lloyd speaks to them in a calm, firm voice and looks them in the eye. Lloyd stands closer to them than he would under normal circumstances. He says, "Gentlemen, we've been standing here in the cold for some time. You've crowded in front of us, and we'll be out here a few more minutes. You'll need to move to the back of the line and wait your turn." Sharon is pleased with Lloyd's assertive communication skills. Lloyd is also pleased, and he and Sharon are able to get into the theater quicker. Lloyd stood for his rights without being defensive, critical, or judgmental.

66 Sometimes your body language speaks so loud, others cannot hear what you are saying. 99

Passive people are usually unhappy because they cannot state what they think and feel. Aggressive communicators get their ideas, thoughts, and feelings heard; but they usually create more problems for themselves because of their aggressive tactics. The ability to be assertive takes thought and practice.

Listening Is Part Of Communication

Listening is the process by which we make sense out of what we hear. Hearing alone is not listening because hearing only means that

Listening skills are essential to good communication.

you recognize that a message is being sent; you may or may not be translating the information and attempting to bring a common understanding between you and the sender of the message. Have you had the experience of watching an entire television program and, at the end, you realize you remember nothing that has been said? If so, your listening skills may need to be sharpened.

Listening is an art that needs to be practiced in order to be perfected. If you were to measure the amount of communication that you are involved in each day, you would find that more time is spent in listening than in speaking, reading, or writing. Yet you have probably spent a good share of your educational time learning to speak, read, and write.

Barriers to Listening

Many roadblocks can stop you from receiving a message. Let's review some of those roadblocks so that you can eliminate them from being barriers to your listening skills.

Noise. Too many sounds at one time or unusual sounds can be barriers to your listening. Focus in on what you are listening to. Block out what is not important. Avoid the distraction of reacting to the unusual attire of a speaker, the pronunciation of a word, or a unique voice quality or dialect. These can be considered "noise" because they can take your thoughts away from the message.

Thinking Ahead. In a conversation people take turns speaking and listening. Sometimes you may take your time for listening to think about what you will say next. If this happens, you are hearing but not listening. Your reply may not make sense because you did not listen to the words of the speaker. He or she may have moved the conversation to a new topic and you missed it!

> **"** The reason why so few people are agreeable is that each is thinking more about what he intends to say than about what others are saying, and we never listen when we are eager to speak. **"**
> —LaRochefoucauld

Illustration 8-2
Eliminate noise from your conversation.

Mind Moving Too Fast. People think at a much more rapid rate than they speak. Most speakers talk at a rate of about 125 words per minute. Most receivers listen at a rate exceeding 500 words a minute. If you are listening at the normal rate of 500 words per minute, you are ahead of the speaker. Thus, your thoughts can wander while you are listening. You may begin to daydream or think about what you need to do later. When this happens you miss the points of the speaker because your mind is elsewhere. If you find yourself ahead of the speaker, use this valuable time to review what the speaker has said. But try to keep your mind focused on the speaker!

Lack of Attention. Good listening requires keeping one's thoughts on what is being said. When you do not pay close attention to the speaker and his or her message, you are not listening. Paying attention will

66 Nature has given man one tongue and two ears, that we may hear twice as much as we speak. 99
—Epictetus

Lack of attention is unprofessional and can cause you to miss important information.

prevent you from missing important information. For example, if you are being given directions on the job and you are not paying close attention, you may do something wrong and cause injury or expense to your employer or a coworker.

Poor Attitude. A poor attitude can also prevent you from receiving a message. For example, if you think a conversation between two of your coworkers is boring, you stop listening. Your thoughts turn to noise that is around you. You miss the conversation because you took on the attitude that it was uninteresting. A poor attitude can be dangerous because it can be a barrier to hearing important information.

Good Listening Skills

Listening takes practice. Work on the following techniques of good listening skills:

1. Prepare yourself to listen.

2. Learn to shift from speaker to listener.

3. Listen actively.

4. Avoid emotional responses.

Prepare Yourself to Listen. Your efficiency as a listener will improve if you prepare yourself to listen both mentally and physically. Block out miscellaneous thoughts that are running through your mind. Attempt to erase those competing thoughts, such as what was said in the carpool on the way to work, the dentist's bill you need to pay, and your plans for Friday night. You cannot act on any of these thoughts now, so eliminate them and prepare your mind to listen. Do some self-talk: *"I'm going to concentrate on what's being said. I need to listen to this information."*

Prepare yourself physically to listen. Sit or stand in a way that is comfortable and will help you listen. Be alert. Look at the speaker as you prepare yourself. A visual bond between speaker and listener is important in effective listening.

Shift from Speaker to Listener. Keep in mind that one of the barriers to good listening is planning what you are going to say next rather than listening to the speaker. Spend your time listening and not preparing your next speech. Avoid the following:

1. Thinking about what clever thing you are going to say next.

2. Planning the next question you want to ask.

The next time you are the listener in a conversation, ask yourself: "Am I preparing a speech or am I listening?"

Listen Actively. Since a person is capable of listening at a rate approximately five times faster than a person can speak, you can use the "extra time" as "think time." Use your extra moments to paraphrase and interpret what is being said. This is called **active listening**.

Active listening is hard work, but the rewards are great. An active listener will make better decisions—decisions based on more information, plus the opinions and experiences of others. The active listener:

1. Takes the time to listen.

2. Shows the speaker that he or she is interested by looking at the speaker and using body language to indicate that listening is taking place.

3. Blocks out noise.

4. Jots down the main ideas (when appropriate).

5. Listens with an open mind.

6. Provides feedback.

Critical Thinking

Think about...

how many examples of an active listener you can find in the scenario.

Jun wants to tell Cheri about his fishing trip to Canada. Cheri knows this trip was important to Jun, and she and her spouse are planning a similar trip next fall. Cheri sits down to listen. Jun says, "The best fishing time seemed to be in the early morning." Cheri asks, "How early?" Jun says, "My biggest thrill during the trip was when I brought in a 22-pound northern pike." Cheri replies, "Wow! That would be a thrill!" Cheri ignores the conversation going on at the table next to them. Cheri takes out a small notebook and says, "Now let's make sure I have this correct." She begins to jot down notes as she asks, "Was the name of that lake Wagbegon or Waybeegon? How many miles south of Dryden is that?" Cheri has exercised active listening skills.

Now look at points 5 and 6 again. When you are in the listening role, keep an open mind. An open mind is one that will listen to ideas and opinions with which you disagree. You are willing to hear the other side and learn. Do not judge the speaker's message. Absorb the information and formulate your opinions later. Disregard looks, actions, or personality. Attempt to understand the speaker's feelings and respect the speaker's thoughts.

When the speaker has stopped talking, provide feedback. Feedback will help you seek more information from the speaker. Asking questions or making comments also shows the speaker that you were listening. Provide the speaker with nonverbal feedback as you listen. Use eye contact, a smile, or a nod to let your speaker know you are an active listener. If you frown, yawn, or turn your eyes away, you indicate that you are not interested.

Avoid Emotional Responses. Many times as you listen it is difficult to control your emotional responses to the speaker's message. Each of us has a list of words that trigger emotional responses—whether positive or negative. What are some words that cause an emotional reaction in you? Perhaps some of the words on your list are *feminist, democrat, republican, racist,* or *liberal.* Poor listeners spend their time reacting to "red flag" words and frequently miss the message.

Separate Facts from Opinions

At times you will need to separate facts from the opinions of those who are speaking to you. This is called **critical listening**. A critical listener determines the accuracy of the message and identifies the main ideas and details being imparted. You will need to evaluate each message by deciding what is fact and what is opinion. This is done with respect for the opinion of the sender of the message.

As a critical listener, you will want to play detective. Your game will include separating facts from opinions. Separate that which can be proven, which are called **facts**, from opinions. **Opinions** are what the speaker says based on his or her personal beliefs or feelings. Opinions may not always be based on fact. Facts and opinions are illustrated below.

FACTS	OPINIONS
—It's 95 degrees outside.	—It's hot outside.
—It can print 15 pages per minute.	—The printer is fast.
—The car is the latest model.	—The car is good looking.
—The laptop computer weighs 5 pounds.	—The laptop computer isn't heavy.
—The dog bit her on the leg.	—The dog is vicious.

Critical Thinking

Think about...
a time when you have heard someone's opinion and assumed it was a fact. What were the results?

66 Where there is much desire to learn, there of necessity will be much arguing, much writing, many opinions; for opinion in good men is but knowledge in the making. 99
—John Milton

Summary

Good communication is essential in the workplace. The sender of information produces the thought or idea that is to be sent to the receiver. The thought or information is called the message. Messages may be verbal or nonverbal. There are several barriers to watch out for as you communicate in the workplace:

1. Poor choice of words.

2. Selective communication. (Hearing only what you want to hear.)

3. Use of jargon.

4. Physical or distance barriers.

Strive to keep the channels of communication open by keeping a friendly attitude, using positive persuasion, helping others feel important, rewarding the positive and ignoring the negative, and being aware of the pitfalls of gossip.

Recognize the importance of assertive communication: standing up for your rights and feelings without stepping on the rights and feelings of others. People who use assertive communication

1. Establish good eye contact with the receiver of the message.

2. Do not use gestures that are threatening or aggressive.

3. Position themselves at the eye level of the receiver.

4. Speak in a normal voice tone.

Listening is the process by which you make sense out of what you hear. The barriers to good listening include

1. Noise.

2. Thinking ahead.

3. Mind moving too fast.

4. Lack of attention.

5. Poor attitude.

Good listening skills take practice. The good listener

1. Prepares to listen.

2. Avoids thinking about what he or she is going to say next.

3. Listens actively.

4. Avoids emotional responses.

The critical listener separates facts from opinions.

End of Chapter Activities

Questions and Projects

1. What nonverbal messages have you observed other than those listed on page 116?

2. What does the following statement mean to you? A good conversationalist is not one who remembers what was said, but says what is worth remembering.

3. Why is it important to be careful in your choice of words when working with someone from another cultural background?

4. List three ways you could make others feel important as you communicate with them.

5. List three ways you could appropriately respond to this compliment: "The paper you wrote about the significance of the Fourth of July was inspirational."

6. List five changes that took place in the "gossip" channel in the opening scenario of this chapter.

7. Describe an experience you have had in which you were a passive communicator. How did you feeling following the experience? How could you have changed your style to being an assertive communicator?

8. Why do you think it is so difficult to learn to listen?

9. List the noises in the workplace setting that you think could interfere with communication. List the noises in the typical schoolroom setting that might interfere with quality listening.

Case Problems

1. Accept a Compliment

Ruth and Helen had been friends for many years. However, because of their busy schedules, they had not had the opportunity to meet for several weeks. They finally arranged to meet for lunch. During lunch Helen said to Ruth, "The feature article you wrote on child nutrition was excellent." Ruth responded, "Did you read the piece I wrote on traffic violations?"

    a. What would be an appropriate response for Ruth following Helen's compliment about the child nutrition article?

    b. How do you think Helen felt when her comment on the child nutrition article was ignored?

2. Impact of Aggressive Communication

Ernie is a medical records clerk in a large metropolitan hospital. He takes his job very seriously. He knows that a mistake in a medical record could be physically damaging to a patient's health. Teresa, one of the emergency room nurses, states that the left thumb of an emergency patient was crushed in a workplace accident. As Ernie is putting the records together for this patient, he notices that the doctor and the emergency paramedic had noted that the patient's right thumb was injured. Ernie rushes out of his office, locates Teresa, and begins yelling at her and shaking the medical records in front of her. He says, "How could you be so stupid? Don't you know left from right? Do you realize the jeopardy you put a patient in when you record misinformation? Where did you get your license to be a nurse, out of a catalog? Don't you care about the reputation of this hospital?" This outburst takes place in the family waiting room outside of the emergency room.

    a. Was Ernie's style of communication passive, aggressive, or assertive? What characteristics of the style were demonstrated in Ernie's outburst?

    b. Who may have been embarrassed by Ernie's choice of communication? What damage may have been done because of where he chose to share his message with Teresa?

    c. How could Ernie have communicated his message to Teresa?

3. Damaging Conversation

Dale, an African-American, is the senior foreman at the Bruning Circuit Breaker Manufacturing Company. He has 25 men and women working on his team. One afternoon Dale asks one of the team members, Henry, to redo two completed units because he thinks that the units will not meet the standards required by quality control. The worker says, "They look okay to me. Why don't you ask one of your soul brothers to redo them?"

    a. Dale is upset by the racial remark made by Henry. What should he say to Henry?

b. What would motivate Henry to use such inappropriate language?

c. Why was the term *soul brothers* totally inappropriate in this setting?

Getting Your Message Across

Harley and George were busy attempting to solve a problem involving a programmable logic controller. Meg was walking through the area and hesitated as she passed them. Meg had considerable experience in working with pneumatic equipment, but she hesitated to offer advice because she did not know Harley and George very well. Harley noticed Meg and said, "Hello." Meg responded by saying, "Hi." Meg then moved out of the work area. Harley said to George, "She sure isn't very friendly. I hear she's real sharp, but I can't seem to get more than a word or two from her." George replied, " I think she thinks she's too good to talk with other employees. I'll bet she comes on strong with conversation when management is around."

Speaking up in the workplace can be a challenge. The challenge is greatest when you are a new employee who is meeting many new people, learning new procedures, and hoping to please everyone with the quality of your work. It is normal to be uncomfortable in conversation with someone who is new to you. In the workplace this level of discomfort can be lessened by studying how to get across your message. You will take part in conversation, give information, and perhaps even be asked to speak before a group of people. In order to share your knowledge and get across your message, you will want to prepare yourself for these challenges. However, do not think of

Objectives

After completing this chapter, you should be able to:

1.
Demonstrate the ability to get a message across to others.

2.
Participate in a conversation.

3.
Present a speech before a group.

your speaking opportunities as difficult challenges. Consider these challenges as opportunities to share your knowledge, get acquainted with people, and help others to know your capabilities.

General Rules For The Sender Of Communication

As you communicate with others, you may be the speaker or the listener. The following rules to communication apply specifically to the sender. You are a sender when you speak or write.

Be Clear

Your message will be received accurately only if you make your statement or request so clear that it cannot be misunderstood. In an effort to make your message clear, be brief, use variety, and itemize.

Brevity. Typically, your communication will be clearer if you use short words, short sentences, and short paragraphs. Brevity is the key to clear communication. The receiver of your message will understand five words better than ten, a two-syllable word better than a six-syllable word, and a six-line paragraph better than one containing twelve lines.

However, be sure that in your attempt to be brief, you do not omit some important part of your message.

Variety. Your communication will get attention if you use variety in your speaking and writing. One way to put variety into what you say or write is to avoid using the same words or phrases over and over. Avoid using trite and meaningless phrases like "you know," "in terms of," and "at this point in time." Also, avoid the tendency to write several sentences in succession that start the same way or that are the same length.

Itemization. Clarity is also improved if you itemize steps or lists that you wish to communicate. Notice how difficult it is to understand the following written instructions:

> "Please locate the records of David Thorton, a patient we saw in March. Make two copies of his medical records, and send one to Doctor McKenzie in the Medical Arts Clinic. Send the other one to the Arthur Clinic on Madison Road. Attach copies of the release forms that Thorton signed when he was in for his last checkup."

If these instructions were written or said in an itemized fashion, they would be much easier to follow:

1. Make two copies of the medical records of David Thorton. Attach the release form signed by Thorton to each copy.

2. Send one of the copies to Doctor McKenzie in the Medical Arts Clinic.

3. Send the other copy to the Arthur Clinic on Madison Road.

Note that when you itemize, you tend to eliminate unnecessary words.

Be Positive in Saying No

In previous chapters you have learned the importance of being *positive*. However, there are times when you must say "no." Thus it is important in your study of getting your message across to learn how to say "no" in a positive manner.

Imply the Negative. In some circumstances you can say "no" or send a "no" message by simply implying it. For example, if a coworker asks you to clock in for him because he is going to arrive at the plant late, you might answer, "Because our company policy is that everyone must clock in for himself, you'll need to clock in for yourself."

Note that you never said you would not clock in for him.

Say What You Can Do. To avoid being negative, you can say what you can or will do without saying what you cannot or will not do. If a customer asks you to ship an order by December 1 and you realize this is impossible, rather than saying "no," this is not possible, say, "We'll have that order on its way to you by December 5."

Use Sentence Structure. When you must say "no," remove the sting of the word by putting the "no" part of the sentence in a dependent clause of the sentence. For example, rather than saying "You failed to identify the color for your new sweater," say, "If you'll let me know what color sweater you want, we'll get it to you within seven days."

Impersonalize the Negative. Make the "no" part of your sentence relate to a thing rather than a person. If you say "This dress appears to have a faulty zipper," the listener will more willingly accept your statement. But if you say "What did you do—jerk on this zipper?" your statement sounds accusatory, and your listener will resent it.

Conversational Skills

Conversational skills are important in the workplace! Take advantage of conversational opportunities to get to know your supervisors and coworkers better. If this opportunity frightens you, that is normal. Take a deep breath, and start a conversation whenever it is appropriate. The secret of being a good conversationalist is to just *be yourself*. If you try to impress others by attempting to be someone you are not, you will be uneasy and guarded. This will make you and the receiver(s) of your message uncomfortable. Such a statement, however, is certain to raise the question, "How can I improve my conversation?" The following paragraphs give you suggestions; after that, you will need to *practice*.

Voice Qualities

Part of your conversational ability will be based on your voice qualities. Your voice qualities are a part of your personality. Work on good voice qualities. There is no one right way to speak. Listening would be very dull if everyone spoke and sounded alike. There are, however, several characteristics of a good voice that you will want to work on as you develop your skills as a speaker and as a conversationalist. They are as follows:

1. good pitch
2. appropriate volume
3. good inflection
4. enunciation
5. pronunciation

Pitch. **Pitch** is the high or low sound of your voice. Pitch is determined by the length, tension, and thickness of your vocal cords. You have no control over the length or thickness of your vocal cords, but you do have control over the tension you exert on them. When your vocal cords are too tense, they produce high squeaky tones. Your listener then realizes that you are tense. Relax and take a deep breath; your pitch will be smooth and improved.

Volume. **Volume** is the loudness or softness of your voice. Have you ever noticed how tiring it is to try to hear someone who speaks too softly? Speak up so that others can hear your message. Do not exhaust others by forcing them to strain to hear you or miss your message because they could not hear what you were saying.

Listening to a very loud voice can also be annoying. Adjust your voice so that others can hear you clearly. If you are unsure of your volume, ask the help of others. Say "Can you hear me?" "Am I speaking loudly enough?" or "Am I speaking too loudly?"

Inflection. **Inflection** is the rising and falling of your voice. If you speak with no inflection, you speak in a **monotone**. A monotone is a voice with no expression. It always sounds the same. Use your voice to help express the meaning of your words. Be sure your voice is not always the same. Ask others for help: "Is my voice flat?" "Does my voice always sound the same?" Put the enthusiasm in your voice that you feel inside.

Critical Thinking

Think about...

what you would do if you were told by your supervisor that your voice qualities needed work.

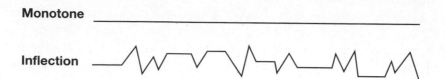

Monotone

Inflection

Illustration 9-1
Conversation is improved when your voice shows emotion.

Read these sentences and put feeling into them. Work at using inflection in your voice.

Martin, did you have a good trip?

The match is over! I won!

Sure, I want to be a part of the project.

Enunciation. Enunciation is pronouncing each part of each word clearly. The more carefully you enunciate, the more likely you are to be understood. Be careful to speak clearly and not run your words together. Avoid the sloppiness of running frequently used phrases together, and take special care not to leave out part of a word.

If you do not enunciate, your speech will be sloppy and difficult to understand.

Pronunciation. Pronunciation is saying a word correctly. Pronunciation requires that you know how words are supposed to be pronounced. If you mispronounce words, you *should* know you make a bad impression or fail to communicate your meaning. Good pronunciation will give you one of the qualities of an articulate person.

Don't Talk Too Fast

Good conversation is meant to be relaxing, so do not talk too fast. When you speak very rapidly, your receiver will sense a feeling of tenseness. Put some pauses into what you have to say. This will slow down your speaking tempo. Do not be afraid of silence in conversation. Constant chatter can be extremely wearing, and an occasional pause or short silence can be refreshing. As you slow down the speed of your conversation, you will enunciate more clearly. It will be easier for your listener to understand your message.

66 The trouble with people who talk too fast is that they often say something they haven't thought of yet. 99

Learn to Listen

You read about the importance of being a good listener in Chapter 8. Good listening is also a very important part of being a skilled conversationalist. If you think of your conversational group as a basketball team, for example, it may help you see the necessity of giving each player a chance at the basket. Throw the conversational ball to others, listen actively, and show interest with your face and body language. Performing this skill will make others think you are a gifted conversationalist. You will not need to say much yourself if you make the conversation of others seem important. A good listener must avoid criticism too. If you have a negative thought, "This person doesn't really know what he is talking about," your face or body language may give you away, defeating all you have been trying to accomplish.

Pass the conversation around.

Dean Abramson/Stock, Boston

Respect the Space of Others

The distance between you and your listener has an impact on how well you get across your conversational message. Have you noticed how people react in a crowded elevator? They stand rigid, do not talk, and stare at the indicator above the door or at the floor. This reaction demonstrates a discomfort because in a crowded elevator, people are "in your space." This also happens in conversation. If you get too close when talking to someone, your message may be lost and the conversation will soon terminate. Our need for space is culturally determined; therefore, what an American would consider acceptable conversation distance may be different from what a Japanese person or persons from the Middle East would find acceptable. You will know you are too close when the listener steps back. If you work with people who are culturally diverse, ask them about the space needs from their culture or do some research on your own.

Achieve Eye Contact

Eye contact is important if your listeners are to take your message seriously. If you are talking to several people, you will need to establish eye contact with each person. This will make each of them feel included. It may be hard to move your eyes away from someone who seems to be responding to you; but if you are to get across your message, you must make an effort to do so.

Some ethnic groups show respect by dropping their eyes. Recognize this act as a cultural characteristic.

Let Others Speak

Keep your comments brief. If you tell a story, keep it short. If you explain the way you think about something, give the highlights only. You need to work at this so you will leave time for others to speak. When you are talking, you are not listening or learning. Give others a chance to speak.

Avoid Being Shy

If you are a shy person, having a conversation is easier said than done. If you feel comfortable fading into the background, fight it. Your shyness or lack of conversation may make others think that you are cold, disinterested, or unfeeling. People may become uncomfortable in your presence. If you start by showing an interest in what others are saying, it will not be long before you will want to participate in the conversation. Your ideas need to be shared!

Conversation—What Do I Say?

So far this chapter has focused on how you should act and what you should do in conversation. Now you need to concentrate on what to say.

Keep Your Statements Pleasant

As you begin thinking about your conversational skill, remember to avoid unpleasant topics, criticism of others, sarcasm, and pessimism. In fact, it would be a good idea to avoid these conversations entirely. Refrain from derogatory remarks for two reasons: (1) Others do not

A competent worker...

■ works well with men and women and with people from a variety of ethnic, social, or educational backgrounds admire the person who makes such remarks. (2) They destroy the spirit of cooperation that can be built by good conversation.

Get Involved

Be prepared to talk as you move to a conversational setting. A good starter may be to compliment one of the speakers. You might want to use a phrase such as, "How interesting. I had never thought of that." This is complimentary to the person speaking because it shows you are thinking about what has been said. Another way to involve yourself in a conversation might be to ask a question. Speakers are always glad to have a question because this gives them a chance to talk to a definite point. If someone has been talking about his or her child, you might ask, "How old did you say your child is?" A question is another sincere form of flattery. It is an easy way, too, to get involved in a conversation.

If you are attempting to get a conversation started, the questioning technique may again be tried. Your question will encourage a response. If your first question does not work, just keep trying until you hit on an interest of the person with whom you want to converse.

Critical Thinking

Think about...

the techniques Roberto used to start a conversation. How can you use similar techniques to communicate with others?

Roberto wanted to establish a good working rapport with a new coworker, Mitch. Roberto said, "Good morning. How was your weekend?" Mitch replied, "Restful!" Roberto did not give up; he kept going. "Great. Did you hear the final score of the Yankees game?" Mitch said, "I don't follow baseball." Roberto responded, "Sorry, I forget that not everyone is a baseball nut. What sports do you enjoy?" Mitch replied, "Oh, my sport is hockey. I grew up in Wisconsin where hockey is very popular, and I've never lost that interest." Roberto thought, "Aha. I finally asked the right question." He said, "It's a small world, Mitch. I grew up in Milwaukee and played hockey in high school and college." The conversation was off and running.

When you use a question to begin a conversation, be careful to choose one that cannot be answered with a single word. For example, "Do you like your job?" The answer you will likely get from this question will be "yes" or "no." You might try a question like, "What do you enjoy about your work?" If you get a one-word answer, "nothing," do not give up. Follow up with "Why don't you tell me what kind of job you would like to have?"

Some questions should be avoided. These include personal questions, particularly those involving health, religion, politics, and money. If you are in doubt as to whether a question is too personal, put yourself in the other person's shoes. Would you like someone to ask you if you have gained weight or what you paid for your car?

Keep an Open Mind

A good conversationalist keeps a tolerant attitude. If you preach, if you dictate, if you pass judgments, others will not enjoy listening to you. Keep an open mind. A conversation should be a free exchange of ideas. Do not try to dominate the conversation or have the final word on every subject. This will permit others in the group to add what they think, and the conversation will flow.

Avoid Total Disagreement

A good conversationalist avoids putting a sudden halt to the conversation. If you take a sudden opposite viewpoint to the one being expressed or contradict the speaker, you are guilty of being rude. Even more unpleasant, however, is that you will usually stop the conversation dead. A mild remark is much more effective and may eventually open the door for you to make your point without being offensive. A remark like "Do you really think so?" is much more tactful than "You're completely wrong!" Work to eliminate all feelings of competitiveness in conversation. There is no winner or loser; instead, there should be a feeling of friendliness and open exchange among the talking group.

Encourage Feedback

If you can show with a nod or a smile that you understand the message presented in a conversation, you will be using a good conversational technique. There are several other ways to encourage feedback. The good conversationalist creates a climate in which others feel comfortable in giving feedback.

Give Reinforcement. If you have asked for feedback, give reinforcement to the listener who responds to your request. For example, suppose you ask a coworker how he or she likes the new health insurance plan. The listener responds, "I think the new program is too expensive for the employee with children." If you say, "Well, you're lucky you even have insurance," your coworker will probably terminate the conversation. To encourage feedback you might say, "I understand it is more expensive for employees with families, but don't you think the benefits for quality medical care for your kids makes it worth the extra cost?" This comment might encourage and continue the dialogue.

Outline the Kind of Feedback You Are Seeking. Try not to ask general or vague questions about feelings, ideas, or behaviors; phrase your questions specifically. Rather than saying to a coworker "Let me know if there is any way I can help you," try being specific. "Do you want help with the inventory of the cosmetics department?"

Speaking Before Groups

In the workplace or in your personal life, you may have the opportunity to speak before a group of coworkers, a committee, or an organization. You may be asked to give a speech. A speech is an occasion when a speaker sends a message to cause some change in the people who are listening. A speech may be given to

1. give information to others.

2. persuade others to do something.

3. entertain others.

4. inspire others.

Some people have a great deal of anxiety about speaking before others. This anxiety can be eliminated if you prepare for the speaking experience. Your preparation includes selecting the subject, preparing your message, and preparing to deliver the speech.

Selecting the Subject

Often the subject you are to talk about has been determined for you. Many times, however, you get to select the subject based on your own purpose for giving the speech. Whichever is the case, you need to review three rules of selecting the subject to help you tailor your subject to the audience and prepare the speech.

1. Consider the interests and needs of the audience. This is step number one. Direct your comments, examples, and stories to the audience. Be sure your audience can understand what you are talking about. A speech should make each listener feel that you are really talking to him or her. No speech should be given without relating what is being said to the listening audience.

2. Consider what you know about the subject. As you begin, jot down what you know about the subject. Determine what you want your audience to know. Allow yourself time to research and verify your information or seek new information to present to your audience.

3. Do not make your topic too broad. You will want to cover your selected topic in the time you have been given. Topics like

Good presentations require good research.

Joseph Schuyler/Stock, Boston

"weather," "art," or "gardening" are too broad. Break the topic into manageable pieces. "Tornadoes in the Midwest," "Work of Monet," or "Growing Roses" would be more reasonable topics to present in one presentation.

Preparing the Speech

Good preparation begins early. Give yourself time to prepare a quality presentation.

Decide the Specific Purpose of Your Speech. Refer to the purposes of a speech listed on page 146. If you decide what it is you wish to tell the listener and why you wish to tell him or her, the rest of the organizing will be easier.

Use an Outline to Organize Your Speech. The speech should have three basic parts:

I. Introduction

II. Body

III. Conclusion

The introduction must be designed to get the attention of the listener. You might want to tell a story, use a shocking statement, use an example, ask a question, or share a series of interesting facts.

The body simply tells the audience what it is that you want them to know. The important thing is to organize your information into logical points so that it is easily understood.

The conclusion will give you the opportunity to give a brief summary of what you have said. The conclusion is the last chance you will have to get across your message to the audience. What do you want them to remember? You might use a personal example that shows your audience the value of the information presented. You could tell a story or a joke that will reinforce your message. You could use a bold statement that shows the audience what will happen if the information you presented is not used. Try to repeat a portion of your opening so that the listeners will have the feeling that they have heard a complete, well-planned presentation.

Now all you need to do is fill in the blanks of the outline.

Let's see what an outline might look like for a speaker who is about to talk about an employee wellness program for a company.

EMPLOYEE WELLNESS PROGRAM

   I. Introduction--The Bon Agra Company instituted a wellness program and reduced absenteeism by 31 percent in the first year of the program.

  II. Body
     A. Why we need a wellness plan?
     B. Who will be involved in planning the wellness program?
     C. Who will be eligible to participate?
     D. What activities will be involved?
     E. What costs will be absorbed by the employee? the company?

 III. Conclusion--We, too, could reduce absenteeism by instituting a wellness program. Review points made in body of presentation. Tell story about how one woman at Bon Agra discovered a dangerous cholesterol level through the wellness program. Her doctor has proclaimed that the program may have saved her life.

Illustration 9-2

> " If you can't write your idea on the back of my calling card, you don't have a clear idea. "
>
> —David Belasco

The best way to write your outline is on index cards. The cards can be easily held in your hand. Do not be concerned about the audience being aware of your cards; the cards signal to them that you are prepared. You will want to write out and memorize your opening and closing remarks. You should choose the exact wording of the rest of the talk as you are speaking. That way you will not need to keep your eyes glued to your notes, and your audience will feel like you are talking with each of them individually. Your index cards are simply a security device for you to keep your comments organized. Of course, you will have planned carefully, thinking through what it is you want to present.

Presenting the Speech

If your speech is well prepared, there is no reason for you to be anxious about the delivery of your message. You have something to share that your audience wants to hear. If they did not want to hear you, they would not be present. Consider the following suggestions to help you prepare.

1. To reduce your anxiety, practice giving your speech before a mirror or before family or friends.

2. Learn to relax your throat. Yawn. Notice how your throat feels. When you yawn, your throat is open. Try to keep this feeling when you are speaking. If you learn to relax, you will benefit in another way. That same sense of relaxation will be conveyed to your audience, helping them to hear your message.

3. When it is your turn to speak, walk quickly and confidently to the front of the room and wait for everyone's attention before you begin. Look at the audience, smile, take a deep breath, and share your thoughts and ideas.

4. As you present your speech, keep in mind your message is important and everyone will want to be able to hear you. Speak to the people in the back of the room, and your voice will be heard. You will lose your audience in a hurry if they cannot hear you.

Practicing a speech before friends or family will reduce anxiety.

5. If as you are talking you find yourself stuck for a word or thought, glance down at your notes, think about what you just said, and just wait for the word or thought to come. Silence is acceptable. Silence may be used to emphasize a point as well as provide you with a few seconds to regroup your thoughts. Do not fill in the time with "ah, uh . . ." Do not apologize to the audience if you get stuck. Just go on with the speech.

6. Be careful not to allow your body language to interfere with what you are saying. Avoid meaningless and repeated gestures like scratching, fiddling with your clothing, or pulling on your ear. Do not lean against the speaker podium or a wall. Stand on both feet, and do not rock from one foot to another.

7. Look at your listeners. Glance at your note cards only as you need to. Pick out four or five people in different parts of the room and speak to them, shifting your eyes from one to another.

8. As you approach the end of the speech, do not drift off or allow your voice to decline in volume. Give your last thoughts with force. Smile. Say thank you for listening. Sit down. Do not end with a meaningless phrase such as "I guess that's all I have to say" or "I think that's it."

Summary

Getting your message across is important in the workplace. You need to be comfortable in order to convince others to accept your ideas. A study of how messages are best transmitted will help you feel more comfortable as you converse and communicate with others.

Your conversation should be clear. Clarity can be achieved by being brief, using variety in your sentences, and itemizing points and steps. Good conversation requires that you

1. Be positive even when it is necessary to say no.

2. Use good voice qualities.

3. Be a good listener.

4. Respect the space of others.

5. Achieve eye contact.

6. Let others speak.

7. Avoid being shy.

As you participate in conversation, it is important to concentrate on what you say. Strive to keep your statements pleasant, get involved in the dialogue, keep an open mind about what is being said, avoid total disagreement with others, and encourage feedback from others.

You may have the opportunity to speak in front of a group. This experience may be challenging to you, but if you adequately prepare and practice for your opportunity, success will be yours.

End of Chapter Activities

Questions and Projects

1. List on the left side of a blank page the words and phrases that you or others use that are trite and used too frequently. On the right side of the page, list phrases that could replace the overused words.

2. How would you tell a customer that the size blouse she desires is out of stock?

3. List the five voice qualities that are desirable for good communication.

4. What body language might you observe if your listener is losing interest in what you are saying?

5. Why is silence important and acceptable in conversation?

6. Explain why the following comments should be avoided.

   a. I can't stand being around a gum chewer.

   b. How can you say that you don't approve of the President's budget?

   c. That's a dumb idea.

   d. You're wrong. I saw the incident.

   e. You should wear brighter colors.

7. Rewrite the items in number 6 so that they would be acceptable in good conversation.

8. Write an opening paragraph for a speech to persuade an audience to support your candidacy for city mayor.

9. Prepare an outline for a presentation you are asked to make about purchasing a new office copier.

10. The following topics are too broad for acceptable speech topics. Give an example of a topic from each broad area that would be an acceptable speech topic.

    a. Food Preparation

    b. Cars

    c. Meat

    d. Housing Industry

    e. Politics

Case Problems

1. Tough to Get Acquainted

Laura was a new employee at the Madison Upholstery Factory. She was eager to get to know her coworkers, but Laura was a shy person. Fran and Allison were fabric cutters, Alexis was a frame builder, and Laura was a finish worker. Fran and Allison had been at the factory for many years, and they were good friends. Alexis had been on the job for only a few months; however, she had worked in the upholstery business for 20 years. Laura's coworkers were friendly, but Laura did not feel she was included in some of the conversations.

    a. How could Laura become involved in the conversations?

    b. What specific techniques could she use to be a part of the conversations?

    c. What will Laura want to avoid in her effort to get acquainted through conversation?

2. Terrified

Larry Williams has worked for Smith and Fields Industry for several years. An opportunity came up for Larry to be promoted to a division director. Larry felt qualified for the position and was excited about the opportunity. His one concern was that he would be expected to give monthly oral reports to upper management. The thought of speaking to a group of 20-25 people terrified Larry.

a. Would you suggest that Larry turn down the promotion if he does not feel comfortable with accepting all of the duties of the position?

b. Who could Larry talk with about his concerns about speaking to groups?

c. What suggestions and support would you give Larry if he came to you for help?

3. Newsletter Dilemma

Louie works in a small company that publishes newsletters for companies too small to hire staff to write, edit, proof, and send newsletters to their customers. One of the customers, Christensen, Inc., is owned by Doug Christensen. Christensen insists on writing the copy for the newsletter and does not like to have his work edited. Louie is assigned to the Christensen account and is really struggling with the copy submitted. Christensen uses trite, overused phrases. He writes sentences that ramble, and nearly every paragraph begins with the word *I*.

a. Based on the human relations skills you have read about early in this text and the information you have just studied about the importance of getting your message across, how would you help Louie?

b. What communicating techniques would you specifically recommend to Doug Christensen?

c. Would you print the newsletter as you think it should be? Or would you just print it the way Christensen wrote it? Explain your reasoning.

Communicating To Resolve Conflict

Grace is a hardworking employee at a large hotel. She works in the catering department and prides herself on planning elegant and unique menus for customers. Her supervisors have expressed their satisfaction with her work. The local paper has written feature articles about Grace and her special attention to the needs of customers. Howard joins the staff of the hotel. He has worked in catering in some of the finest hotels in Paris. Howard stops by one of the special dinners that Grace has planned for a wedding party. He comments to several of the waiters that the production is shabby compared to what he has observed at other hotels. A conflict is brewing in the catering department. Can it be solved? What kind of a conflict is it?

Conflict is something you learn about at a very young age. As a child you may have had conflicts with a sibling or experienced conflicts with friends. You have seen conflicts settled in court, and you have probably experienced or heard about labor conflicts.

Conflict is a communication concern as it can stop the flow of information.

What Is Conflict?

There are many definitions of conflict. The one supported in this chapter states that **conflict** is a difference of opinion caused by

Objectives

After completing this chapter, you should be able to:

1.
Define conflict.

2.
Identify the types of conflict and their causes.

3.
Explain the stages of conflict.

4.
Identify positive and negative ways of dealing with conflict.

opposing attitudes, behaviors, ideas, needs, or goals. The word *conflict* is usually associated with negative thoughts, unpleasant situations, or unpleasant memories. Everyone has his or her own likes and dislikes, unique ideas, habits, and personalities. Conflict may result from these differences. There will be no end to conflict in your life; but the good news is that there are many ways to cope with conflict, avoid conflict, and sometimes change a conflict to a positive situation. Conflict forces choice; and making a choice can help you test the merits of the certain attitudes, behaviors, needs, or goals in conflict.

Types Of Conflict

You will be better able to deal with conflict if you understand the types of conflict and recognize the basic causes of conflict.

Simple Conflict

Have you ever had a disagreement with a friend about a fact that was insignificant but nevertheless caused a conflict between the two of you?

ary Sue is a history buff. She especially enjoys sharing her knowledge about American history. Mary Sue's coworker Gayle, who majored in American history in college, also likes to discuss American history. At lunch, after a particularly stressful morning in the office, Mary Sue and Gayle were talking history. Mary Sue said that Big Hole, Wyoming, was the site of the major battle with the Nez Perce Indians. Gayle said, "No, you're wrong. That battle took place in Montana." They argued back and forth for several minutes, and the conflict was soon intense. They sought the opinions of coworkers. Finally, Ken suggested that they call the local library and ask the reference librarian to check the *World Almanac and Book of Facts* to settle the simple conflict. Gayle was right. The site of the major battle with the Nez Perce Indians took place at Big Hole, Montana. Mary Sue said, "Okay, you won that one." Gayle said, "Yes, but you had me thinking I might be wrong."

The **simple conflicts** are usually over a fact, such as these: What is the tallest mountain in North America? What is the largest animal on the continent of Africa? Where is the Danube River? What day did you and a friend visit Disney World last year? A conflict over facts can easily be solved by consulting a source of information that is considered "expert" on the part of those involved in the conflict. When you find yourself in conflict over a fact, end the conflict by checking a source

---

In the left margin:

❝ . . . But as the most beautiful light is born of darkness, so the faith that springs from conflict is often the strongest and the best. ❞
—R. Turnbull

immediately. If you are right, do not gloat. If you are wrong, simply say, "Well, you were right. That's a fact I won't forget." Do not allow a simple conflict to harm a relationship or the flow of communication.

Ego Conflict

Ego is your feeling of self-worth. Conflicts involving egos are probably the most damaging to relationships. This is because in an **ego conflict**, the persons view "winning" or "losing" the conflict as a measure of their expertise and personal worth. Ego conflict escalates when one or both parties introduce personal or judgmental statements. When conflict is tied to your personal worth, the conflict becomes an ego conflict. Once your ego becomes involved in conflict, your ability to behave in a rational manner is jeopardized. Ego conflict is difficult to resolve without bringing in emotions. You must be careful to separate the content of a conflict from your potential ego involvement.

 ulio and Nicole were discussing the Pulitzer prize winners in the field of music in the 80s. Julio said that John Harbison won the award in 1987. Nicole insisted that Harbison won the honor in 1983 for his work, "The Flight into Egypt." The discussion became heated when Julio mentioned that he was a music major in college and had studied the prize winners in a music appreciation class. He said he knew what he was talking about. Nicole replied, "Are you saying that I don't know what I am talking about because I don't have a college degree?" Julio said, "I do have an advantage over you." The conversation escalated to name-calling and severely damaged the relationship of Julio and Nicole.

The conflict between Julio and Nicole could have been solved when it was a simple conflict. A call or trip to the library would have settled the matter before egos got involved.

False Conflict

There are situations when you think a conflict exists, but in reality it does not. This type of conflict is called **false conflict**. For example, suppose you are a supervisor and one of your staff does not show for work on Monday morning. You are concerned and angry because you were counting on this person to help you with a specific project. A few minutes later you see the person walk into her office with a stack of papers. The employee says, "I came to work a few minutes early this morning so I could use the quality copy machine on the fifth floor. I thought that would give us a head start on the day." This situation was a false conflict.

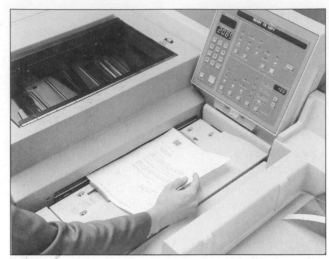

A supervisor who assumes an employee has not arrived to work when the person actually arrived early to copy paperwork is an example of false conflict.

Photography courtesy of Eastman Kodak Company

The first thing to do when you feel a conflict coming into place is to determine whether that conflict is real. Do not jump to conclusions. The energy devoted to getting upset over a false conflict is wasted. In the example above, how was positive communication saved? What do you think might have happened if the supervisor spoke first?

Values or Beliefs Conflict

You have determined what is important to you. The values or beliefs you have about certain aspects of life may not be the same as those of others. When the differences are brought into focus over a particular issue involving one of your values or beliefs, **values or beliefs conflict** can occur. For example, maybe you feel that society should take care of those people who are in need in the form of a welfare system. A coworker is opposed to any type of welfare program. If you and your coworker are to get along, you should probably talk about topics that do not include welfare or agree to debate the topic for fun. Do not risk unnecessary conflict with someone who has different values or beliefs than yours. Recognize that you are not likely to change the values or beliefs of others. Perhaps you can agree to disagree.

 Jerry and Sandra had worked together for several months. They had a good working relationship. Sandra shared with Jerry that she was having very bad headaches. Jerry told her that he believed in the use of herbs and natural cures for headaches. He offered to go on his lunch hour to the health food store and pick up a helpful powder. Sandra laughed and said, "Get real. I don't believe those health foods will make any difference." Jerry was offended by her remark and walked away from her. He told others in the work area about their conflict, and soon the workers were taking sides with Jerry or Sandra. Jerry and Sandra were both uncomfortable about the conflict that had occurred.

Stages Of Conflict

Simple, ego, false, and values or beliefs conflict may occur in the workplace. Conflicts among coworkers are very destructive because they can destroy the morale of the people involved, divert energy from the important tasks that need to be performed, reduce the cooperative spirit of the work team, increase stress, and harm positive communication. It is important to review the stages of conflict further so that it can be prevented. Regardless of the cause or kind, conflicts typically pass through a series of stages.

Stage I—Taking Sides

A conflict in the workplace may begin with two individuals; however, it does not take long for others to learn about the situation. The first step of a conflict in the workplace is *taking sides*. It seems to be a natural phenomenon for others in the workplace to take the side of one of the persons involved in the conflict. Taking sides is harmful as it can split the workforce, destroy teamwork, and cause a great deal of tension and stress.

Stage II—Keeping Score

The second stage of conflict is *keeping score*. The teams that have now developed often keep track of what the other team "does to them." During this phase each side tries to prove the other side is unreasonable. The "score keeping" may not even be related to the original conflict. If you know of an office or a family that has a long record of keeping score, chances are they do not even remember the original source of the conflict.

Stage III—Showdown

The most dangerous and volatile phase is the *showdown*. The people involved in the original conflict, or the teams that have developed, will decide that they "have had it" or they "just can't take it anymore." They then decide to confront the other person or team. This confrontation can be a constructive activity involving talking over the situation with everyone involved and coming to a compromise or an agreement.

Critical Thinking

Think about...

how Jerry and Sandra could have resolved this conflict and avoided their mutual discomfort.

Critical Thinking

Think about...

what Ben could do to better understand Ted's need to worship on Saturday.

Ted and Ben have been in conflict for several weeks over the fact that Ted refused to help Ben with a special work-related project on a Saturday morning. Ted belongs to a church that worships on Saturday. Ted considers Saturday a day of rest and a day to spend with his family. Ben was aware of Ted's religious practices, but he could not understand why Ted would not make an exception and work on a Saturday morning to complete the project they needed to present on Monday. The tension between Ted and Ben was building up, and it was affecting their ability to work together. Finally Ted said, "Ben, we've got to talk about the animosity that's building between us." Ben replied, "Yes, I agree." They talked for several minutes about the incident that had caused the conflict. The value conflict was settled after Ben explained that he felt you could worship any day and Ted explained how important Saturday was to him and his family. They agreed that they would not discuss religious practices in the future. Ted promised to respect Ben's opinion. Ben vowed to respect Ted's feelings. This constructive conversation was a positive showdown.

All showdowns may not be constructive. A showdown can be a destructive experience when the people threaten each other physically or verbally or use some other negative techniques of handling conflict. This destructive type of showdown should be avoided.

Stage IV—Adjustment

After the showdown one or both sides may decide to make some changes in their behavior. In the scenario above, you read about Ted and Ben. Their adjustment was that they would each respect the other's opinions and feelings. The adjustments that people make determine how well the conflict is settled. For example, if only one side makes the adjustments, the conflict may start all over again. The adjustment can also be made so that the conflict is settled in a constructive manner. Opening up and discussing issues can usually lead to a satisfactory adjustment agreeable to both sides. A positive result from a conflict can be that it helps build a spirit of teamwork among people as they share the conflict, celebrate its settlement, and learn more about each other in the process. The adjustment stage is a good time to build open and positive communication channels in the workplace.

Handling Conflict Adjustments

The adjustment phase of conflict needs further exploration. Stage IV would lead you to believe that positive or acceptable adjustment always follows a showdown. This unfortunately is not true.

Negative Conflict Adjustment

There are three negative ways to handle conflict; they are withdrawal, delay, and aggression. As you read the following scenarios, think about the reasons why these are not constructive methods of dealing with conflict.

Withdrawal. A common way of handling conflict is to avoid it or withdraw from it. You choose to remove yourself physically or psychologically from the situation. This is typically done by avoiding the person, refusing to think or talk about the conflict, changing the subject when the conflict is brought up, or maybe even doing something as drastic as quitting a job. Withdrawal can be very frustrating to those involved in the conflict in the workplace. You may find it very difficult to focus on your work when you spend most of your time thinking about avoiding a situation or an encounter. The conflict needs to be faced, and a suitable solution or adjustment needs to be determined.

Martha told Carol that she was disappointed with her because she refused to be the department representative for the United Fund Drive. Carol respects her superior, Martha, but Carol has served as the department representative for several years and feels that it is someone else's turn to do this job. Martha, however, told Carol it was necessary for everyone to support this community effort and continued on about civic responsibility, etc. Carol now avoids Martha. If Carol sees Martha coming toward her, she gets involved in a phone conversation or moves to another area of the department. If Carol arrives at the restroom at the same time as Martha, she uses the restroom on another floor. Carol has started parking across the street so that she does not see Martha in the parking lot before or after work. Carol has rearranged her schedule over a conflict that needs to be discussed and resolved.

66 What man does not alter for the better, time alters for the worse. 99
—Francis Bacon

Delay. Another way to handle conflict is to delay it. You may settle a small part of the conflict but not handle the critical important issue. The excuse you use is that you are "cooling off" the situation temporarily. This method is not entirely negative. Sometimes postponing a discussion over a conflict gives it a new perspective and allows people to calm down and reach a rational compromise, adjustment, or solution.

Randall and Goro work in the pressroom of a newspaper and know the importance of getting the paper out to the delivery people. On Thursday evening Goro is especially eager to leave the pressroom to see his son play football. A breakdown in the equipment occurs about 3:30 p.m. and will take a couple of hours to repair. Everyone will have to work late to get the papers out for delivery on time. Goro says, "I'm tired and have worked my share of the overtime. I'm going to leave at 5." Randall replies, "We need you. You have to stick it out and help." Some unkind remarks fly back and forth between Randall and Goro. The supervisor, Mac, steps in and offers to help Randall, and Goro leaves at 5. The conflict was temporarily settled, but the initial conflict is still in need of attention.

Aggression. The poorest way to handle a conflict is through aggression. Through aggression you attempt to force another to accept your ideas. **Aggression** is an emotional response to conflict. Verbal aggression can be emotionally damaging to those involved in the conflict, as well as to those in the area where the conflict takes place. Physical aggression is the absolute worst way to handle a conflict. It can cause injury and will not bring about a suitable adjustment to the conflict.

 im and Nathan work in a chemical plant. Proper care of the chemicals is a constant safety issue. Tim asks Nathan if he has secured some of the chemicals as they are about to leave for the day. Nathan responds, "I can't remember. Why don't you check them for me? I want to call my girlfriend." Tim responds, "It's your job. Why don't you check yourself? " Nathan jumps up and says, "Get off my back!" Nathan shoves Tim. Tim takes a swing at Nathan. This act of aggression causes the chemicals not to be checked and creates a conflict that will need to be resolved between Tim and Nathan if they are to continue to work together. Also, such aggression could cause Tim and Nathan to be dismissed from the workplace.

Positive Conflict Solving

None of the conflict-solving techniques described above are appropriate for positive conflict solving. The trick to handling conflict is to

*Physical aggression is **never** an acceptable way to handle conflict.*

put the emotional energy generated by the conflict toward a constructive solution.

If you are involved in a conflict or if you are attempting to mediate a solution, you must first establish the correct frame of mind.

Conflicts can be solved only when both people

“ Cooperation is a one—way street. Make sure you are going the right way. ”

1. Agree to cooperate.

2. Believe the problem has a solution.

3. Recognize that a difference of opinion is not a personal attack.

4. Respect the opinions of all involved.

5. Make an effort to be patient.

Once these attitudes are in place, a step-by-step solution can be attempted.

The basic problem-solving technique is often referred to as the scientific method as it has been used successfully in solving scientific problems. The **problem-solving technique** leads to the solution of a conflict by answering five key questions.

FIVE-STEP PROBLEM SOLVING

1. **What is the conflict?**

2. **What are the facts?**

3. **What is the overall objective?**

4. **What are some possible solutions?**

5. **What is the best solution?**

Illustration 10-1
Five-step problem solving.

Let's go through each of the steps listed in Illustration 10-1.

What Is the Conflict? This sounds like a simple question, but as you try to put into words exactly what the conflict is, you will realize that this might take some work. It has been said that a conflict well stated is half solved. As you put the pieces of the conflict together, you may begin to find some solutions. You may know something is wrong—you are in a conflict with another—but you cannot quite describe what the conflict is. As you attempt to state the conflict, take care

1. not to be judgmental

2. to be objective

3. not to favor anyone

Just state the conflict in specific terms.

Charles and Amy are engaged in a discussion. Amy says, "Let's buy a new house." Charles agrees, "Yes, I think the market is right." Amy replies, "I've always wanted a ranch-style house. Let's call a realtor and tell him or her we're in search of a ranch-style house."

Charles says loudly, "What do you mean a ranch-style house? You know I like contemporary designs."

What Is the Conflict? Charles and Amy do not agree on the type of house they want to buy.

You will notice in this statement there is no attempt at a solution. There is no right or wrong in the statement of the problem.

What Are the Facts? The answer to *"What are the facts?"* is important to write down. Notice you are writing down facts, not opinions or value judgments. The facts listed must relate specifically to the problem. Drop any "oughts" or "shoulds." There are several facts in the Charles and Amy scenario: (1) They agree it is time to buy a house. (2) Amy wants a ranch-style house. (3) Charles wants a contemporary house. (4) Charles and Amy need to discuss what they want in a house.

What Is the Overall Objective? This answer can be difficult, but it does not have to be. Perhaps you have never really thought about the main objective involved in a conflict. Again, it helps to write down exactly what the overall objective is going to be. Charles and Amy's objective is not difficult to see. The overall objective is to find a house that is pleasing to both of them.

What Are Some Possible Solutions? The answer to this question is to write down as many solutions to the conflict as you can think of. One method of clearing the way for a good solution is to write down the extreme solutions first. Charles and Amy's extremes might be as ridiculous as buying two houses or getting a divorce so that they can each live in the house they like. After the ridiculous is written, it is time to devote your attention to solid possibilities.

(1) Look for a ranch-style house with a contemporary flair or design. (2) Look at houses that are neither contemporary nor ranch. (3) Design their own house with features they both like. (4) Stay in their present house.

nay occur when there is a
ego, values, and beliefs
at you perceive only as
go through several phas-
and adjustment.
ve or positive way. The
:lude withdrawing from
nflict, or attempting to
'e approaches do not find
.evate the level of the
the scientific five-step
) find a resolution to a
ng technique direct the
five questions.

Activities

sing
> by
:st
ot
ay is
com-

ou have withdrawn from
How did you feel? Was

>ed
so
of the
to
s-
l
ition.
ature

beliefs conflict in which
olved. How was the con-

iality
onal

our personal life or work
e news. Describe each of
alse, values or beliefs, or
.)

the

Summary

Conflict will appear in your life. Conflict simple disagreement over a fact; when you are questioned; or when a situation arises t conflict. Conflicts in the workplace typically es: taking sides, keeping score, showdown,

Handling conflict can be done in a negat negative techniques are often used. They in the conflict, delaying the solution for the cc solve the conflict aggressively. These negati an answer to the conflict. In fact, they can e conflict. The positive approach of following problem-solving technique is the best way t conflict. The five steps of the problem-solvi settling of a conflict by preparing answers t

1. What is the conflict?

2. What are the facts?

3. What is the overall objective?

4. What are some possible solutions?

5. What is the best solution?

End of Chapter

Questions and Projects

1. Explain in writing an example of when y a conflict. What were the circumstances the conflict ever solved?

2. Describe an ego conflict or a values or you or someone you know has been inv flict resolved? Or has it ever been resolved?

3. List three conflicts you are aware of in y life or a conflict that you read about in th the conflicts and determine if they are simple, ego conflicts. (There may be some combination

4. Identify whether the following conflicts are examples of simple conflict, ego conflict, a values or beliefs conflict, or a false conflict.

_____ Jack says to his African-American friend, D. J., "It's all right here in 'black and white.'" D. J. is offended by the use of the phrase "black and white." Jack tells him he is being overly sensitive. A conflict follows.

_____ Suki says, "Why don't you answer that phone?" Her coworker, JoAnne, says, "Why don't you? If you've got time to tell others what to do, you have time to answer the phone!"

_____ Emma says that the quote, "Silence is a true friend who never betrays" belongs to Shakespeare. Niki says, "You're wrong; the quote comes from Confucius."

_____ Clarann is a vegetarian. James, her coworker, laughs at her and tells her that she is going to die early because she needs meat to live.

_____ Biff regards himself as a football star, and when Winston challenges his ability, a conflict follows.

5. List three resources you could check to solve a simple conflict over who pitched the winning game of the World Series in 1989.

6. Why is the conflict step of taking sides detrimental to the workplace?

Case Problems

1. Two Talents

Tara is an assistant in the art department of a major publishing company. Dan is an assistant in the editing department. Both employees are well known for quality work and are highly praised by their supervisors. Dan takes some copy to Tara and asks her to fit the copy into the caption of an illustration that she has designed. Tara says, "You expect me to destroy the message of this illustration with a trite line like that in the caption?" Dan retorts, "The caption supplements the meaning of the illustration. By the way, it isn't a trite line. Not everyone sees what you see in an illustration." Dan is upset by Tara's attitude. Tara is annoyed with Dan's comments. They must continue to work together, but after this confrontation, adjustments will need to be made.

a. What type of conflict is this?

b. What is the conflict?

c. Is this the type of conflict that may lead quickly to the stage of taking sides? Why?

d. Why would the negative technique of withdrawal not be an option in this situation?

e. What are the facts?

f. What is the overall objective?

g. What are some possible solutions?

h. What do you think is the best solution?

2. New Job

The branch bank of First Trust at Summerville has been closed. The employees at the closed branch have been transferred to the Timmon branch of First Trust. Vicki has been a loan officer at the Summerville branch for nine years. She is pleased that she was able to transfer her experience to the Timmon branch. After being on the job for several weeks, Vicki takes time at home one evening to make a list of the procedures used at Summerville that she feels work better than the ones currently being used at the Timmon branch. Vicki knows that she needs to be careful not to spring the entire list on her fellow loan officers all at once, but she makes a mental note to bring up one or two procedural recommendations at each staff meeting.

At the staff meeting, Vicki says, "I'd like to recommend that we check the credit ratings of all loan applicants before we process any paperwork. This will save time and paperwork." Mick, another loan officer, says, "That's not the procedure we follow at this branch. You aren't at Summerville." Vicki replies, "I realize that, but I do feel my suggestion is worthy of consideration." Mick says, "Let's move on to the next item of business." Mick gives Vicki a glare that says "Keep quiet." Mick has been with First Trust for 15 years, and he is in line for a promotion to vice president of the loan division.

a. Is there a conflict? What is the conflict?

b. Would you recommend that Vicki continue to present her procedural suggestions at future meetings?

c. Should Vicki attempt to discuss Mick's remarks to her after the staff meeting with Mick?

d. What advice do you have for Vicki in the future?

e. What additional information would you like to know about this situation?

3. Conflict over a greeting

Glen, an African-American joins the staff at Jones, Wiebert, and Jones Law Offices. Glen is a second-year law school student who has a goal of being a top-rate trial lawyer. Glen will work at the law office as a clerk for the summer. Carl is also a summer law clerk and just happens to be the son of the senior law partner.

Glen and Carl work together on the research for several cases. One case involved several interviews with African-Americans. Glen greeted the African-Americans with comments such as, "Hello, brother," "Give me five," or other greetings often used in the African-American community. Carl is a European American, and he was offended by these greeting methods. After one of the interviews, Carl said to Glen, "You're almost an attorney. Why can't you just shake hands with the people we interview like a white man?" Glen was hurt by the comment. After this situation Carl and Glen continued to work together, but the quality of their work suffered as it was difficult for them to communicate.

   a. What is the conflict? What type of conflict is it?

   b. Was Glen's greeting appropriate?

   c. Were Carl's remarks out of line?

   d. What are the facts?

   e. What is the overall objective?

   f. What are some possible solutions?

   g. What solution would you recommend to the problem?

4. Not Always Funny

Jason Andrews has worked at Hy-Gain Electric for 15 years. Over the years Jason has been crowned the practical joker of Hy-Gain. Jason jokes with everyone from the plant manager to the janitor. Most people enjoy his humor and find his antics day brighteners. Kim Le has been with Hy-Gain for only a few months and, of course, has met Jason. Jason tells Kim a joke that includes racial slurs about Asian-Americans. Kim is proud of her heritage and feels that no joke is funny that puts down a group of people. Kim says, "Jason, in the future I'd prefer that you stay away from me and keep your jokes to yourself. Please leave me alone." Jason is hurt by Kim's remark because it is important to him that he be liked by everyone. He doesn't understand what he did to offend her. He attempts to apologize, but Kim walks away. The next morning Jason and Kim are assigned to work on a project together.

a. What is the conflict? What type of conflict is it?

b. Is there more than one conflict in this case?

c. How might this conflict impact on the workplace?

d. Was Kim within her rights to say what she did to Jason? Why?

e. How can Kim begin to adjust to the new work situation?

f. How can Jason begin to adjust to the new work situation?

g. Is there a solution to this case problem?

Unit 4

Developing Your Productivity

Units 1, 2, and 3 have concentrated on helping you improve your personality so that you have the self-esteem, positive attitudes, interpersonal skills, and communication skills needed to fit in and get along on the job. This unit is concerned with another important aspect of your preparation—the ability to get the job done. Part of that ability is the result of your education, technical training, and experience in doing the work you are hired to do. Another part has to do with how well you are able to apply yourself. To apply what you know and to use your skills effectively, you must be motivated. You must not only be able, but also willing, to work hard. You must be able to think. The days when many jobs required only mindless application of muscle are gone forever. You must have good work habits, and you must be able to cope with the stress and pressure that can sometimes prevent you from being productive. Your study and participation in the learning activities of this unit will help you effectively use your job knowledge and skills. In addition to developing a pleasant personality, you will be learning to become a good worker.

Contents

Chapter 11
Motivation

Chapter 12
Work Habits

Chapter 13
Thinking Skills

Chapter 14
Managing Stress

Motivation

C raig was a student in a cooperative education program. The telephone rang in the office of his teacher-coordinator, Ms. Cardona. "This is Georgette Wilson, Craig's training sponsor. Can we talk about a problem we're having with him?" "Of course, " Ms. Cardona said. "What's going on?" "Well, as you know, in this kind of business, we can't always hover over our people and tell them every little thing to do. But when Craig comes to a slack period or when he completes an assigned job, he disappears. Usually I find him in the coffee room or out having a smoke." " I understand, " Ms. Cardona said. "We'll have a talk." Later, in discussing the matter with his teacher, Craig said, "But, Ms. Cardona, I always do what I'm told, and they tell me I do good work. What do they expect?"

Be Self-Motivated

Self-motivation is a drive within you to get things done. How can you acquire this drive if you do not possess it now? As your needs change, the spark that motivates you will change also. Right now you may be working for grades—a passing grade or a high one. Or you may be interested in the approval of someone whose opinion is important to you. The term psychologists use for this is **external motivation**. This means that the drive to achieve comes from outside yourself. In time, external motivation may be partly replaced by

Objectives

After completing this chapter, you should be able to:

1.
Demonstrate ways to improve self-motivation.

2.
Develop the ability to show initiative.

3.
Explain the meaning and importance of going beyond what is expected.

internal motivation. Internal motivation is the kind that comes from within, such as the satisfaction that comes from doing a good job.

Be Willing to Work

When a person is hired to do a job, the employer expects the employee to be willing to work. However, many workers appear to spend their time in other ways. Being self-motivated means that you have overcome the desire to just relax and avoid hard work. Here are four clues that tell your supervisor or employer how willing a worker you are:

- You willingly perform the tasks that are assigned to you.

- After the assignments have been made, you arrange your duties so that the work is completed on time.

- Because mistakes can be costly, you take great pains to be accurate.

- You take pride in your work.

Take On Unpleasant Tasks

Any job contains a certain amount of drudgery. This is especially true in entry-level jobs that require little training and experience. These jobs consist mainly of routine work that may not be challenging or interesting.

If you are faced with a job that is messy, dull, or physically exhausting, the natural reaction is to find some excuse to avoid or delay getting down to work. You may get a drink of water or adjust the ventilation. You welcome distractions and interruptions and find it

Take on all tasks with a smile.

hard to return to where you left off. The way to overcome this natural tendency and to develop self-motivation is to exercise self-control. Simply force yourself to face the task at hand. Save that drink of water as a reward at the end of your first completed task. Adjust the ventilation after completing another task. If you use self-control the first few times, you will form the habit of concentrated effort. With this habit, you will find yourself becoming a much more productive worker.

The following list contains suggestions for evaluating your self-motivation. If you find traits in this list that you would like to acquire, begin now to try to make them a part of your personality.

Ask yourself: Most of the time do I . . .

- accept the challenge to work at a task that doesn't appear to offer immediate interest or pleasure.

- choose to postpone pleasure rather than postpone work.

- avoid procrastination by not waiting until the last minute to start a task.

- concentrate by learning to work in the presence of distracting influences such as noise, physical discomfort, and interruptions.

- persist in finishing a task even when I'm weary and work late if the occasion demands it.

> Perhaps the most valuable result of all education is the ability to make yourself do the thing you have to do when it has to be done, whether you like it or not.
> —Huxley

Show Initiative

Your first job may call for following orders implicitly, doing what you are told to do without question. There may not be many opportunities for acting on your own—for showing **initiative**. In time, however, you will grow through experience and practice and will then be given greater responsibilities. You may be called upon for more independent thinking and action.

Act on Your Own

As a newcomer in the world of work, you may find it hard to know just how far you should go in showing initiative. Sometimes the rules of the organization make it necessary to follow a set pattern in everything that is done. In most cases, however, the follow-the-rules phase lasts only a short time.

When you are not expecting it, you may be faced with a crisis. For example, the manager who is to sign all orders may be in the hospital or out of town. When something like this happens, the only thing you can do is weigh the matter carefully. What will happen if you simply

Think about...

a situation in which the plant manager has given strict orders that his home phone number not be given to anyone under any circumstances. He is at home with the flu. A production supervisor calls in a panic. "I need him to make a decision. I can't take responsibility for it, and I need that decision NOW! Otherwise the whole production run could be ruined," he says. What should you do in this situation?

follow the rules? Would you lose an order? If the consequences of following the rules are worse than acting on your own, you must have enough initiative to take action. The only requirement is that you think the situation through carefully and make your decision on the basis of the best information you can get.

Occasionally you will have the opportunity to show initiative when you cannot be sure your actions will be appreciated. You may face possible disapproval whether you act or not. Failure to act in a crisis when there are no rules to guide you may be the worst thing you can do.

Use Good Judgment

Using initiative requires good judgment. It will help to put yourself in your employer's place. Ask yourself how you would expect an employee to proceed. For instance, if you see a lot of clutter around your work area, it is likely that taking the initiative to clean it up would be appreciated. Or perhaps you have an idea for a more efficient way to perform a routine task. Doing the task a different way without first checking to see if it is all right may be viewed by some supervisors as showing too much initiative. A good strategy is to explain your idea to someone in charge and be sure you have approval to proceed.

There are times when you cannot avoid a difficult decision—when you must use your best judgment and take action right then and there. For instance, suppose a customer is upset because he received the wrong merchandise. As a salesperson you should certainly show your concern. You should promise that something will be done about the situation—whether you have been previously instructed to do so

Demonstrate a concerned, helpful attitude when dealing with customers who are dissatisfied.

or not. There is the possibility that what you promise may not be what your supervisor would want, but it would be worse to lead the customer to believe that the store does not stand behind its merchandise.

Admit Your Mistakes

It takes courage to show initiative. It also takes courage to admit your mistakes when you have used your initiative with poor judgment. Having admitted your mistake, your path will be much smoother. If you cover up your mistakes, you will spend much time making excuses, blaming others, and depending on an alibi. If you admit an error in judgment, you may feel ashamed (or you may even be punished), but eventually you will be respected for your honest admission.

G regory is a trainee in a bank. One of his jobs is to check the computer overdraft report and call the customers to notify them that they are overdrawn. Usually he is instructed to transfer funds from a savings account, but in this case a customer asks Gregory to transfer funds from another bank electronically. This is the first time he has heard of electronic transfers, and Gregory hesitates. Then he asks, "Can you withdraw the funds and bring a cashier's check to be deposited in your account?" The customer responds with "You mean you want me to make a trip to the other bank and then to yours when it would be so much easier to just let the computer and the telephone do it?" There is another pause. Then Gregory says, "Let me call you right back after I talk to my supervisor."

Be Open to Something New

Do not let new and unfamiliar situations upset you. Instead, let them be stepping-stones to learning. A beginner does have a lot to learn. People know that, but they do not expect the learning process to go on forever. The beginner who needs to be told something only once is considered unusually bright. The one who learns new routines with minimal instruction is rare indeed. Everyone makes mistakes, but the beginner with a good work attitude seldom makes the same mistake twice.

The person who is enthusiastic about putting new ideas into effect does not say, "It can't be done." Instead, he or she will have an "I can" attitude. A person with this attitude will not always wait to be told what to do. Nor will the person need to have work laid out or be told repeatedly how to perform a task. He or she will listen carefully the first time (and probably take notes) so that the task can be performed the next time with little or no assistance.

Learn on Your Own

Another way to show initiative is by learning all you can about the business and your place in it. You also show initiative by taking courses to prepare yourself for promotion and by learning how to do work that must be done even though it has not been definitely assigned to you. Learn how to think and act swiftly in emergencies, and do more than you are told to do. If new and unusual situations arise, learn how to handle them.

Take advantage of opportunities to learn on your own.

©Ulrike Welsch/Photo Researchers

Another valuable benefit of learning on your own is that you may be able to fill in for a coworker who is absent. Being able to apply what you learn in one situation to a different set of circumstances is a valuable skill. You can plan and carry out new duties with minimal help from others. You are better prepared to attempt new things and to be creative. In the long run, your employer and your coworkers will benefit from your increased capacity for doing your job and helping them with theirs.

Go Beyond What Is Expected

A valuable key to success is to do *more* than your employer expects of you. Another is to set higher standards so the quality of your work *is better* than expected. When the work that you do is outstanding, you look good to your employer; you are recognized as an outstanding performer. This also makes your supervisor and your working team look good.

Here are some examples of going beyond what is expected:

- performing the difficult, tedious, or unpleasant task when you might be expected to leave it for someone else

- performing your work with poise, dignity, and patience although conditions at work or in your private life may be distressing

- setting high standards and working hard to reach them

- paying attention to details

- displaying a high level of concentration

- working late to complete a job

- making an extra effort to please a dissatisfied customer

Like the rewards for many other positive qualities, the reward for going beyond what is expected may be delayed. If you see no immediate benefit for your extra effort, your own satisfaction will be reward enough. You will know that you can cope with whatever you need to do. However, it is very likely that your employer will recognize and appreciate what you have done. He or she will think of you as a person who is a self-starter and as someone who can be depended upon to get the job done without much supervision. In the long run, you may have an advantage as you compete for a raise, a promotion, or a better position. Eventually others will notice that when there is a need for someone to "go the extra mile," you can be depended upon.

Summary

Motivation can come from outside yourself—external motivation—or you can be motivated from within. Your self-motivation is reflected in your willingness to work hard, especially at tasks that may not be pleasant. Developing and using self-control will help you emerge victorious over drudgery. Some helpful ideas include

- postponing pleasure in order to finish a task,

- avoiding procrastination,

- learning to concentrate,

- learning to persist in working even when tired.

Critical Thinking

Think about...

the fact that you *can get by* when you do what your employer expects, and no more. Why should you do *more* than that?

Your employer and coworkers expect you to show initiative. However, good judgment is essential if you are to avoid mistakes. Showing initiative includes taking advantage of every opportunity to learn on your own, making decisions, and acting independently without always being told what to do. Self-motivation will inspire you to go beyond what is expected.

End of Chapter Activities

Questions and Projects

1. What is the difference between *external* motivation and *internal* motivation? Give examples of each. Under which type of motivation is the most work likely to be accomplished? Explain your answer.

2. You ride the bus to work. The schedule allows you to arrive either 25 minutes early or three minutes late. What would you do?

3. List several ways you could improve your self-motivation. From the list, select those you could start working on now.

4. Assume you have been promoted to supervisor. One of the people with whom you formerly worked is now working for you. She is habitually late for work but is doing a good job otherwise. It is your duty to talk to her about her tardiness. What will you say? Write down your exact words.

5. Shannon works as a receptionist. A customer calls during the lunch hour asking for the new price on a rechargeable battery pack for his power drill. He says that the catalog price is wrong and wants an up-to-date price quotation. Should Shannon

   a. leave the switchboard and go into her supervisor's office to look for the new price on his computer?

   b. tell the customer to call back after lunch?

   c. promise that the supervisor will call back after lunch?

Choose a response from those listed above or one that you think is more appropriate. Explain what Shannon should do and why.

Case Problems

1. Job or Career?

Laura is a salesperson in a clothing department of a department store. The sales staff in the store is paid a weekly salary. No commission is paid for the amount of goods sold. Laura is very industrious and is usually the first to greet a customer. After serving her customers, Laura returns the clothing to the racks. She then keeps busy arranging merchandise or studying new items that have been recently put in stock. She is always pleasant and courteous. Dale, who works with her, tells Laura she is foolish to work so hard when she receives no extra pay. Laura knows that Dale's attitude is characteristic of the feeling of many of the members of the salesforce.

   a. Is it profitable for Laura to work as she does?

   b. Do you feel that Laura may be rewarded for going beyond what is expected?

   c. If Laura is promoted, can you think of any advantages her attitude will have in a position of greater responsibility?

   d. Why do you think the other salespeople feel as they do about their work?

   e. If you were in charge of Laura's department, how would you handle this situation of indifference on the part of some of the sales personnel?

2. How Much Is Too Much?

Sonia supervises the shipping and receiving department of a university library. She has several part-time student helpers. Usually they are able to keep up with the flow of incoming mail. However, after weekends or holidays the books and magazines pile up, and it may take several days for Sonia and her crew to get caught up. Most Mondays and days after holidays Sonia works from one to three hours overtime to catch up.

   a. Because Sonia works on a salary, she gets no overtime pay. Should she continue working overtime? If not, how should she handle the situation?

   b. Sonia catches the flu and misses three days of work. When she returns, she finds the backlog of undelivered mail so great that she has to work 11 hours per day for a week. Her supervisor does not seem to know about Sonia's overtime work. What should she do? At what point do you think Sonia should refuse overtime work?

3. Price Check

A customer brings a pair of sandals to the cash register. The price is clearly marked $9.99. Alvin, the checker, remembers having sold several pairs identical to these at $19.99. His supervisor is not available, and Alvin must decide what to do then and there without consulting anyone.

a. What risks must Alvin face if he makes a decision in this situation?

b. Considering the best interests of his employer, what action should Alvin take?

Work Habits

G reg and Ramona were talking after a staff meeting. They had been advised that productivity was slipping and that top management was expecting supervisors to encourage workers to be more conscientious. Ramona said, "Some of my people are unproductive simply because they don't know how to work. They have bad work habits." "Well, maybe they could learn how to work more efficiently from someone who has good habits. Who's your best worker?" Greg responded. Ramona thought for a moment and said, "Jean, the receptionist and file clerk. She concentrates on the job at hand and isn't distracted. She doesn't spend time chitchatting. She's very task-oriented, but flexible; when something new comes up, she adapts to it. She's not a clock watcher. You never have to remind her to find something to do when she's caught up on her work. When I ask her to do something, she does it immediately, and she does it well." Greg smiled. "Maybe I could entice her to come to work in my section. I'll trade you two stock clerks for her."

Responsibility

To be **responsible** means to be answerable or accountable for something within one's power to control. The definition includes being dependable and reliable.

Employers expect responsible behavior. They try their best not to hire irresponsible individuals as employees. Employers look for

Objectives

After completing this chapter, you should be able to:

1.
Define and explain the importance of responsibility.

2.
Define and explain the importance of being conscientious.

3.
Develop the ability to work under pressure.

4.
Exhibit self-control and maintain professional composure.

5.
Define and explain the importance of orderliness in the workplace.

6.
Develop a realistic, workable schedule for efficient time management.

7.
Explain the importance of efficient management of material resources.

SCANS
Focus

A competent worker...

■ ensures that the work schedule is followed (determines his or her appropriate shift for the week)

■ coordinates with the shift supervisor to keep him or her informed of any changes

■ finds suitable replacement if unable to come to work

■ arrives at work well-groomed, prepared, and on time

evidence of responsible behavior in reports of education and work experience. Also, they expect to see this trait mentioned in letters of recommendation from former employers and other references. Part of being responsible includes:

■ working hard

■ paying attention to details

■ concentrating on your work, even when it is unpleasant

■ showing effort and perseverance toward goal attainment

These suggestions were presented in Chapter 11. Other important elements of responsible behavior are presented in this chapter.

Be Dependable

If someone describes you as **dependable**, consider it a great compliment. In most cases it means you do what you say you will do. It sounds simple, and yet workers with the best of intentions are often labeled as undependable. They hate to disappoint someone by saying no, so they say they will get a report out by five o'clock even though they know they will not be able to do it. Truly dependable people, however, do not say yes unless they are certain they can carry out their promises.

In effect, when you say you will do something, you create a contract. A written contract might seem more important to you, but a spoken promise is just as important. If you are a dependable worker, you will do your work well and not rely on excuses.

Be on Time for Work. Being dependable also means that you will be at work at the time you are expected to be there. Consider what happens when you are late for work. Everything you do becomes shaded by the fact that you were late. You are behind with your work, so you hurry to catch up; because you hurry, you make mistakes; making mistakes causes you to become flustered, so you hurry more. This circle of hurry and errors goes on all day. On the other hand, if you come to work on time or early, you are relaxed when you start your first task. Relaxation helps you work rapidly and accurately. Working in this way brings you a feeling of satisfaction, and this feeling helps you with the next task at hand. The result is a circle of excellence that works for you all day.

Punctuality is easily controlled. First, examine your situation and identify the possible causes of tardiness. Is it difficult for you to wake up? Do you allow too little time for all that you have to do before you leave for work? Do you have transportation problems, such as unexpected traffic congestion or unreliable bus service? After determining

Oversleeping can spark a series of events that ruin your workday.

Photo by Jim Whitmer

Critical Thinking

Think about...

what happens when you are late for work. What will your supervisor and coworkers do? What will they think? After you arrive what will you do and how will you feel that is different from what happens when you are early or on time?

the potential causes of tardiness, take action to eliminate or avoid them. For example, you might set the alarm clock for an earlier time or place it across the room so you will have to get out of bed to shut it off. Plan your early morning activities the night before to ensure that you will have plenty of time—with some to spare. Some things, such as setting your clothes out, mixing your orange juice, and feeding your pet, can be done before you retire. Attendance and punctuality form an important block in building your success.

Call In If You Expect to Be Absent. Worse than workers failing to show up for work is failing to show up without giving any warning ahead of time. Consider what happened to Neil in the following example.

eil worked as a dishwasher in a restaurant about five miles from his home. On the way to work on his bicycle, Neil had a flat tire, which took nearly an hour to repair. While he was at the service station fixing the tire, he could have telephoned to let his supervisor know he would be late. But he was somewhat shy, and the prospect of explaining his problem over the phone made him feel uncomfortable. So Neil was nearly an hour late as he approached his place of employment. Now the anxiety he felt about facing his employer was even greater. Not having the courage to go to work late, Neil did not show up at all. To make things worse, he did not call to explain his absence. The next day Neil's worst fears were realized. When he arrived at work, his supervisor had a termination slip waiting for him.

Was the supervisor's reaction too severe? Perhaps so. However, one of Neil's problems was not realizing how his supervisor would feel about unexpected tardiness or absence. When you understand the problems this can create on the job, you may not think the supervisor's action was unreasonable.

Be Conscientious

Being **conscientious** suggests following the dictates of one's conscience. In a work situation, it suggests one who is **meticulous**—who is concerned and careful about details. It also suggests that the worker stays with a job until it is done well. The conscientious worker would not deliberately waste time or avoid work. His or her conscience would not allow the employer's time, resources, or money to be wasted.

Following are 15 examples of employee behavior that might not be considered conscientious. Which of these behaviors would cause you to have a twinge of conscience? In the space provided, write yes, no, or ? if you are uncertain about whether or not the behavior violates your conscience.

1. ___ Waiting 10 minutes for someone to help you proofread 10 pages.

2. ___ Delivering a package that could be mailed instead.

3. ___ Going to someone's office for a conversation instead of using the telephone.

4. ___ Beginning coffee breaks and lunch periods early or finishing them late.

5. ___ Carrying on social conversations (on the phone or in person) during working hours.

6. ___ Doing your personal work (without anyone else knowing about it) during working hours.

7. ___ Working fast (and carelessly) so there will be time after the work is done to read, sleep, play cards, etc.

8. ___ Working slowly to make the work fill up the time available for it.

9. ___ Causing a situation that will bring the work to a halt (a broken machine, shortage of materials, etc.).

10. ___ Daydreaming when you should be concentrating.

11. ___ Performing a task yourself when it could (and should) be done more efficiently by someone else.

12. ___ Wasting time preparing for or talking about doing a job instead of getting to work and doing it.

13. ___ Refusing to do something that you could do because "It's not my job."

14. ___ Wasting a lot of time kidding around, playing jokes or pranks.

15. ___ Pretending not to notice customers waiting to be served.

Some of these actions, when you see respected workers participating in them, may appear to be normal and acceptable. But they are not. Any of them, when carried to the extreme, can cause both employers and coworkers to label a person as someone who wastes a lot of time.

The actions described above are intentional. They are ways of slowing down or avoiding work. As you review the results of this self-test, ask yourself if the motives behind the action are something you are proud of. You may justify the action by saying "It's okay. Everybody does it. There's no rule against it." This behavior may not be against the rules. However, it *does* violate the norms of the workplace.

In the world of business time is money. Employers appreciate the worker who does not waste time. In addition to conserving and using time well, the conscientious worker is not content with mediocrity. Doing a good job without wasting time is what your employers will expect and what you should expect of yourself.

Self-Management

Sometimes, because of work pressures and frustrations, a person can "blow up" and lose emotional control. Here is an example.

B ill was a first-line supervisor in a plastics molding department. After arriving at work 30 minutes late, he found that Joe, a new employee, had set up a production run incorrectly. Joe did not start the run, but if he had, it would have taken several hours to correct the mistake. Bill lost control of his temper, used abusive language in reprimanding Joe, and threatened to have him fired. Later Bill discussed the problem with the plant manager, a trusted and caring friend. "I blew up at Joe because it was the last straw," he said. "I had just come to work after a series of terribly frustrating experiences. My neighbor had a loud party last night, and I couldn't get to sleep. So I phoned and asked him to tone it down. When I finally did get to sleep, I overslept and was late for work. On my way to the garage, I noticed that about three feet of my new hedge had been torn out. Obviously I thought it was done by one of the drunks at my neighbor's party.

When I confronted him about it, he denied everything and accused my wife of ruining the hedge when she went to work earlier. He threatened to knock my block off if I didn't apologize, and he's big enough to do it. Then when I finally got to work worrying about the deadline, I saw that Joe had the setup wrong. I just lost it."

Develop Self-Control

Self-control is the ability to direct the course of your behavior; it is the capacity to manage your own thoughts, feelings, and actions. In the example above, Bill allowed his personal problems and frustration to affect his behavior on the job. Employers expect and appreciate employees who are able to leave their personal problems at home. This can be difficult. Self-control is evident when you are in control of your emotions and actions. It requires mental discipline and personal willpower, but it is vital if you are to do your best on the job.

Work requires self-control. Most people want to work, but doing the job well sometimes requires personal discipline. When a supervisor oversees the work, external motivation helps you to settle down to work. However, if you have a job you must do without direct supervision from others, you must have the self-control to work efficiently.

6 6 Lack of willpower has caused more failure than lack of intelligence or ability. **9 9**
—Flower A. Newhouse

SCANS Focus

A competent worker...

■ exhibits self-control and responds to feedback nondefensively

■ demonstrates self-control when customers disagree with his or her ideas

■ prepares mentally to handle customers (maintains professional composure throughout the day)

When you have to work under pressure, learn to maintain self-control and avoid taking your frustration out on coworkers.

Bruce Peterson/H. Armstrong Roberts

Learn to Work under Pressure

Another valuable self-management trait is the ability to work under pressure or unusual conditions. You need to learn to meet deadlines, keep several jobs going at once, resolve any problems that come up, and do extra work without panic. When the pressure mounts, you can relieve it. Relaxation is the key, and most people must train themselves in relaxation. Here are some relaxation tips:

- Stop for a moment (especially when you feel your muscles tightening up) and take a few deep breaths.

- Do a relaxing exercise: Swing your hands at your side and stretch.

- Take a "power nap." Lie down and totally relax for five minutes.

- Find time outside your work to do some of the things you enjoy.

- Learn meditation techniques or yoga.

- Leave your workplace for a brisk walk or other vigorous exercise.

- Find a quiet place and read a magazine or novel during lunch or a break.

Organization

andra met Gloria at the water fountain, and they paused to talk. "I can't imagine how Randy gets anything done," Gloria whispered, nodding in his direction. "He has stuff all over the place, and he seems to be in a dither half of the time just trying to keep track of what he's doing." " I know, " said Sandra. "And I overheard the supervisors talking about it. I don't know how much longer he can keep it up."

If you are an **organized** person, your behavior is methodical, logical, and directed toward goals or outcomes that you have clearly in mind. You have both the motivation and the ability to be orderly, efficient, and systematic in your personal life and in your employment. This includes organizing the things around you at home and at work. It also includes organizing your time.

Orderliness

It seems natural for some people to be very tolerant and accepting of disorder in their surroundings. At home you will find their clutter everywhere—in the kitchen, the bedroom, the garage, the closet. Others are very orderly and cannot tolerate clutter. Being extremely sloppy and disorganized leads to serious problems at home, at school, and especially at work. On the other hand, being driven to extreme orderliness in every aspect of living can create problems. Perhaps you have had the experience of living or working with an excessively orderly person and with someone who is totally disorganized. If so, you will understand that for a person to fit in and get along, it is essential to strike a balance between the two extremes.

While disorderly habits may be tolerated in one's private life, it is unusual to find a workplace where they are considered acceptable. What is your reaction when you see evidence of disorganization and everything in disarray?

Critical Thinking

Think about...

what might have caused what you see in this scenario and look for evidence to answer the questions.

You take your car in to have the electrical system checked. The sign over the door to the work area reads, "Customers not allowed in the shop." The door is ajar, and out of curiosity you look in. You see grease and dirt everywhere. There is a puddle of oil under the lubrication area. Dirty rags are lying around, and a rack for wrenches and hand-tools is nearly empty. The tools are on the workbench in disarray or on the floor. There is a large stack of old tires in one corner and piles of boxes with used parts in another. A mechanic wearing a grimy baseball cap backwards walks across the shop and kicks several empty cardboard cartons out of his way. He calls out, "Larry, where's my 17 millimeter socket?

- Are the mechanics going to be careful and conscientious as they check the electrical system in your car?

- As they do the work, are the mechanics going to be efficient? Will they waste any time (at customer expense) because of their disorderly shop?

- As you think about the places where you do business, how often do you see this kind of disorganized work environment? Is this situation typical of the efficient, productive, successful workplace?

In business being disorderly is usually unacceptable, and some employers think it is intolerable. Would you like to work in a situation where everything is in total disarray? Probably not. Lack of organization is the cause of tremendous waste of time in the workplace. It can cause frustration and chaos for customers, employees, and managers.

On the other hand, there are many benefits that come from **orderliness**. It encourages efficiency and helps to eliminate mistakes and inaccuracy. Orderliness also helps to prevent wasting time, materials, and other resources. The ultimate benefit is productivity and profit for your employer. This in turn benefits your customers and *you*.

A disorganized work area can cause you to waste a lot of time.

Photo by Jim Whitmer

In addition to material and financial benefits, being orderly and well-organized on the job has psychological benefits. A major source of frustration is eliminated; and praise, rewards, and promotions are more likely. Finally, there is the reward of self-satisfaction. Being orderly just makes you feel better about yourself.

Efficient Time Management

Efficiency is appreciated and rewarded in the world of work. Part of the meaning of efficiency has to do with how well a task is performed. Know-how and skill contribute to efficiency. Dependability, conscientiousness, self-control, the ability to work under pressure, and orderliness contribute to efficiency. However, if you were to ask supervisors and managers to identify the most important efficiency factor, most would probably choose time management. Inefficient time management, more than anything else, paves the way for wasting time and, therefore, reducing productivity and profit.

What *is* efficient **time management**? What does one do to manage time? The process is similar to money management. With money management you have income that makes money available, and you use the money by spending it. The written plan for allocating money to various uses is a *budget*. With time management you look at time as the resource to be used. A calendar and a clock tell you how much of this resource is available, and a *schedule* is used to show how it will be used. Following is a step-by-step procedure for efficient time management.

66 Well arranged time
is the surest mark of a
well arranged
mind. 99
—Pitman

1. Identify Tasks to Be Completed. When job analysts study an employment position, they start by conducting a job and task analysis. The position under study is subjected to a **job breakdown**, which results in a specific list of tasks to be performed. The analyst will continue the process by considering each task, one at a time, to determine what the worker needs to know, what personal qualities or traits are required, and what training or skills are needed. All the tasks with this analysis make up a job description. The job description for your position can be very helpful in identifying the tasks to be completed.

If you are employed now and do not have a job description available, here is what you can do to identify the tasks to be completed. Review what you have been assigned to do. If possible, ask your instructor or work supervisor to help by going over your various assignments to determine exactly what you are expected *to do*—not what you are supposed to know, what skills you need, or how the job is to be done. Simply list the tasks in no particular order. Keep in mind that tasks consume time. If there is something on the list that is not time-consuming, cross it off. To make it easier to use the information, prepare a 3" x 5" file card for each task. Write a brief description of the task at the top of the card. You will use space on the front and back of the card to record information produced later.

2. Rank the Tasks in Order of Importance. Now that you have an inventory of the tasks that you are expected to accomplish, review them to evaluate their importance. With all the tasks in view, ask "Which is the most important?" If there are some that appear to be equal in importance, ask "Which should be done *first?*" If that question does not help you choose one that is clearly most important, choose one at random and label it number one. Then follow this procedure until all the tasks have been assigned a number. Finally, sort the cards so that they are arranged in order.

3. Determine Time Requirements. To determine the time requirements for each assigned task, you must carefully consider the following questions:

How much time is required to accomplish the task?

How much time is available for it?

What is the deadline? If there is not a specific deadline, what would be a reasonable, acceptable time for completion?

Now write the results of your analysis on the card for each task.
George Northcote Parkinson, after analyzing the efficiency of the Royal Navy, concluded that WORK EXPANDS TO FILL THE TIME AVAILABLE FOR ITS COMPLETION. This conclusion became known

as "**Parkinson's law**." Here is an example: You are expected to mow the lawn. If you have just an hour before you are to meet some friends to go play golf, you get the job done in time. But if you have three hours on a lazy afternoon, the job somehow takes that long (including time out for lemonade and two telephone conversations).

4. Develop a Workable Schedule. You now have a stack of cards. Each card has information about a task: its importance, the time it will take to complete it (assuming Parkinson's Law has no effect on it), the time available for completion, and task deadlines. With this information you can develop a schedule showing what you will do and specifically when you plan to do it.

There are many different ways to go about scheduling. One way is to prepare a daily list of "Things to Do Today." You may also make such a list on a weekly or monthly basis. Following is an illustration of a weekly work schedule. Elaborate and detailed systems for scheduling are available in most bookstores. Whatever system you choose, it is important to use accurate estimates of time requirements and to be conscientious and realistic about including important deadlines. You should think of a deadline written in your schedule as a commitment—a promise to do something according to your schedule.

Your schedule should be flexible. Pencil in new items as needed. Adjustments are made occasionally based on an accurate evaluation of your progress. Along with maintaining your schedule, you may also revise and update the card file as an ongoing record of progress and accomplishments.

Illustration 12-1
A weekly work schedule.

Using a schedule to plan and monitor your activities can help you to be efficient and make the best use of your time. But you should not become a slave to the schedule. Occasionally (sometimes all too often) you may be swamped with work. Unexpected and unplanned demands will be made on your time. The time you planned to use for a specific task may have to be used for something else; you will have to "make time" for the task, squeezing it into the schedule sometime in the future. The best that you can do under such circumstances is to use the information that appears in the schedule and revise it using your best judgment.

Make compromises, adjustments, revisions, and continue monitoring and making new plans.

Efficient Resource Management

The most important—and probably the most expensive—resource your employer has is *you*. You, your coworkers, supervisors, and management personnel are the *human* resources of the enterprise. Everything in this chapter up to this point has been concerned with the efficient management of human resources. This brief concluding section is concerned with efficient management of material and facility resources.

In any position of employment, you will have responsibility for resources that can be expensive. If you have a job, think about what

Employees expect efficient resource management.

Elizabeth Hamlin/Stock, Boston

you see all around you in your workplace. Imagine a workplace that might be in your future. Is there a building that is heated, air-conditioned, and well lighted with facilities such as restrooms, a cafeteria, and more? Are there cars, trucks, computers, filing cabinets, product displays, and machines or equipment for production? Do you see supplies and materials that are to be used (and possibly wasted) in getting the job done?

All these resources are available to help you do your job well. They are provided to help you keep your productivity and the quality of your work within accepted standards. You will be expected to conserve these resources and make good use of them. Remember, from your employer's point of view, "time is money." The material and facility resources for which you are responsible represent money as well. Waste and misuse have negative effects on productivity and profits.

Summary

Good work habits are an important qualification for success in the world of work.

A sense of responsibility that includes being dependable and reliable leads to habits that make you more productive. Being on time for work and not wasting time are important. You should also be sure to call in when you are going to be late or absent from work.

When time and material resources are wasted, the impact on your employer is the same as if money were taken. A conscientious worker would not deliberately avoid work or use any tactic that leads to inefficiency and less productivity.

Self-control is important in the workplace. It requires self-discipline and willpower. You should make an effort to be sure that problems and frustrations in your private life are not allowed to affect your performance on the job. Finally, you should expect your work environment and the demands of your job to create pressure. To be successful you must learn to cope with the pressure of the work environment and not let it reduce your productivity.

Some people have a natural inclination to be organized and meticulous; others seem naturally disorganized and disorderly. Employers value order. Being orderly in your work can lead to better job performance, rewards on the job, and self-satisfaction.

Efficient time management includes analysis tasks that consume your time. To manage your time efficiently, rank the tasks in order of importance. Consider the time available, how much time the task requires, and deadlines for completion of the work. Use this information to develop a realistic, workable schedule.

A competent worker is expected to manage facility and material resources efficiently. Waste and misuse can have negative effects on productivity and profits.

End of Chapter Activities

Questions and Projects

1. Wherever you work you are likely to be involved with others as a member of a working team. This means that you interact with coworkers: What they do affects you and what you do affects them. If someone is undependable or irresponsible, it can hamper the team effort. Following are three examples. For each, explain how the incident might have influenced the productivity of the team.

    a. At a fast-food restaurant that opens for business at 9 a.m., the person responsible for turning on the french-fry cooker arrived at 8:45 a.m. In the rush to get ready for customers to arrive, she forgot to switch it on. It takes 20 minutes to heat up.

    b. A salesperson working in the women's shoe department finds several pairs of shoes in the stockroom and takes them out on the sales floor for a customer to try on. Instead of returning the unsold shoes to their proper location, he leaves them on a convenient top shelf. (He plans to put them where they belong after the "rush hour.")

    c. One of the two people in an automotive service shop who is assigned to install and balance new tires fails to show up for work because he could not get his car started on a cold, snowy morning.

2. Workers in a copper mine are allowed to take materials and supplies as needed from the supply room. During deer hunting season, the purchasing agent notices that the supply of flashlight batteries is used at three times the normal rate. When the purchasing agent presents this information in a staff meeting, one of the supervisors comments, "It's no big deal. Why make an issue of it?" What should the purchasing agent say and do in response? Why?

3. Find something in your life that is disorderly. It might be a cluttered garage, basement, or if you are less ambitious, refrigerator.

If you are a very orderly person, you may need to ask a friend to allow you to take on this project for him or her. Review the situation, develop a plan of action, and create order out of the chaos. After completing the project, prepare a written explanation of the procedure you followed. Was there a logical step-by-step process? Share your experience in group discussion.

4. Develop an efficient time management plan for one week. If you are attending school, if you are employed full-time or part-time, or whatever your routine might be, include all your important, time-consuming activities. Follow the procedure as explained in this chapter to develop a schedule, showing how you will use your time over the seven-day period.

Case Problems

1. Working under Pressure

A coworker and close friend works as a secretary/administrative assistant for five real estate agents. She also answers the phone and greets potential clients when they drop in at the agency office. She shares her feelings as follows: "It seems like I'm in a swamp with a bunch of alligators. The agents are constantly bringing in work that they want done immediately. They always seem to expect me to drop everything to do their work. When the work load slacks off, I feel so disorganized; it seems impossible to get caught up. I can't concentrate on anything for very long because clients keep coming in and interrupting me. Then there's the telephone—the worst interruption of all. I think I'm going to scream!"

a. As a trusted friend and someone who cares, what advice would you give?

b. If your advice is followed, what might happen to improve the situation?

2. Up the Ladder

Helen and Marilyn were seated together on an airplane trip to a travel agency managers' convention. Helen started the conversation. "How's business, Marilyn?" "Best ever, Helen. But I'm a bit worried about how it's going to be after next week. My best agent has been hired away by your agency." Helen smiled. "I know. And I expect my business to improve. We're lucky to get Mei-ling. In your letter of recommendation, you shouldn't have been so candid about her ability." "I wish we could have offered her a management position," Marilyn responded. "Mei-ling is the most efficient agent we have. Not the most intelligent. Not the best educated. Not the most experienced. But the most efficient!"

a. What do you think are some of the work habits that might have helped Mei-ling succeed?

b. As Marilyn interviews candidates for the vacant position, what are some questions she might ask? Make a list of six questions, and for each tell what useful information she might obtain.

Thinking Skills

T he personnel manager of a large department store is talking to the cooperative education teacher-coordinator. The purpose of the teacher's visit is to find potential training stations for marketing students. The personnel manager is saying, "We need good people for sales positions. We do NOT need salesclerks. We do NOT need management trainees. Under our new management philosophy, everyone has to be a manager. We expect those we hire to be able to do what we used to expect only of supervisory personnel. In fact, we don't think of our merchandising managers as supervisors anymore. And the people they used to supervise are no longer called salesclerks. They're now called sales associates. They are paid better now than they were when we expected them to work in the shadow of a supervisor. But more is expected of them. When a problem comes up or when decisions have to be made, they handle it. Now we expect them to do the work and to manage themselves as well. They no longer have someone they can go to for direction. They have to do their own thinking. Are you training your students to think?"

Employers Want People Who Can Think

The demands of the workplace are changing. One of the changes that is of concern to employers and to educators is a renewed emphasis on higher-order thinking. Leaders in

Objectives

After completing this chapter, you should be able to:

1.
Explain the importance and value of being able to think critically and creatively.

2.
Describe higher-order thinking abilities and skills.

3.
Describe the specific abilities that contribute to critical thinking.

4.
Describe the specific abilities that contribute to creativity.

5.
Explain procedures for evaluation, decision making, and problem solving.

6.
Identify and explain when and how to use logical inference and creativity in analytical problem solving.

7.
Plan and work toward improving your higher-order thinking abilities and problem-solving skills.

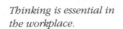
Thinking is essential in the workplace.

H. Armstrong Roberts

" The new emphasis in education for the workplace of the future is on the three R's. . . READING, WRITING, AND REASONING. "
—Former U. S. Labor Secretary Elizabeth Dole

Critical Thinking

Think about...

the meaning of Elizabeth Dole's statement for your education and preparation for employment. What new challenges and opportunities might you face in school and at work?

education and business agree that **higher-order thinking** is difficult to define but easy to recognize in the workplace. The U.S. Department of Labor Secretary's Commission on Achieving Necessary Skills (SCANS) conducted in-depth interviews with employers across the nation. They also analyzed a wide variety of jobs. As a result they determined that the thinking abilities and skills most in demand in the world of work are

- reasoning

- creative thinking

- problem solving

- decision making

Thinking Defined

Over the past 50 years, there have been several scholarly research projects to determine exactly what thinking abilities are. For example, J. P. Guilford, author of *Personality*[1] and many journal articles on the

---

[1]J. P. Guilford, *Personality* (New York: McGraw-Hill Book Co., Inc., 1959).

200 *Thinking Skills*

"Structure of Intellect," defined thinking in terms of five components. These components are

- memory
- cognition
- evaluation
- convergent thinking
- divergent thinking

Memory is recognized when a person is able to "play back" what has been learned. With **cognition** a person can recognize and pick out bits and pieces of information. **Evaluation** is more complex and difficult than memory and cognition. Therefore, evaluation is one of the "higher-order" thinking abilities. Evaluation is used when a person makes judgments. Another component of higher-order thinking is **convergent thinking**. This ability is involved in reasoning, analytical problem solving, or critical thinking. Finally, the third kind of higher-order thinking is **divergent thinking**. This is the kind of thinking that is involved in creativity or creative problem solving.

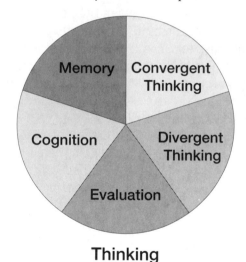

Thinking

Illustration 13-1
Components of thinking ability... J. P. Guilford.

Characteristics of Higher-Order Thinking

Psychologists have not succeeded in finding a clear, systematic explanation of exactly what happens when a person is engaged in thinking. The process of higher-order thinking is especially complicated; the paths of reasoning and analysis are seldom obvious. What happens in creative thinking is even less apparent. However, psychologists do understand and agree about several characteristics that describe higher-order thinking. These characteristics are evident in critical thinking and also in creativity.

Higher-order thinking requires

- Reflecting thoughtfully upon the knowledge that you have. This involves consideration of a resource of information, which is turned over and over in the mind, a process called **incubation**, to create new knowledge.

- Being sensitive to slight variations in meaning and shades of interpretation. This is called **nuanced judgment**.

- Using words effectively to communicate the results of higher-order thinking. This is called **rhetoric**.

- Creating order out of what appears confusing. This is referred to as **discovering structure** in apparent disorder.

Critical Thinking

Gregory is someone who appeared to be very smart. He had scored in the top 5 percent on the Stanford-Binet IQ test, the Miller Analogies test, and the ACT. He had a 4.0 grade point average in high school, including some college courses he was allowed to take during his senior year. All this was supported by excellent letters of recommendation. Gregory had everything that smart college students are supposed to have, and he was invited to enroll at Yale as a top selection. In a conversation with the school counselor, Gregory's college advisor said, "There's no doubt that this was Mr. Real Smarto. And he performed just the way the tests predicted he would. During his first year at Yale, he did extremely well on multiple-choice tests and was great in class, especially at analyzing other people's arguments and evaluating other people's work. But it didn't stay that way. Gregory wasn't even in the top half by the time he finished. It just didn't work out. I wonder what went wrong?"

A popular term that includes evaluation and convergent thinking, the abilities with which Gregory was gifted, is **critical thinking**. Another term for critical thinking is *reasoning*. Specifically, what does one *do* when reasoning or thinking critically? Following is a list of critical-thinking activities. A person with critical-thinking ability is able to

- distinguish between verifiable facts and value claims

- determine the credibility of a source of facts or value claims

- determine the accuracy of a statement of fact

- distinguish between warranted or unwarranted reasons or conclusions

- distinguish between relevant or irrelevant facts, claims, or reasons

- detect bias

- identify stated and unstated assumptions

- identify ambiguous or equivocal claims, reasons, or arguments

- recognize logical inconsistencies in an argument

Creativity

E lena's performance in high school and the first year of college was not impressive. In a conversation with her high school counselor, Elena's college professor explained, "Her grades weren't great. Her IQ, Miller Analogies, and ACT scores were really low by Yale standards. When I interviewed her, I wanted to admit her, primarily because she had absolutely superlative letters of recommendation. But I was outvoted by the selection committee. So in order not to lose her, I hired Elena as a research assistant. In addition to working full time, she took classes. Her

Creativity is important in many work situations.

Blumebild/H. Armstrong Roberts

work and ideas proved to be just as good as the letters said they'd be. She was extremely creative, had really good ideas, and did exceptional research. Some of the most important work I've done was in collaboration with her. After she proved herself, she was admitted to Yale and is doing great."

Finding a clear, specific definition of creativity is not easy. Alex F. Osborne, author of *Applied Imagination*[2], defined **creativity** as "The ability to visualize, to foresee, and to generate ideas."

E. Paul Torrance, author of *Guiding Creative Talent*[3], suggested that creativity is "the process of sensing problems or gaps in information, forming ideas or hypotheses, testing and modifying these hypotheses, and communicating the results." He contributed more than any other person to the development of creativity tests. The Torrance tests measure the following specific creative thinking abilities:

- **Fluency**—the ability to produce many ideas quickly.

- **Originality**—the ability to produce ideas that are unusual.

- **Flexibility**—the ability to produce a variety of ideas.

- **Elaboration**—the ability to add interesting detail to ideas.

- **Curiosity**—the ability to ask revealing questions.

- **Imagination**—the ability to make wild guesses.

In addition to the abilities listed above, the highly creative person has an attitude of self-confidence. One way to identify the creative people in a group is to simply ask, "Are you creative?" Those who say "yes" probably are.

Other characteristics of creative people are

- strong motivation to use their creative potential

- open-mindedness to the ideas of others

- unusual curiosity

- awareness of the excitement and challenge in life

- sensitivity to the problems—an attitude of "constructive discontent"

The SCANS report shows that employers place a high value on workers who demonstrate creativity, especially in the use of **visualization**, or "seeing things in the mind's eye."

*Critical
Thinking*

Think about...

your own creative thinking abilities. How capable are you with respect to the creative thinking abilities listed above? What might you do to challenge and improve your creativity?

[2]Alex F. Osborne, *Applied Imagination* (New York: Charles Scribner's Sons, Inc., 1963).

[3]E. P. Torrance, *Guiding Creative Talent* (Prentice Hall, Inc., 1962).

Critical Thinking and Creativity Are Equally Important

One might expect highly intelligent people to be more likely to be highly creative. Not so. There have been many careful research investigations over the past 40 years concerning the relationships between intelligence and creativity. The evidence shows that creativity and IQ test scores are unrelated. So you should realize that few people are both highly intelligent and highly creative. And few are neither. There are many who score high on IQ tests but earn average scores on creativity tests. Also, there are many who score high in creativity but average on measures of intelligence.

Elena, in the scenario presented before, is an example of someone of average intelligence who is highly creative. Several decades ago—during the 1950s—intelligence testing was fashionable, and creativity testing was just emerging. It was generally believed that the IQ test measured everything that was important in human thinking. At that time Elena would have been considered to be an "overachiever." No one would have expected her with an "average" IQ to outperform someone like Gregory, who scored far above average on intelligence tests. But Elena is not an overachiever. Her high level of creative ability suggests that she has the thinking power to achieve at a very high level even though her critical thinking ability is just average.

Higher-Order Thinking Strategies

Despite the earlier comment about the notion that there are no reliable step-by-step procedures for higher-order thinking, something worthwhile can be accomplished by following logical problem-solving procedures. Following is a closer look at several procedures or strategies for solving problems using critical thinking and creativity.

Evaluation

Evaluation is a term that was used by J. P. Guilford to describe one of the three higher-order thinking abilities. An example of evaluation applied as a problem-solving strategy is the judging at a county fair. The judge examines an animal, a piece of art, or craft work and makes decisions about the quality of the object. Another example is in a young artist's competition in music or dance, during which a panel of judges evaluates individual performances.

A competent worker...

■ sees things in the mind's eye

■ is able to organize and process symbols, pictures, graphs, or other information (for example, sees a building from a blueprint, a system's operation from schematics, the flow of work activities from narrative descriptions, or the taste of food from reading a recipe)

Critical judgment and evaluation require higher-order thinking.

Bob Daemmrich/Stock, Boston

The procedure for evaluation is to

1. Identify or develop appropriate **evaluation criteria**. A criterion is an indicator of quality.

2. Identify or develop appropriate **standards** for each criterion. Standards tell how much quality is required or the level of quality that is required.

3. Determine the extent to which standards are met for each of the evaluation criteria.

Decision Making

A variety of decision-making strategies are presented in management textbooks. They all require the application of critical thinking and creativity where information is gathered and logical analysis of the information is used in reaching a good decision. Here is an example.

The procedure for decision making is to

1. State the desired goal or condition. What do you want to happen, or how will things be different if the decision is a good one?

2. Identify possible obstacles to realizing the goal or condition. What might prevent the attainment of the desired goal or condition?

3. Develop ideas for dealing with each obstacle. What are some effective ways of preventing or overcoming the barriers that stand in the way?

4. Evaluate the ideas considering costs, benefits, and consequences. How much will each idea cost? Will the benefits justify the costs? What might happen as a result of implementing the idea?

5. Choose the best idea. Considering all of the information available, which idea will be best in terms of the desired goal or condition? Sometimes more than one idea or a combination of ideas will be selected.

As you study the procedure for decision making, you should note that evaluation comes into play in Step 4 and in Step 5. Also, the skills of critical thinking and creativity are applied every step of the way.

Problem Solving

The problem-solving procedure outlined by the SCANS researchers can be visualized as a funnel, as shown in the following illustration. At the top is an assortment of information that is logically processed, then narrowed down to a conclusion or solution to the problem. In other words, the information is used to reach the conclusion by using convergent thinking, or logical analysis. Therefore, this strategy for solving problems is referred to as **analytical problem solving.**

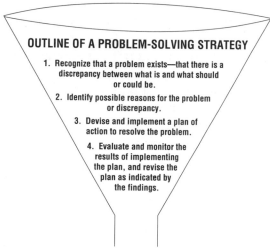

OUTLINE OF A PROBLEM-SOLVING STRATEGY

1. Recognize that a problem exists—that there is a discrepancy between what is and what should or could be.
2. Identify possible reasons for the problem or discrepancy.
3. Devise and implement a plan of action to resolve the problem.
4. Evaluate and monitor the results of implementing the plan, and revise the plan as indicated by the findings.

Illustration 13-2
Outline of a problem-solving strategy.

Just as convergent thinking, or critical thinking ability, gives one the power to do *analytical problem solving*, divergent thinking, or creative thinking ability, gives one the power to do **creative problem solving**. There is a step-by-step procedure for analytical problem solving, and there is a very similar procedure used for creative problem solving. The distinction between creative problem solving and analytical problem solving is in what happens at the point where possible solutions to the problem are needed. Following are the specific steps:

Analytical Method	Creative Method
Step 1 Identify and clarify the problem.	*Step 1* Identify and clarify the problem.
Step 2 Gather pertinent information.	*Step 2* Gather pertinent information.
Step 3 Use **logical inference** to determine possible solutions.	*Step 3a* Use **brainstorming** to produce possible solutions.
	Step 3b Develop and refine the ideas for solution.
Step 4 Evaluate the alternative solutions.	*Step 4* Evaluate the alternative solutions.
Step 5 Choose the best solution.	*Step 5* Choose the best solution.

You will notice that in one case **logical inference** is used to come up with various ideas for solving the problem. When a person draws inferences, critical thinking and logic are used. For example, if a person shows up for work moving slowly with a "glassy stare" and slurred speech, one might infer that he or she is under the influence of drugs or alcohol. Another logical inference might be that the person had been in an accident or did not get enough sleep. However, if you ask the question "What are some possible causes and consequences of what you see in this person's behavior?" you would be using a brainstorming technique.

To help you visualize how problem solving works in employment situations, study the following examples that take you through the steps of problem solving. One shows how a travel agent might use this strategy in resolving a problem with a dissatisfied customer. The other is an example of a construction supervisor using the same problem-solving strategy when timber piles break.

As you study these examples, keep in mind that analytical skills come into play at various steps in the process and that creativity skills are needed for others. When logical, convergent thinking is needed, we see critical thinking being used. When new ideas—clever, interesting, and unusual ideas—are needed, **brainstorming** and other creative thinking techniques are used. Test yourself by indicating in the margin where analytical thinking (AT) is used and where creative thinking (CT) is used.

The Travel Agent's Problem

1. *Recognize that a problem exists—that there is a discrepancy between what is and what should or could be.*

A customer comes into the travel agency with a complaint. She is obviously dissatisfied with her travel experience.

2. *Identify possible reasons for the problem or discrepancy.*

The travel agent talks with the customer to determine the nature of the problem. She asks questions and looks for clues in the answers. She reviews the customer's file. At the conclusion of her investigation, the travel agent decides what should be done to satisfy the customer.

3. *Devise and implement a plan of action to resolve the problem.*

The travel agent contacts a representative from the company at fault to notify them of the customer's complaint. She negotiates compensation for the customer with a company representative and notifies the customer of the compensation offer.

4. *Evaluate and monitor the results of implementing the plan, and revise the plan as indicated by the findings.*

The travel agent makes a follow-up contact with the customer to learn the results of the negotiations between the company and the customer. When the customer and the company express satisfaction, the case is closed.

The Construction Supervisor's Problem

1. *Recognize that a problem exists—that there is a discrepancy between what is and what should or could be.*

   The construction supervisor discovers that timber piles are breaking before they reach the specified bearing.

2. *Identify possible reasons for the problem or discrepancy.*

   The construction supervisor analyzes how and why the timber pilings break during the piling operation. He reassesses the strength of the materials, the equipment specifications, and the skills of the workers under his supervision.

3. *Devise and implement a plan of action to resolve the problem.*

   The construction supervisor evaluates and selects the appropriate equipment to accomplish the project. He chooses the right kind of timber pilings based on the strength, diameter, and cost to meet project specifications.

4. *Evaluate and monitor the results of implementing the plan, and revise the plan as indicated by the findings.*

   As the new equipment setup and timber pilings are used, the construction supervisor carefully observes the work being done. He inspects the completed work and is satisfied that the new pilings will not break under the stress they are required to bear.

Your Thinking Skills Can Be Developed

C elia's former high school counselor was talking with her Yale professor. The professor said, "Her grades, letters of recommendation, IQ, Miller Analogies, and SAT scores were good but not great. She was accepted at Yale, and the first year she did average work. Surprisingly, however, she turned out to be the easiest student to place in a good job. And this surprised me. Celia lacked Gregory's super analytic ability and Elena's super creative thinking ability, yet she could do a job while others were having trouble. Celia, it turns out, had learned how to play the game. She made sure she did the kind of work that was valued by her employer. She had savvy—a kind of practical grasp of things. And that doesn't show up on IQ or creativity tests."

Having the *ability* to think is of no value unless you learn how to use it. You also need thinking *skills*. Developing these skills can give you the power to *use* your thinking abilities.

The dictionary defines skills as "technical expertness" and "proficiency." It includes ". . .using one's knowledge effectively. . ." and "a learned power of doing a thing competently—a developed aptitude or ability." The distinction between abilities and skills is that abilities are like the tools you use for thinking. Skill is what you need to develop if you are to make good use of the tools. For example, a camera is a tool for a photographer. To take good pictures, the photographer must have a good camera. But that is not enough. He or she must also have picture-taking skills, including the desire to photograph something of interest. You must develop your thinking skills if you are to take advantage of your thinking abilities.

It is important for you to understand that whatever thinking abilities you have, those abilities can be improved. And most importantly, the skills required to use those abilities can be learned. Knowledge is acquired by reading, listening, etc. Attitudes develop under the influence of emotional experiences. Physical (or psychomotor) skills are developed through coaching and practice. It is the same for intellectual skills, such as reasoning and creative problem solving. Knowing what to do and having the benefit of coaching and repeated practice—these are the keys to learning to think.

66 Like most behavior, creative activity probably represents, to some extent, many learned skills. There may be limitations on these skills by heredity; but I am convinced that through learning one can extend the skills within those limitations. 99
—J. P. Guilford

Summary

More than ever before, employers look for and appreciate employees who are able to think on their own. They seek out and reward workers who can make decisions, solve problems, and handle critical and creative thinking activities that were traditionally in the domain of supervisors and managers.

Critical thinking is an intellectual skill that is needed and used in the workplace. It is based on two higher-order thinking abilities—evaluation and convergent thinking. Creativity is based on divergent thinking. Higher-order thinking is complex and requires thoughtful reflection, nuanced judgment, and the ability to discover structure in apparent disorder.

Critical thinking skills allow a person to do analytical problem solving, to make logically sound judgments and decisions. Creativity helps a person to visualize, to foresee, and to generate ideas. Fluency in producing ideas, flexibility, originality, elaboration, curiosity, and imagination are factors in creative thinking. Both creativity and critical thinking are important, and a person can be highly gifted in one kind of thinking and only average in the other.

Procedures or strategies for higher-order thinking allow for a clear step-by-step process of evaluation, decision making, and problem solving. The problem-solving procedure is essentially the same for analytical problem solving and creative problem solving. The distinction is that creative problem solving requires brainstorming techniques to produce a variety of good alternative solutions while analytical problem solving requires logical inference at that stage of the process.

Improving your higher-order thinking abilities skills is worth the effort. It takes some coaching and repeated practice, but it can enhance your value as a worker and make you more effective and productive.

End of Chapter Activities

Questions and Projects

1. John Mansfield said, "Man's body is faulty, his mind is untrustworthy, but his imagination has made him remarkable." To what extent do you believe this to be true? Discuss.

2. Think about your past experiences at work and in school. Write down three instances where creativity on your part either improved or actually saved a situation.

3. Are students with the highest IQs necessarily the ones who can produce the most original ideas? Discuss why or why not.

4. Test your creative thinking abilities. Either working alone or in a small group, have a brainstorming session for exactly ten minutes. In that time write down as many clever, interesting, and unusual ideas as you can think of for using empty plastic beverage containers.

Evaluate the results of your session by

   a. counting the number of ideas, regardless of quality. Over 50 is excellent, 30 to 50 is good, and less than 30 suggests you need to suspend judgment, try harder, and be more creative.

   b. considering how many of the ideas are really unusual. This is a measure of your originality. If at least 10 percent of the ideas appear to be so unusual that probably no one else would think of them, your originality score is excellent. Five percent is good. Less than that shows a lack of originality.

c. counting the number of times you changed categories in responding. When this happens you are showing flexibility. You sort of "shift gears" mentally. For example, in 15 responses you list five as containers, seven as decorations, and three as floating objects. Your flexibility score would be 3. A flexibility score of 12 or more is excellent, 7 to 12 is good, and less than that suggests that you have a tendency to get in a "mental rut" and stay there.

5. Try out your problem-solving skills. Either working alone or in a small group:

a. Look around your school, your workplace, or your community. Find a problem that is important enough to motivate you to work on it. Write one or two paragraphs to describe the discrepancy between what is and what should or could be.

b. Identify the possible reasons for the problem or discrepancy. Use logical inference—analyze the situation the way you would if you were trying to unravel a mystery. Then have a brainstorming session to use creative thinking to come up with a variety of interesting ideas about possible causes of the problem or discrepancy. Make a list of your ideas, and arrange them with the best ideas at the top of the list.

c. Devise a plan of action to resolve the problem or remove the discrepancy. Again, use logical inference and creativity as you did in Step b above. Write the plan in terms of 1) objectives or goals to be accomplished, 2) strategies and implementation plans, 3) ideas about how the achievement of objectives or goals will be evaluated, 4) a time schedule, and 5) an estimated budget.

6. Either working alone or brainstorming with a small group, make a list of as many ideas as you can think of for improving your critical thinking and creativity. Take 15 minutes (suspending judgment and letting the wild ideas flow) and make the list as long as you can. Then choose the best ideas and write a plan of action.

Case Problems

1. Career Transition
Mercy has been enjoying a professional career in interior design. Her husband Paul is doing well as a truck driver hauling freight for a food wholesaler. Their first baby is on the way, and Mercy faces the possibility of leaving an interesting job that she has been devoted to for several years. Their second-story apartment is small, their parents live out of

town, and most of their friends work all day. The prospect of Mercy having to interrupt her career is discouraging because of her strong creative urge and enjoyment of dealing with people. However, the possibility of being a full-time parent is appealing.

a. Specifically, what are the problems Mercy and Paul need to solve?

b. Identify three possible solutions, and outline the advantages and disadvantages of each.

2. Tired Out

Merlin's Tire Shop has been in business for 17 years. Tire sales have been steady, and Merlin has been collecting about 20 worn-out tires per day, hauling them to a vacant lot in the suburbs. A new city ordinance classifies the pile of tires as a fire hazard, and the city manager orders that they be removed. The community trash disposal site has a policy of charging one dollar per tire, and Merlin calculates that his cost for using the trash disposal site would put him out of business.

a. Specifically, what are the problems Merlin needs to solve?

b. Make a list of clever, interesting, and unusual ideas for using old tires to make something useful.

c. Outline a plan that might allow Merlin to dispose of his used tires without going out of business.

Managing Stress

R oberto recently started working as a grocery checkout clerk. He has set for himself a goal of being an assistant manager within a period of three years. He works extremely hard at his job and strives to learn everything he can by observing others and asking questions about the grocery business. After one year Roberto is promoted to assistant produce manager. He is thrilled. In his eagerness to continue to climb toward his goal, he puts in voluntary overtime, helps everyone in his department, and provides special services for preferred customers. He ignores the fact that he has not taken any vacation time. Some nights he is unable to sleep because he is thinking about some phase of his new position. He is losing weight and frequently feels tense. His stomach is often upset, and he experiences a burning sensation. After checking with his physician, Roberto learns that he is developing a gastric ulcer.

What Is Stress?

Dictionary definitions do not quite capture the meaning of **stress** as it is seen and experienced in the world of work. One of the *Webster's* definitions describes it as an ". . . emotional factor that causes bodily or mental tension. . . ." A practical way of defining stress is the feeling one gets from prolonged, pent-up emotions. If the emotions you experience are pleasant and desirable—joy, elation, ecstasy, delight—you usually feel free to let them show. They are not suppressed. Therefore, positive emotions do not usually cause stress. Negative emotions, on the other hand, are more often held inside. They are hidden. You suffer quietly and you experience stress.

Stress Effects

Just as there is great variety in the range of emotions you might experience, there are many possible manifestations of stress—in your private lives and in your working lives. Here are some words that describe the effects of stress.

■ anxiety	■ strain	■ tension	■ burden
■ pressure	■ anger	■ slump	■ dejection
■ misery	■ despair	■ anguish	■ gloom

Prolonged stress can be devastating. *Burnout*, *breakdown*, and *depression* are some of the terms used to describe it. By wearing a mask, you may expect to hide stress caused by problems in your personal life and not let it influence your performance on the job. This will probably not work. The more you try to hold your emotions in, the greater the pressure build-up will be.

Stress Follows You. There is simply no way to survive the experience of long-term stress without damage to your private and work life. It is almost impossible to insulate one from the other. If you are under stress because of something that is going on in your work situation, it

Work overload can create stress.

H. Armstrong Roberts

will be very difficult to maintain your positive attitudes and productive work habits. The most tranquil and satisfying personal life will be upset by the effects of stress that may occur in one's working environment. Similarly, being under emotional strain and having stress in one's personal life is bound to have a negative effect at work.

Stress Can Help. Sometimes stress can have desirable side effects. You may have heard someone say, "I like to work under stress. If I have a deadline to meet, I work harder." Physical stress builds muscle. For some people "test anxiety" improves performance; for others it hampers their performance. The problem is to be able to avoid crossing the line between improved performance and harmful stress.

Stress Affects the Body. For most people the body seems to adjust to stress. At least it does so in the short run. But sustained and increased stress may cause harmful physical changes: insomnia, irritability, headaches, stomach pain, skin rash, and more. It is also clear from medical research that stress can influence heart function, cause high blood pressure, and raise levels of blood cholesterol.

Another dramatic effect of stress in some people is **hysterical conversion**. This means that a person who is unable to cope with a highly stressful emotional experience simply converts the stress to a physical symptom. For example, a soldier in combat may "freeze." He is actually unable to move when faced with what he views as an impossible task. Few will encounter such extreme stress, but you cannot eliminate it totally from your life. Before you look at ways to manage and alleviate stress, it will be helpful to understand some of its causes.

Stress Build-Up

What are some of the underlying causes of stress build-up? Many negative emotional experiences are potentially stressful. Following are some examples.

Everyday Frustrations. From the time you wake up until you go to sleep, you may be confronted with a succession of depressing emotional situations. Managing to get yourself (and possibly a spouse and children) out of bed and ready to face the day can be a challenge to your patience and ingenuity. Driving to school or work can be harrowing. You may experience frustration in arranging to get the car repaired. You may face conflicts in school or at work, such as coping with unrealistic deadlines, equipment failures, or unexpected bad weather. If part of your job is selling, you may experience feelings of rejection when most of your customers say "no."

A series of stressful and frustrating experiences throughout the day can cause you to lie awake at night in an emotional turmoil—unable

Think about...

a person in your life who has shown evidence of being under stress. What are some physical signs and effects that were apparent? What are some attitudes and behavioral evidence that you noticed?

to get needed rest. You face the next day with less emotional and physical stamina. After another stressful day and another night without rest, you may have even less emotional strength and stability. Therefore, stress build-up continues day after day.

Problems in Your Personal Life. Surviving the normal, everyday stress described above can be difficult. But far more serious and painful circumstances can create long-term stress. More serious stressful circumstances may include separation from loved ones, personal illness or illness of a loved one, death of someone you care about, or conflict with a spouse or close friend. Other major causes of stress are problems with drug and alcohol abuse, domestic violence, care of elderly relatives, chronic mental illness, physical handicaps. The list goes on and on.

Managing your personal finances can be another stressful experience. This can be a problem no matter what your income level, but it is especially difficult if you must support a family and do not earn enough to live comfortably. Unpaid bills, unwise use of credit, and budget limitations can make life difficult.

Changes. A common cause of stress is dealing with life's transitions—changes. This is especially true when a person must cope with too many transitions all at once. For example, Sue Ellen has just completed a program in fashion merchandising. She is eager to get started on her new job. Her mother is ill and requires care. Her father died a few months ago. Sue Ellen's new job requires that she relocate to a town 100 miles from home. The move, a new career, and a change in family relationships may cause excessive stress for her. Too many changes have arrived at the same time.

Work Adjustment. In some jobs the work itself may cause stress or tension. One factor that causes stress is **monotony**, or doing a task repeatedly. Another is being expected to do more work than your skills and the allotted time will allow. In contrast, sometimes not having enough to do can create stress.

A change in jobs or new job responsibilities, such as a promotion or a different assignment, can cause stress. There may be too many kinds of tasks for which you are not well prepared. You may be subjected to stressful working conditions—noise, interruptions, temperature extremes, poor lighting, or unsafe situations.

Some jobs are unavoidably stressful because of the nature of the work itself. Some examples are law enforcement, health occupations, fire fighting, air traffic control, news reporting, and many more. Even though most hazardous jobs have many safeguards to protect workers, work that is dangerous is stressful. Wherever you work, some stress is sure to occur.

Some jobs are unavoidably stressful because of the nature of the work.

©Thomas S. England/Photo Researchers

Stress Signals

If you are experiencing long-term stress, you may or may not be aware of it. But even if you are, you may choose to avoid facing up to your problems. When the solutions are not obvious and easy, it may feel better to hide the problem—even from your inner self. Following are some signs and symptoms of stress that you should be concerned about.

Depression. Depression is an emotional disorder that is marked by sadness, inactivity, and a feeling of emptiness. It may cause an over-stressed person to withdraw from co-workers, family, and friends. The depressed person may begin to feel emotionally drained, sick, or numb. If you are experiencing depression, you may lose interest in your work, family, friends, and everything that enriches your life. You are overcome by feelings of hopelessness.

Physical Warning Signals. Physical symptoms are generally one of the first signs of too much stress. The physical warning signals usually listed by medical experts as signs of harmful stress include these:

- pounding of the heart
- dryness of the throat or mouth
- insomnia
- feeling constantly tired
- inability to concentrate
- chronic pain in the neck or back
- stomach pain

- decreased or increased appetite
- nightmares
- an overpowering urge to cry
- dificulty in breathing
- trembling
- an urge to escape
- panic

66 Depression, gloom, pessimism, despair, discouragement, these slay ten human beings to every one murdered by disease. . . Be cheerful. 99
—Dr. Frank Crane

Often stress signs are ignored as they seem to come and go. If these symptoms are totally disregarded, more serious conditions may develop.

Mood or Personality Changes. If you are under a great deal of stress, your behavior may become unpredictable. You may do things that are not typical of your behavior. If you lose your temper or express extreme disgust with others or yourself for no apparent reason, you may be experiencing too much stress. If you are uncomfortable with a new position or additional responsibilities, you may experience personality changes brought on by too much stress. Unfortunately you may be unaware of the changes in your mood or behavior. The changes may have to be pointed out to you by others.

Check Yourself for Unhealthy Stress Symptoms

Rate yourself by checking the appropriate space beside each symptom.

Symptom	Rating		
	often	sometimes	never
constant fatigue or low energy	_____	_____	_____
recurring headaches	_____	_____	_____
chronic skin problems	_____	_____	_____
stomach problems	_____	_____	_____
high blood pressure	_____	_____	_____
inability to sleep	_____	_____	_____
temper outbursts	_____	_____	_____
moodiness	_____	_____	_____
nervous habits, such as nail biting	_____	_____	_____
inability to concentrate	_____	_____	_____
compulsive eating	_____	_____	_____
excessive use of alcohol or tobacco	_____	_____	_____

It is normal to experience a few of these symptoms sometimes, but enduring any of them often over a long period of time indicates unhealthy stress.

Handling Stress

Lois and Arthur started working as desk associates in a hotel in their community. Lois wants very much to please the management staff and has clear goals in mind. She works very hard to accommodate customers. She answers the phone courteously, goes out of her way to get along with everyone, and follows company policies relating to procedures and hospitality. Arthur is often indifferent to guests, ignores special guest requests, and frequently violates company policies by taking shortcuts. Arthur's attitude bothers Lois, and she cannot overlook his shortcomings. She tries to cover for him by doing some of his work as well as her own. She makes tactful suggestions to him whenever possible about his attitude, and she worries about his job performance. She cannot accept the imperfections she has identified in Arthur's work. These imperfections eventually cause her so much stress that she loses her enthusiasm for the position and the goals she has set for herself. Lois finds herself dreading the thought of going to work. She even considers forgetting about a career in the hotel industry. She is generally miserable. Lois has not learned to accept what she cannot change or alter.

Fortunately there are many effective ways to handle stress. The ideal option would be to avoid it. Manage your life so that you survive the emotional down times without allowing stress to engulf you. But if you find yourself under stress, your wisest option is to find ways to reduce or eliminate it. You need not, and should not, live your life in emotional stress and discomfort. You *can* handle it. Here are some suggestions that may help.

Understand the Causes of Stress

Understanding *why* you are under stress is important. This may seem obvious, but it requires a deliberate, conscious effort to pause and simply ponder your situation.

Self-Analysis. Preparing a written assessment of your stress factors can help you to visualize and understand them. For example, you may write "I feel tired most of the time. My lower back seems to ache all through the day and night. I miss deadlines and run behind schedule." After your list of possible stress factors is written, consider each item and ask why. "Why am I feeling tired? Why does my back ache? Why do I run behind schedule?" Careful consideration of the answers to the "why" questions will reveal stress factors such as trying to do too much, managing time poorly, or having no time out for recreation.

It may help to talk things over with someone with whom you feel comfortable and secure. A good friend or a professional counselor

Critical Thinking

Think about...

what might happen if a person simply uses willpower and self-discipline to *ignore or quietly endure* the experiences that are creating stress. Can this strategy work in the long run? Why or why not?

can help you explore possibilities and clarify your thinking about what is causing stress in your life. These talks will release pressure, make you feel better, and help you see a new side of a problem. If you find yourself preoccupied with a difficulty, turn to a good listener and discuss what is troubling you. In the process of describing your problem, you may find a solution.

Deal with the Stress Factors. Develop techniques to deal with the causes of stress. The longer you avoid dealing with the stress factors, the more stress will build up. If tension comes because you have put off an unfinished task, restructure your priorities so you can get the task you have been avoiding out of the way and off your mind. Take the tasks that you have been neglecting, write them down, and check them off as you take care of them. Make it a point to talk with any person causing stress in your life and resolve your differences.

You may find yourself ignoring the causes of stress by simply saying "I'm not feeling well," "I'm just tired," or by taking your frustration and stress out on others with unkind thoughts, words, or actions. This behavior only increases stress.

Control Your Achievement Motivation

It is only natural to want to achieve. For some people this can be almost an obsession. Psychologists refer to these hard-driving people as having **Type A personalities.** More easygoing, relaxed people are described as **Type B**. If you face the challenge of reining in your Type A behavior as you struggle to achieve, you may need to slow your pace. One of the reasons you are under stress is that you put yourself in high gear for long periods of time. These periods may prove to be too much for your emotional and physical health. Stop and reflect on your life. As you are working toward a goal, you will reach points where it is appropriate to stop and reward yourself for a job well done. This reward period will allow you to relax and get away from the pressure.

Take It Easy on Yourself. It is impossible to pay attention to all areas of your life simultaneously. Take care of things as you can. Do not expect perfection in yourself or others. Realize that there are some things that you cannot control. Learn to accept what you cannot change or alter. Ask yourself if you are aiming at the unreasonable or the impossible. If you are trying to live up to someone else's expectations or expecting others to live up to your standards, you may be setting yourself up for failure. Remember, you are only human; imperfections are acceptable.

Manage Your Time Better. Time management can reduce stress, especially if you are a Type A overachiever. You may simply be trying to do too much. When you plan and schedule your work and your personal life, it will be easier to be realistic about your achievement motivation. The suggestions offered in Chapter 12 can be applied here. Strive to work as efficiently as you can and continually seek ways of streamlining your work. Work to complete tasks on time and in an expedient manner. Attempt to break down big jobs into reasonable blocks of work. This is a good way to tackle what seems like an overwhelming task and to feel rewarded as you complete each step. Delegate and share work with others when appropriate and acceptable. Avoid attempting to do everything yourself. Keep your work load under control.

Maintain Good Health

What you need to do to maintain good health depends on the kinds of problems that cause stress in your life. Following are some suggestions for alleviating stress and improving your physical health.

Get Regular Physical Exercise. Exercise can help to relieve stress. An effective exercise program can "burn up" the tension that builds up in your body during a long period of stress. Activity, such as moderate walking, can relieve tension and relax your body. Other activities that provide physical release from stress are playing tennis, running, bicycling, and other forms of exercise you enjoy. If you have had a stressful morning, skip the coffee break and try a walk break.

Get Involved in a Wellness Program. Employers across the country are realizing that stress may be an important factor in reducing employee

Exercise that you enjoy can relieve stress and improve your health.

H. Armstrong Roberts

productivity. They know that stress can contribute to absenteeism, and they understand the negative effect stress can have on alcohol and drug use. Employers know how stress can harm good human relationships. As a result, many companies have started **wellness programs** or joined a local health agency's program. Participation in a wellness program can help you counteract the effects of too much stress before it becomes harmful to you.

Include a healthful diet in your wellness program. Most medical experts agree that cutting down on fatty meats, dairy products, eggs, sweets, and salt will help to relieve stress. It is generally recommended that eating more fruits, vegetables, poultry, fish, and whole grains has a calming effect on a stressed person. Research has also shown that for hard-driving Type A men, artery-damaging cholesterol increases with stress. For easy-going Type B men, stressful experience did not seem to increase blood cholesterol levels.

Be Good to Yourself

If you experience stress as the result of working too hard for too long without a break, you should try to get away from it all. Redirect your thoughts to something pleasant and relaxing for awhile to "recharge your batteries."

Get Away and Have Some Fun. An exotic, expensive vacation can certainly help in coping with stress. Fortunately those of us with less time and money can "get away" simply by changing our pace or taking a break from our routine. Weekends, holidays, and hours after work can relieve stress if you spend some of the time doing things you enjoy. Do you like to meet friends after work? Do you have a hobby such as sewing, reading, woodworking, gardening, hiking, square dancing, or working on restoring your classic car? Plan time to do the things that help you relax and give you pleasure. Reward yourself. Enjoy yourself.

Look on the Bright Side. Attempt to develop a positive outlook on life. Always strive to concentrate on what is positive. Look beyond yourself, and avoid spending too much time thinking about failure. Whenever the opportunity arises, try to turn negative statements made by others into positive ones. If a coworker says, "We'll never get this report done," respond, "If we work together, I think we can do it!" A positive thought will introduce a new spirit and get everyone working hard to achieve. A positive spirit will indeed help reduce stress.

66 Leisure for men of business, and business for men of leisure, would cure many complaints. 99
—Thrale

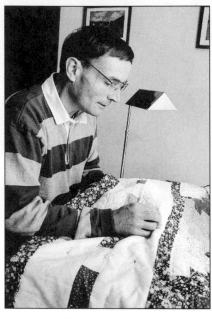

Take time to do something you enjoy.

Photo by Jim Whitmer

Summary

Stress is the feeling one gets from prolonged, pent-up negative emotions. The more you try to hold in your emotions over an extended period of time, the greater will be the stress build-up. The effects of extreme stress can be devastating.

There is simply no way to insulate your working life from the effects of stress in your private life, and stress at work affects your private life as well. Sustained and increasing stress can affect your physical health. Everyday activities can also be stressful, and problems in your personal life can cause extreme stress.

There are many effective ways to handle stress and to help avoid it. The first step is to identify the underlying causes of your stress and carefully consider the possible reasons for allowing them to develop. Talking with a friend or counselor can provide help with this self-analysis.

After the underlying causes of your stress are identified, you will be able to devise plans for managing or avoiding them in the future. Some strategies that have proven to be effective in managing stress are being less demanding on yourself and managing your time better. You should also maintain control of your health with diet and regular exercise and, if possible, by participating in a wellness program.

Finally, you can get away from the personal and work situations that create stress by taking time to play or doing something that you enjoy.

End of Chapter Activities

Questions and Projects

1. Have you had the experience of living or working with someone who was under stress? Think of one case, and

    a. Describe the stressful behavior. What were the signs and symptoms that made the stress apparent?

    b. Consider the person's behavior. Do your best to identify the causes of the stress. What were the emotional events or experiences that, over an extended period, created the signs and symptoms you described in your answer to question a?

2. Review your experiences in school and in your social life. Do you participate in athletics? Do you perform or compete in music, drama, debate, or dance?

    a. Describe the emotions you experienced. Were they positive—making you feel good? Or were they negative—making you feel not so good?

    b. Consider the positive emotions—those that made you feel good. Did you try to hold them inside and hide them, or did you feel free to express them? Did you feel stress build-up? Was there a positive or negative effect on your performance?

    c. Consider the negative emotions--those that made you feel not so good. Did you try to hold them inside and hide them, or did you feel free to express them? Did you feel stress build-up? Was there a positive or negative effect on your performance?

    d. Share and compare your experiences with those of your classmates. In general, were positive emotions more or less likely to cause stress build-up? How often did positive emotions improve performance? How often did negative emotions and stress improve performance?

3. Interview someone you know who appears to be very busy and under a lot of pressure—someone who can make a list of everyday frustrations. Ask this person to share with you his or her ideas about

    a. Some of the physical and mental consequences of keepingup this kind of pace over a long period of time.

    b. Ways of reducing or avoiding stress build-up under these conditions. Share the responses to this question in class, and prepare a poster highlighting the best ideas for stress management.

4. Interview a medical doctor, a counseling psychologist, a nurse, or another health-care professional who is experienced in treating people who are under stress. Ask him or her to tell you about possible consequences of stress build-up–both psychological and physical. Share your findings in class, and prepare a list of all the physical manifestations of stress.

5. Has there been a time in your life when you went through a difficult period involving a lot of change? The changes might have been the result of moving to a different community, the ending or beginning of a romantic relationship, attempting to lose weight or quit smoking, attending a new school, having a new housemate, experiencing the death of someone you cared about, going through losing one job and having to find another, or having a serious illness or injury.

    a. Describe the situation. What happened and how did it make you feel?

    b. What did you do to help yourself cope and adjust to the changes? How well did your coping and adjusting techniques work?

6. Can regular exercise, control of your diet, and other wellness activities help you to manage stress in your life? Analyze your situation. What are you doing about exercise and physical recreation? What are you doing and what *should* you be doing to improve and maintain good health? Prepare a plan and schedule.

Case Problems

1. Overworked
Lisa has been in the position of assistant manager for a fast-food operation for two months. She supervises 15 full-time employees and 10 part-time workers. She does all the food and beverage ordering, takes care of promotional items and advertising, and opens and closes the

restaurant every day. The cleaning crew is often late or does not show up at all, and Lisa ends up cleaning the floor, the equipment, and the restrooms. Lisa finds herself snapping at dependable employees and faithful customers. She often feels tense and has an upset stomach and annoying headaches. Lisa sees her family physician and is told that perhaps she is working too hard and too many hours. Lisa does not see any alternatives. She continues to work as she has in the past.

a. What could possibly be the end result of Lisa's situation?

b. Why do some people work themselves into situations similar to this?

c. Would you recommend that Lisa give up the position? If not, what would you recommend that she do about her workload?

d. What additional information would you like to know about Lisa?

2. Downward Spiral

About two months ago, Julia's parents told her they were getting divorced. They have been very open and honest about their problems but agree their lives would be better in the long run if they divorce now after 30 years. Julia says she understands and will support her parents' decision. However, Julia's work no longer gives her satisfaction or a feeling of self-worth. Her hobbies, recreational activities, and social life mean little anymore. Coworkers annoy her, noise in the office bothers her, and no one can please her. She finds herself lashing out at coworkers, ignoring friends, brooding in frustration, and feeling depressed most of the time. She prefers being alone and doing nothing. Julia is beginning to see her friends pull away. She has picked up clues that her coworkers and supervisor are not supporting her for a promotion for which she is qualified. Finally, Julia begins to take a serious look at what is happening to her life.

a. What are some of the emotional pressures that could be causing stress for Julia?

b. What specific stress signals are apparent in Julia's situation?

c. If Julia decides to "turn her life around," what are some changes that she should make to eliminate or manage her stress?

Unit 5

Developing Your Social Conscience

The three chapters of this unit concentrate on helping you develop beliefs and values that you need to be a good citizen in your community and in your workplace. The content of this unit represents the values and beliefs that your employers and the citizens of your community expect you to have. You are expected to conduct yourself with integrity according to the values and ethics that prevail in the world of work and in our society.

The focus of Chapter 15 is on your basic beliefs and standards with respect to being honest, trustworthy, loyal to your employer, and free from the effects of substance abuse.

In the modern workplace, the potential for misunderstanding, conflict, and unfair treatment is greater than ever. Chapters 16 and 17 are concerned with preparing you to adjust and get along and also to be a positive influence in your place of employment.

The beliefs and values addressed in this unit—your personal ethics and standards of conduct, what you believe, and how you behave with respect to discrimination and diversity in your work environment—make up your social conscience. You are encouraged to develop positive values and beliefs and to let them guide your behavior as a worker and as a citizen.

Contents

Chapter 15
Standards Of Conduct

Chapter 16
Recognizing Discrimination

Chapter 17
Diversity

Standards Of Conduct

N ancy and Marshall, supervisors in a soft drink distribution center, were sharing a table in the lunchroom. Nancy looked around for a moment and said, "Where's Yvonne? Doesn't she work here anymore?" "Well, I doubt that she ever actually worked for *this* company," Marshall said. "She's gone now, and the manager told me it's because she was working for *Yvonne*." "I think I know what you mean," Nancy said. "I hear they were very upset when they found out that she gave a copy of our mailing list to her friend in Houston. And I know she was doing homework for her accounting class during her afternoon break— a very *long* break." "Really?" Marshall responded. "I didn't know about that, but I did see her here when I came in to do some catch-up work Saturday morning. She was working at the office manager's computer, and I saw the printer turning out copies of her yard sale advertising. I wouldn't trust Yvonne to work for *me*!"

Integrity And Ethics

Integrity, as defined by *Webster*, is adherence to a code of moral values. It means that you do not compromise under pressure to do something that you do not believe is right. A person's integrity is a reflection of his or her **ethics**. An ethical person recognizes a moral duty and obligation to conform to accepted professional standards of conduct—the rules of right and wrong.

Objectives

After completing this chapter, you should be able to:

1.
Explain the value and importance of maintaining standards of conduct that are appreciated and accepted in the workplace.

2.
Explain the meaning of personal integrity and ethical behavior.

3.
Discuss the importance of loyalty to your employer.

4.
Explain the meaning of petty theft and identify a variety of typical examples.

5.
Describe various forms of expense account abuse.

6.
Describe various forms of abuse of fringe benefits and privileges.

7.
Explain the importance of avoiding drug and alcohol abuse.

SCANS
Focus

A competent worker...

■ chooses an ethical course of action

■ establishes credibility through competence and integrity

■ can be trusted

■ recognizes when faced with making a decision or doing something that may break with commonly held personal or societal values; understands the impact of violating these beliefs and codes on the organization, on his or her self-esteem, and on others

66 Many people who spend an hour a day in physical exercise to keep fit refuse to spend an hour a week in the cultivation of their morals and their ethics. 99
—Allen E. Claxton, D.D.

It is possible to behave ethically, not because it feels right, but because you know that unethical behavior may have undesirable consequences. The issue of personal integrity comes into focus when you let what feels right guide your behavior. When you do something that does *not* feel right, you have violated your integrity.

Understand Employer Expectations

The values and ethics that set standards for your conduct should be consistent with the expectations of society and the expectations of your employer. When you accept a job and an employer accepts you as a worker, a contract is made. You agree to work. The employer agrees to pay you for your work. But there is more to the contract. You expect to be allowed to learn and progress on the job. You expect good supervision and training. You expect the employer to be honest with you—and fair. You expect a reasonably safe, pleasant place to work. You expect to have occasional rest periods, time for lunch, extra pay for overtime work, and other fringe benefits.

The paragraph above outlines a very substantial list of expectations. But you are not entitled to any of them without meeting an equally substantial list of employer expectations. Many of those expectations are highlighted throughout this book—a positive attitude, productive work habits, initiative and motivation, knowledge and skills, and many more.

Keep Your Standards High

If you have several years of work experience, you realize that some people will have an "anything goes" standard of conduct while others will be strict in their views of what should and should not be done. It is up to you to set moral and ethical standards for yourself. Therefore, you should judge carefully as you develop "rules and regulations" for your personal behavior. Your morality—your integrity—will be defined by how well you conform to the standards of what you personally believe to be right.

You also must recognize that your standards may not match those of your employers and coworkers. What they believe to be right will also be an important consideration as you make the day-to-day decisions regarding your conduct. Obviously if you violate the standards and expectations of your employers and coworkers, you face the possibility of negative consequences. Keep your own standards high, and maintain your integrity by using those standards as guidelines for your behavior.

Loyalty

Among the most important employer expectations is loyalty. Many employers complain that the young people of today do not understand the importance of loyalty in the workplace. In fact, some employers actually prefer to hire and promote older workers who have demonstrated their loyalty. Of course, age and physical maturity do not automatically mean that the worker will be more mature in job performance and attitudes. But as a young worker, you will have to prove yourself with respect to loyalty. Most employers are very intolerant of what they consider to be disloyal behavior.

rturo, a server-trainee in a restaurant, noticed that some of the waiters and waitresses were receiving consistently larger tips than he was. Finally, he discovered the reason for it. Sandy, the person assigned to help train Arturo, explained it this way. "What it amounts to is giving free drinks and salads," she said. "You refill soft drink glasses but forget to add the extra drinks to the check. You serve salads that weren't ordered and tell the customers that they're on the house. Sometimes you just sort of forget to put drinks or salads on the check. Most often what the customers should have paid for the salads and drinks shows up in your tip."

Arturo finds himself in a **dilemma**—a situation where one way or the other he was bound to create a problem for himself.

When accepting a job, you agree to be loyal and dedicated.

Critical
Thinking

Think about...

what Arturo should do.
Should he report this
practice to his supervi-
sor, or should he go
along with the scheme?

To help you understand what loyalty means to an employer, try to put yourself in his or her position. Ask yourself, "How would I feel about this situation if I were the owner or manager of this business?" How would you feel if you were Arturo's employer? What would you deserve and expect in that situation? As Arturo's employer you would probably expect him to tell you what is going on, respecting his obligation of loyalty.

As it turned out, Arturo chose loyalty to the employer over loyalty to his coworkers. When Arturo left his job to return to college, the manager expressed appreciation for his loyalty. Also, Arturo was promised a job in the future and a good recommendation to any other prospective employer.

Honesty

66 There are few, if any, jobs in which ability alone is sufficient. Needed, also, are loyalty, sincerity, enthusiasm and team play. 99
—William B. Given, Jr.

When a supervisor writes a letter of recommendation saying "Lou is an honest person," the message is that Lou can be trusted. A person's honesty is often tested under extreme stress. But the person with integrity and high standards of conduct will be able to resist great pressure and remain honest. Your challenge is to set standards of honesty for yourself that will cause your employers to admire and respect you.

Rather than present a list of rules for honesty in employment, you will study some situations that might challenge your own honesty. As the possible alternatives to the situation are discussed, you will begin to understand what typical employers might expect of employees with reputations for being honest. Then you should be able to measure your own personal standards against those of your future employers. Hopefully, you will want to set high standards of honesty for yourself. In the long run, your honesty will be rewarded.

P at and Jan were sharing a hero sandwich at the deli where they often met for lunch. "I'm amazed at what some people get away with today in business," said Jan. "If you want to, you can get away with anything." "It's the same at our bank. But you could find yourself unemployed—maybe in jail," Pat responded. "I'm not talking about crime, " Jan said. "I mean things like writing letters on company time, using the postage meter for personal mail, taking extra time at the water cooler, showing favoritism to customers who bribe you with gifts, not reporting cash transactions to avoid income tax. I could go on and on—and they get away with it!" There was a pause. Then Pat said, "Do they really?"

Avoid Petty Theft

When you take something from someone else fully intending not to return it to its owner, you are guilty of **larceny**. Larceny is theft and a larcenist is a thief. But any judge will tell you that many convicted larcenists do not think of themselves as thieves. For example, you may know someone who has taken merchandise from a store without paying for it. Do you think of these people who are guilty of shoplifting as criminals? You should since shoplifting is a criminal offense.

There are many kinds of larceny in the workplace. **Grand larceny** is the legal term for stealing something of great value. **Petty larceny** describes the theft of something of a lesser value or importance. The legal penalties are greater for grand larceny, but petty larceny is probably a greater problem for employers. Shoplifting by the employees in a retail business is only one form of the problem, however. Employee theft of supplies, equipment, and materials is another form of petty theft that causes employers great concern.

Knowing what is acceptable behavior and what is not, as your employer sees it, is not always easy. Following are some examples of behavior that some employers may allow. Others may consider such behavior to be dishonest.

It doesn't matter who does it, stealing is stealing.

Test yourself. . .

Study the following examples. In the space beside each item, indicate your judgment as follows:

Honest and ethical = 2   Dishonest but ethically okay = 1

Honest but unethical = 1   Dishonest and unethical = 0

____ Taking small quantities of inexpensive office supplies, such as pencils, file folders, and transparent tape.

____ Writing personal letters on company stationery, using company postage, and using company long-distance telephone lines for personal calls.

____ Taking a small amount of supplies or materials that the company produces or uses in large quantities.

____ Taking things that the employer has no use for and wants to dispose of, such as day-old bakery goods, used packing boxes, surplus or waste building materials, defective or damaged merchandise, scrap paper, and free samples of merchandise or supplies.

SCORING: If your score is above 5, your standards are probably lower than your employer's. A score of 3 or less suggests that your standards of honesty are high.

What you must do to protect your reputation for honesty is find out what your employer's expectations are and be sure your standards of conduct conform to those expectations. You can learn about what is expected by simply asking, "Terry, do you mind if I take a truckload of sand to fill the sandbox I made for my cousin?" Or you might be less direct: "Dan, may I use the company long-distance line to call my parents in Minneapolis, or should I have the call billed to my home phone?"

You may also learn what is acceptable and what is not by observing and talking with your coworkers. But be careful. You may find yourself along with others violating your employer's rules.

Avoid Expense Account Abuses

Many business occupations involve travel, meals, and lodging at company expense. Selling "on the road," traveling to deliver merchandise or to service customers' equipment, and participating in business conferences are examples of business-related travel. Some companies have liberal expense accounting policies. They trust the employee to keep personal records and simply report what was spent. Other employers enforce elaborate rules and regulations. These detailed rules and recordkeeping procedures are designed to protect the employer from employees who might use the expense accounting system to obtain extra income. Here are some examples of questionable uses of expense accounts.

Test yourself...

Study the following examples. In the space beside each item, indicate your judgment as follows:

> Honest and ethical = 2
>
> Honest but unethical = 1
>
> Dishonest and unethical = 0

_____ Reporting more expensive meals than actually eaten.

_____ Asking reimbursement for meals not paid for (such as those received on an airplane).

_____ Including liquor (reported as food) on expense accounts.

_____ Reporting greater automobile mileage than actually driven.

_____ Riding the bus but reporting taxi fares.

_____ Asking for full reimbursement when two people share a ride.

_____ Staying in exclusive hotels, traveling first-class, or eating at the most expensive restaurants.

_____ Asking reimbursement for expenses for vacation time (taking an extra day for recreation at the end of a business trip).

_____ Including personal long-distance telephone calls on a hotel bill.

SCORING: If your score is above 5, your standards are probably lower than your employer's. A score lower than 5 suggests high honesty.

Some of these practices are clearly dishonest and unacceptable. Some appear to be questionable. Others may seem, to most people, to be perfectly acceptable. Your challenge, as always, is to learn what your employer expects of you in a given situation. Then you must avoid abuses that can damage your reputation for honesty.

Use expense accounts in a way that strengthens your reputation for honesty.

©Blair Seitz/Photo Researchers

As an inexperienced worker, you will need to make a special effort to learn your company's rules and policies. Be aware that you may encounter individuals who set a bad example—"bending the rules" or cheating whenever and however they can. Most of the time, however, you will find individuals who live by high ethical standards. For instance, they stay with friends or relatives and pass the savings in hotel bills along to the employer. Or they take advantage of the lowest possible air fare and travel at an inconvenient time to get a lower-priced ticket. They eat inexpensive meals, carry bag lunches, and find ways to conserve on food expenses. In one case a sales representative was found to be reporting unusually low travel expenses. When the expense account auditor investigated, it was found that the representative owned a small car that used very little gasoline. The representative made sure the reimbursement covered only actual expenses, which were considerably less than other representatives driving larger cars or those reporting "inflated" mileage.

You should realize that in the long run, both you and your employer will benefit when you economize and help your employer make a profit. Just as there are people who use the expense account to steal from their employers, there are people who use it to conserve and reduce expenses for their employers. You will probably find most of your coworkers' actions to be somewhere between the extremes. The majority of people are honest in reporting their actual expenses. The chance of losing is greater than gaining; it could mean your job.

Consider this: When employees' personal standards of honesty are high, a relaxed, trusting relationship grows. Employers seldom question or even review the expense accounts reported by trusted employees. When necessary the employees can report unusually high expenses without hesitation. Working in such an atmosphere is a pleasure. But it is far from pleasant working in an atmosphere of insecurity and mistrust that results when employers see expense accounting as a potential tool for petty larceny.

Avoid Abusing Fringe Benefits And Privileges

Critical
Thinking

Think about...

how you would react to Adrian's habit if you were the owner of the restaurant.

Adrian works at a restaurant. He gets an hourly wage plus tips. He also gets free meals for himself and a 50 percent discount on food for anyone else in his family. Adrian decides to have a party. He uses his food discount privilege to buy $40 worth of fried chicken for $20. Also, he is in the habit of ordering the most expensive steak sandwich at closing time and taking most of it home supposedly for his dog. Sometimes he just leaves it on his plate.

Almost any job you can think of has certain fringe benefits and privileges. And almost every one offers some opportunity for exploitation—or dishonesty. Consider the following situations:

- Many retail stores offer employee discounts on merchandise.

- Employees of a small meat-packing plant are allowed to buy tenderloin at one-third of the market price.

- Employees of a large automotive service station are allowed to take any parts that may be discarded when repairs are made.

- Many automobile and motorcycle dealers allow their employees to drive used vehicles that are in stock.

- A television dealer allows service department employees to work on their own sets during evenings and weekends, with parts provided at the dealer's cost.

These are only a few examples. You probably can think of many more. Also, you can probably imagine many different ways to take advantage of such situations to an employer's disadvantage. This is where your good judgment, your sense of fair play, and your basic honesty will guide you.

Test yourself. . .

Study the following examples. In the space beside each item, indicate your judgment as follows:

Honest and ethical = 2

Honest but unethical = 1

Dishonest and unethical = 0

_____ Gordon collects tickets at a movie theater. Pablo, Sue, and Mary Ann go to a movie. Gordon accepts two tickets for three people. After the show Gordon joins Mary Ann to make it a double date.

_____ The purchasing manager has responsibility for obtaining supplies for the hospital. The surgical supplies salesperson wants to sell bandages to the hospital. On Saturday the purchasing manager and the surgical supplies salesperson play two rounds of golf (paid for by the salesperson, who put the charge on his expense account). On Monday the hospital places an order with the surgical supplies salesperson.

_____ The receptionist schedules appointments with the executive. (Appointments with the executive are valuable.) The client (a seafood wholesaler) is willing to pay the receptionist for scheduling appointments for her ahead of other clients. At Christmas time the client gives the receptionist 15 pounds of frozen lobster as a present. (Actually both individuals understand that the lobster is given in return for favoritism in scheduling appointments with the executive. There is no written or spoken contract, but a deal is made.)

_____ The store display specialist has construction skills and materials available to her. (Also, she loves lobster.) The receptionist wants a planter for her office. (She has 15 pounds of frozen lobster from the client.) The display specialist builds a planter for the receptionist's office using company time and materials. She gets 15 pounds of frozen lobster—as a gift.

SCORING: If your score is above 4, your standards are probably lower than your employer's. A score lower than 2 suggests high integrity.

Avoid Drug And Alcohol Abuse

You may be the type of individual who never drinks alcohol or abuses drugs. If so, these standards of conduct will probably be an asset as you seek employment and advancement in the world of work. As with the other personality traits discussed in this chapter, employers have a variety of expectations. Basically, you will find employers having one of the following three points of view:

1. At one extreme is the employer who cares only about one thing—production. In this situation no one will be overly concerned about what you do when you are not on the job. Your private life is your own business as far as your employer is concerned. Whatever you do privately, your employer will only be concerned with how well you do the job you were hired to do. You will be expected to keep your personal life and affairs in control so they have no effect on your work.

2. At the opposite extreme are employers who assume that anyone associated with the company must live by certain moral and personal behavior standards. People employed by a church, local government, or a school or community organization have a public image to protect. Taken to the extreme, employers have been known to fire a person for having been seen near or in an establishment deemed inappropriate.

3. Between the two extremes described above are the employers who expect that personal problems, drugs, and alcohol abuse will not influence job performance. But in addition, they may want to maintain a favorable company image. For example, a bank, a retail store, or a real estate agency might feel that their business would be hurt if customers think the company's salespeople are not of the highest moral character. This point of view is especially common in small communities where company employees are recognized by everyone and where stories of improper behavior get around quickly.

Many employers evaluate and hire employees on the basis of their moral character and reputation.

The employment community recognizes that drug and alcohol abuse threaten the work environment in numerous ways. These abuses can affect the safety standards, productivity, loyalty, and morale. In addition, there are legal issues that address the rights of individuals. As a result some companies and organizations have instituted initial drug testing in their hiring process and subsequent testing throughout the term of employment.

Some of these employers may actually try to help their workers with company-sponsored programs. These programs may provide services such as counselors and doctors who can help with substance abuse and family problems. Most communities also offer programs through their social services, including the sponsorship of a variety of support groups.

Summary

An ethical person who has integrity will sense a moral obligation to conform to accepted standards of conduct. The issue of personal integrity comes into focus when you let what *feels right* guide your behavior. If you violate the standards and expectations of employers and coworkers, you face the possibility of negative consequences.

Among the most important of the typical employer's expectations are loyalty and honesty. Petty theft—larceny—is both illegal and unethical, and you should avoid it. Expense account abuses should also be avoided.

There are many fringe benefits and privileges that challenge a person's integrity and have implications for his or her moral standards. Also, employers expect your standards of conduct to include avoiding drug and alcohol abuse.

You may find it difficult at times to maintain higher standards of conduct. But to the extent that you are successful in doing so, your chances for success and personal satisfaction will be increased. Remember that the higher your standards, the more options you have. Prospective employers will be more interested in hiring you. You will be welcome in a greater variety of employment situations. Your chances for success and personal satisfaction will be increased in the long run, and you will take pride in yourself. You will be the winner.

End of Chapter Activities

Questions and Projects

1. How might you, as a beginning worker, learn the unwritten code of behavior that prevails in your workplace?

2. You have heard it said that "Honesty is the best policy." Yet some successful business owners and managers are accused of dishonesty—in advertising, selling methods, failing to stand behind what they sell, and so on. Is honesty always the best policy in business today? In your opinion, why or why not?

3. Interview several employers to determine their policies for controlling or eliminating problems with employees whose standards of conduct do not meet their expectations. If possible, work with other students. In the interviews you might ask the following questions. Also, prepare a report summarizing the answers.

    a. To what extent is employee theft a problem in your business?

    b. What action do you take when you discover a case of employee theft?

    c. How effective is the action in preventing future theft?

    d. What problems do you have with employees abusing special privileges or benefits?

    e. What actions do you take to prevent or control the abuses?

    f. What are some examples of employee misconduct with respect to ethical or moral behavior in your business?

4. Assume you have discovered that some of the employees in the supermarket where you work are stealing empty soft drink containers and selling them to youngsters in the neighborhood at half their value. You see some of these children returning the same bottles for cash at the check-stand of your store.

    a. What are your responsibilities to your employer? to your coworkers?

    b. What should the store manager do upon discovering the details of this situation?

Case Problems

1. To Draw or Not to Draw

Tim is working part-time in the drafting department of a small manufacturing firm. Since he has access to graphic supplies, materials, and equipment, he decides to use his coffee breaks and lunch periods to design and produce detailed sketches of a family room remodeling project for his home.

a. Should Tim ask permission, or should he feel free to go ahead with the project since he intends to do it on his own time?

b. How do you think his supervisor should respond if Tim asks permission?

c. What reasons might be given to justify refusing Tim's request?

2. The Encounter

Hal worked the night shift as an admitting clerk in a hospital. About 3 a.m. he heard a noise in the pharmacy. He opened the door and saw Mrs. Swann, the hospital administrator, with a beaker of clear liquid in her hand. Mrs. Swann said nothing when she saw Hal. She simply set the beaker on the counter, then walked past Hal and out the door. Hal checked the beaker and found it to contain alcohol. Thinking it was none of his business and fearing that he might be fired if he said anything, Hal said nothing to anyone about the incident. Two months later Mrs. Swann was replaced as administrator with no explanation. But everyone on the hospital staff figured out the reason when Hal admitted Mrs. Swann to the hospital later as an emergency case with alcohol poisoning.

a. Did Hal make the right choice in keeping quiet about the incident? If not, what should Hal have done?

b. If Mrs. Swann had caught Hal in the pharmacy with a beaker of alcohol, would she have overlooked the incident? If not, should she have overlooked it?

3. No Personal Calls

Ruth McDonald is busy with her work when she receives a personal telephone call from her friend, Harry, who wants to find out about a weekend trip that is being planned. Harry is working at his first job. Ruth knows Harry does not realize that the office is no place for personal calls. Ruth does not want to hurt Harry's feelings, so she tries to be tactful. Finally, she says, "Harry, I must go now. Mrs. Maxwell is buzzing me. See you Friday."

a. Do you think Harry was made aware that he should not call Ruth during office hours?

b. Should Ruth have been more honest with Harry so he would understand how to behave in the future?

c. Can you think of a tactful way that Ruth could have informed Harry of the general rule regarding personal telephone calls during business hours?

4. Business within a Business

Bertha works as an assembler in a sash and door factory. Scrap wood accumulates as the window and door frames are produced, and the owner of the business allows the employees to take the discarded wood for use in their fireplaces at home. Bertha's neighbor, Mr. Larson, offers to pay Bertha for fireplace wood and makes it clear that he will not mention the fact that he is paying Bertha for the wood. Bertha reasons that this is okay. She thinks, "The boss doesn't need to know. Anyway, I'm underpaid on this job, and I can use the extra cash."

a. Do you agree with Bertha's reasoning? Explain your answer.

b. Under what circumstances, if any, would you expect Bertha's employer to approve of this arrangement?

Recognizing Discrimination

A rlene has been working as a designer for a clothing manufacturer. Her record as an employee is excellent, but she has a tendency to worry about her job. During dinner with a friend, Arlene said, "I think I'm in for real trouble." "What's the problem?" her friend asked. Arlene replied, "They've added another designer in my division— a young Korean woman. The boss probably wanted someone who will work 24 hours a day and all weekend. You know how those foreigners are. She'll probably work for next to nothing," Her friend responded, "I don't know why you're so concerned. You're very talented and constantly complimented on your work." Arlene said, "And her accent is ridiculous. You'd think that if she were going to live here, she could learn to speak the language. I don't know why they couldn't have hired one of the hundreds of local designers who are dying to get into the business."

Prejudice And Stereotyping

Everyone has an inner sense of fairness, and when it is violated, they feel uncomfortable or angry. **Discrimination**, according to the dictionary, simply means to recognize differences. However, it has taken on a negative meaning as a word used to describe unfair treatment of a particular person or group due to race, gender, religious affiliation, or physical disability. The treatment is unfair because it is not based on what is *real*, but on stereotypes and prejudice.

Objectives

After completing this chapter, you should be able to:

1.
Explain the meaning of discrimination, prejudice, and stereotyping.

2.
Explain a person's rights in employment as a result of the Civil Rights Act and the Americans with Disabilities Act.

3.
Recognize and deal appropriately with sexual harassment in the workplace.

4.
Recognize and avoid subtle discrimination, prejudice, and stereotyping.

5.
Avoid being subjected to discrimination, prejudice, and stereotyping in the workplace.

6.
Demonstrate tolerance and understanding for others who might be subjected to discrimination, prejudice, and stereotyping in the workplace.

Prejudice means prejudging someone based on the fact that she or he is a member of a particular group.

Discrimination is a behavior which is often based on an attitude. If you, as an individual, think that a particular race of people tend to be lazy, you display a discriminatory attitude. If you were an employer and refused to hire people of that race, you would be guilty of discrimination.

Prejudice

A term that is often used in connection with discrimination and whose meaning can be the underlying cause of discrimination is **prejudice**. It means to prejudge or form an opinion without taking the time or effort to judge in a fair manner. Prejudice leads to treating a person unfairly. If you have decided that people belonging to a particular minority race are inferior, you will likely prejudge all people you meet belonging to that race. If you meet William, a member of that minority group, you will prejudge him based solely on being a member of that minority. You will be guilty of discrimination against William based on your prejudice toward his race.

Stereotyping

Whenever you judge others based on beliefs about a group as a whole rather than as unique individuals, you are guilty of **stereotyping**. If you stereotype an individual, you assign to that person a set of characteristics that may be unfair and undeserved.

Stereotyping can also work in reverse. You may give people an unfair advantage by assigning them very positive traits because of stereotyping. For example, you may choose Edna as a friend because she wears famous-label clothes, looks like a fashion model, and lives with her parents in a luxurious home. If you take a look at Edna as an individual, you may find a discrepancy between Edna's real personality and the image you have because of the stereotype. Stereotyping is not only unfair, it is likely to be inaccurate.

People should be judged on their abilities in the workplace.

Photo by Richard Younker

Avoid Prejudice and Stereotyping

Discrimination, prejudice, and stereotyping can become so much a part of your life that you hardly notice them. All too often prejudices feel comfortable. You do not think about them. You may even endure the discomforts of prejudice in order to keep a job. Today, however, there is an effort to make people conscious of their prejudices and the damage that can be done by those feelings.

When prejudice becomes a part of your personality as a worker or when you learn to accept unfair treatment based on prejudice, a type of decay sets in. Work becomes less satisfying. Conflict becomes a part of each day of work. Often your productivity will decrease. In order to be a better worker, you should remove these barriers to productivity and job satisfaction. You need to learn to recognize and not accept discrimination in the workplace. You must be sensitive to what is going on around you and recognize your personal prejudices in order to change them. Prejudice and stereotyping can be very difficult to overcome.

The first step in dealing with unfair discrimination in employment situations is to become aware of it. As you become aware of and sensitive to discrimination, opportunities to take positive action will

> ❝ To keep the Golden Rule we must put ourselves in other people's places. If we had the imagination to do that...fewer bitter judgments would pass our lips, fewer racial, national and class prejudices would stain our lives. ❞
>
> —Harry Emerson Fosdick, D.D.

appear. Here are some suggestions about how to take advantage of those opportunities:

- Speak up and challenge those who make negative comments based on prejudice or stereotypes. Usually this can be done tactfully. For example, "I understand your point of view on this issue, but it really isn't fair to judge an individual because she is Native American."

- Express your disapproval or walk away when someone tells a joke or story that makes fun of someone on the basis of prejudice or negative stereotypes. For example, "I know you don't intend to be unkind, but if I were Polish, I'd be offended by jokes that make Polish people look stupid."

- Bring up the subject of discrimination. When you see the opportunity in casual conversation at work, share what you are discovering and learning about prejudice and stereotyping. You may influence others to be more aware of and sensitive to these problems. For example, "Isn't it great that more women are being promoted to management positions in the banking industry? Now I realize what Ellen was trying to say when she complained about having to train the young man who was to become her supervisor."

- Avoid using a person's minority group label to identify him or her. For example, say "Deliver the package to the receptionist" instead of "Deliver the package to the Oriental woman at the front desk."

- Learn and use the preferred terms for identifying minority group members. For example, use "persons with disabilities" instead of "handicapped" and "Native American" instead of "Indian." Be very careful not to use unacceptable nicknames for nationalities and ethnic groups.

- Resist and expose prejudice when you discover it. In almost every working group, you will find someone who presents an image of being tolerant and fair-minded when actually he or she is motivated by intolerance and prejudice. It may be difficult or impossible to change the attitudes of such a person, but you can refuse to support or agree with acts of discrimination. Also, you may be able to express your disapproval and call attention to the discrimination in an effort to stop it.

What The Law Provides

The Civil Rights Act became law in 1964. The strongest federal legislation in the area of job discrimination ever passed was the 1972 amendment to that legislation. It was called Title VII.

Equal Employment Opportunity

According to **Title VII of the Civil Rights Act of 1964,** employers are not allowed to discriminate in any area of employment. Employers cannot discriminate in recruiting, hiring, promoting, discharging, classifying, or training employees. The agency responsible for enforcement of Title VII is the Equal Employment Opportunity Commission (**EEOC**). The EEOC receives and evaluates complaints either by trying to work out the problem or referring the complaint to the courts. This agency also develops guidelines to help organizations write and put into practice legal hiring programs.

The EEOC is supported and used by state and local government entities. For example, cities and counties may have Community Action Boards, Human Relations Commissions, Human Rights Officers, and Citizen's Review Boards concerned with discrimination by employers and government agencies.

Affirmative Action

Affirmative action is a hiring policy many private and public employers use to correct the effect of past discrimination against minorities and women. Under affirmative action plans, employers list the discriminatory barriers in their organization that are limiting to minority applicants and current employees. Then plans are set up to eliminate those barriers. In the past some employers were legally required to develop and follow affirmative action plans. Now affirmative action is encouraged on a voluntary basis.

As employers changed their policies for recruiting, selecting, and hiring, a problem with **reverse discrimination** emerged. The most common objective of affirmative action is to create a work force with fair representation of women and minorities. The obvious strategy for achieving this goal is to give preference in hiring and promoting to workers who would have been subjected to discrimination in the past. When this preference is used, it can result in reverse discrimination toward those who would have been given preference in the past. While it may seem to be fair and reasonable as a solution to problems created by past discrimination, reverse discrimination is still discrimination and is unfair.

Critical
Thinking

Think about...

situations in which reverse discrimination might be a good thing. Do you know about or can you imagine an example of reverse discrimination where everyone concerned received fair treatment?

Race, Color, and National Origin

In the process of recruiting, selecting, and hiring workers, employers are prohibited by law from asking certain questions concerning race, color, or national origin. The law makes it very clear that your race, color, or ethnic background should not be determining factors in whether or not you will be hired. Any employer may ask whether the applicant is a citizen of the United States. Questions regarding an individual's ability to speak or read a foreign language are also permitted. However, questions regarding ancestry or native language are not allowed. Asking "What language did you speak at home as a child?" is illegal.

Religion

eon applied for a job as a retail clerk with a local department store. Based on the area of town where he lived, the personnel officer, Gladys, asked if Leon was a Seventh-Day Adventist. Gladys gave him no further consideration because the store was open on Saturday. Gladys knew that Adventists observed Saturday as their day of worship.

The religious discrimination described above is not fair and obviously not legal. Over the past few decades, much of the discrimination against certain religions has diminished although it has not completely disappeared.

As a job applicant, you should be advised concerning normal hours or days of work required by the employer. An employer may ask if you are willing to work the required schedule. An employer may not, however, quiz you about your religious denomination, religious practices, religious affiliations, or religious holidays.

Gender and Family Status

The language of Title VII indicates that you cannot be discriminated against because of your gender. This type of discrimination has been and continues to be a major issue in our society. As the traditional role of women has changed, more and more women are entering the work force. Men, too, have taken a look at the roles assigned to them and are discovering that they have additional options. These redefined roles have caused some concern on the part of employers.

Employers are concerned about the following:

- How much time will family obligations take?

- How often will the employee be absent for family commitments?

- How much time will be required away from the workplace if a new baby becomes a part of the family?

- Who is responsible for child care in the home?

Even with these concerns, the law does not allow asking questions about family status. An employer may not ask your marital status; and you do not need to provide information about whether you are single, engaged, married, divorced, or separated. Employers may not ask questions about a spouse's income or questions regarding the number and ages of children or plans for pregnancy. As an applicant you may be asked if it will be possible to meet specific work schedules or if there are any activities, commitments, or responsibilities that may hinder you from doing your job.

Other questions that may allow the employer to learn about your family status (without asking directly) can relate to expected duration on the job or anticipated absences. These questions may only be asked if they are asked of all applicants and weighed equally in evaluations for both sexes.

Age

Discrimination because of a person's age is referred to as **ageism**. Younger workers are often hired because they are less expensive and are stereotyped as more flexible and willing to learn. Younger workers can also be placed at a disadvantage because they have little experience. Older workers may be hired because of their experience, knowledge, and maturity. However, they may be discriminated against because their understanding of methods and technology is considered dated. By law it is illegal to discriminate against hiring a person based solely on age. While employers may require a work permit (issued by school authorities) providing proof of age for younger workers, an employer may not require a birth certificate as proof of age before hiring.

Character

Traditionally there has been discrimination and prejudice in the workplace against those whose character does not meet with the general standards of society. Criminals, members of subversive organizations, those who are poor credit risks, and others who are considered to be "undesirable" are often not hired to work even though they have the abilities to perform in a given occupation. In many cases, however, the law requires that such individuals should have equal opportunity in employment with people of "acceptable" character.

An important regulation helps prevent discrimination against people who may have been arrested for, but not convicted of, a crime. It prohibits inquiry as to whether a job applicant has ever been arrested. Questions concerning an applicant's conviction (and if so, when, where, and the disposition of the case) are allowed. No questions may be raised regarding your credit rating, charge accounts, or other financial matters. You may be asked about the type of education and experience you obtained in military service as it relates to a particular job, but you may not be asked about what type of discharge you received from the service.

The Rights Of Persons With Disabilities

There are approximately 50 million persons with disabilities in the United States. There has never been a time when these people have been free from discrimination in the workplace. However, in July of 1990, the **Americans with Disabilities Act** (ADA) was passed to make such discrimination and prejudice unlawful. Title I of the act deals with employment.

The ADA prohibits discrimination in hiring by not allowing the employer to specifically ask if the job applicant is disabled. The person *may* be asked if he or she is able to perform the essential tasks and functions of the job. However, that is a fair question and should be asked of everyone. The employer is not required to hire a person who is not competent to do the job.

Another important provision of the ADA is that employers are not allowed to give special treatment or make special requirements of disabled persons. For example, a physical examination may not be required unless all job applicants are required to have one.

After the disabled person is hired, the employer must *make reasonable accommodations* so that the employee will be able to stay on the job and perform effectively. Some examples are these:

- The job may have to be restructured, or reassignments may have to be made.

- Special equipment may have to be acquired, or modifications may have to be made to existing equipment or devices.

- The entire workplace and its facilities must be accessible. For example, if the door to the lunchroom is too narrow to accommodate a wheelchair, it may have to be widened.

It is possible for the employer to avoid making some of the accommodations if it can be shown that being expected to make them is unreasonable. The employer must show that the accommodations would entail "undue hardship, difficulty, or expense."

©Renee Lynn/Photo Researchers

With the passage of ADA, disabled people conquered one more hurdle in their struggle against discrmination.

©Paul Fortin/Stock, Boston

Sexual Harassment

Thus far some of your legal rights in employment have been discussed. This section is concerned with another type of legal right—the right to be free from **sexual harassment.** Sexual harassment is coerced, unethical, and unwanted intimacy. It is not only an issue of sex; it is also an issue of power. Sexual harassment can occur at any level of an organization. Supervisors may be harassed by subordinates as well as vice versa. Men may harass women, and women may harass men.

The Supreme Court has ruled that remarks, gestures, and even graffiti can be considered forms of sexual harassment. Rude sounds, whistling suggestively, jokes about sex, derogatory rumors, notes or signs posted in a person's work space, brushing up against bodies, and unwelcome touching are forms of sexual harassment.

Sometimes the perpetrator is not aware that his or her behavior is considered harassment. What may be intended as friendly teasing can come across to the victim as bullying. Flirting may come across as sexual harassment. The key to recognizing the difference is how the victim *feels* about it. Most acts of sexual harassment are power plays that are degrading in nature. Nobody has the right to harass another person.

The consequences of sexual harassment can lead to a good deal of personal sacrifice. A victim may feel obligated to quit a job due to the harassment or may expect to be fired from the job for resistance. If you feel that you are the victim of sexual harassment, you *should* resist. First, and most importantly, you should confront the person who is harassing you. Tell him or her how you feel about what is happening and make it very clear that you want the unwanted behavior to stop.

Next, if the harassment continues, explain the situation to your supervisor. If the perpetrator *is* your supervisor, then go to his or her supervisor. If that fails to resolve the problem, you have several options for taking legal action.

The equal opportunity laws and civil rights agencies can provide help for those who feel they are being sexually harassed. Some forms of harassment (such as physical assault) are crimes. Do not hesitate, in that case, to go to your local police department. If the form of harassment you encounter is not specifically a crime, there are other remedies. Unions and personnel departments can provide internal contacts. You may also file complaints on a federal level with the EEOC and on a local level with human rights agencies.

People who are being sexually harassed sometimes fail to speak up. Ignoring or tolerating the situation can often lead to a cycle of ongoing harassment and victimization. They may need to learn to be assertive and establish strong personal boundaries. They should tell coworkers to stop when their behavior is offensive and inappropriate. Bystanders, too, must speak out against harassment when it occurs, or they can become moral spectators. If you feel you are being harassed on the job, remember that you have the right to be free from pressure or abuse. You have the right—and you owe it to yourself—to resist!

If necessary, tell someone in a position of authority when you feel you are the victim of sexual harassment.

Subtle Discrimination

S ix years ago Elizabeth had been a very successful receptionist in a utility company. She had enjoyed her work and now was ready to return to the job market after taking time off to care for her elderly parents. She refreshed her professional skills by taking a computer class and a human relations class at a local community college. She prepared a resume, updated her references, and began the interviewing process. But things seemed different now. It seemed people were talking down to her—treating her with less respect. When she finally obtained a position, she found herself in the back office of the company doing data entry work where she had little contact with the public. After several weeks on the job, she explained to her boss that she would like to be moved to a position where she could meet the public. He mumbled something about "We like to give the public an image of being a young, forward-looking company." Her coworkers did not seem to enjoy the "goodies" she brought to break time. They made comments about the importance of being trim and fit. Elizabeth was aware that she had put on quite a few pounds over the past few years.

Critical Thinking

Think about...

what Elizabeth's problem was. Is there discrimination?

The United States Constitution offers many kinds of protection from prejudice and discrimination. Many federal, state, and local regulations also contribute to the protection of our rights. But peoples' attitudes cannot be entirely controlled by legislation. Your attitudes and those of your coworkers will still be controlled by emotional reactions to the social environment.

Discrimination not entirely covered by law may be just as harmful as the types of discrimination previously discussed in this chapter. This type of discrimination is often referred to as **subtle discrimination**. Subtle means not obvious and seldom brought out in the open. Subtle discrimination includes discrimination based on appearance, values, lifestyle, or some other personal factor.

In this category you find discrimination against overweight people, short people, tall people, single people, divorced people, and recovering alcoholics, to name a few. You may be a victim of this type of discrimination, or you may be guilty of subtle discrimination against others.

If you find yourself a victim of this type of subtle discrimination, what should you do? If you wish to stay in a company, you need to find out if the discrimination factor holding you back can be changed. If the difference is not something you can change, or something you choose not to change, you can only strive to excel in another area to make up the difference. Sometimes the change is easy and worth the effort. If your future or happiness is blocked by subtle discrimination and it is something you cannot change, you may want to consider looking for employment in a new environment where you feel more accepted. Most importantly, do not let discrimination injure your self-esteem and thus limit your potential.

Avoiding, Resisting, Or Fighting Discrimination

To this point we have considered the many different aspects of discrimination and prejudice in the work world. You have been encouraged to be alert and sensitive to discrimination and prejudice. This section is concerned with what you might actually do if you are faced with discrimination.

Keep in mind that prejudice and discrimination are destructive and can often be offset by developing tolerance and understanding for other individuals. Tolerant people are those who are secure and can separate the important from the unimportant. For instance, does it really make a difference to you if Phyllis eats bean sprouts at break time? Should her eating habits really make a difference in how you feel about her? A willingness to accept and try to understand others as they are will go a long way in helping you preserve good working relationships.

There are several options available to you if you feel you are a victim of discrimination.

Turn and Walk Away

There may be situations where you consider the costs of confrontation too high when dealing with discrimination. You may feel that the least painful choice is to walk away from the pressure. It may seem best to resign your position or ask for a transfer to free yourself from a situation. You may even refuse a job offer, feeling that the pressure of prejudice from your subordinates or coworkers will be too great.

Simply turning and walking away may, at times, seem like the least painful option, but it leaves you with little hope or satisfaction. In the long run, it can affect others who may be in your position. Prejudices will not be brought to light. Unfair practices will continue. By leaving, you will be helping to maintain that prejudice. Keep your own rights in mind. Then turning and walking away may not seem so painless.

Positive Resistance with Patience

Occasionally you can overcome prejudice with time and patience. The very nature of prejudice—based on stereotypes of the individual or the group—is unfair. Often it is not an accurate picture. Demonstrating that you do not fit the image by doing your best can do much to reduce or eliminate the prejudice. For instance, when Anna, a woman in her late fifties, reorganized the entire filing system, eliminating the problem of misplaced files, her coworkers began to seek her advice. They no longer allowed the difference in age to keep them from including her. They no longer avoided contact with her.

Positive resistance does not mean that you should ignore or endure the prejudice. **Positive resistance** means clearly recognizing and confronting the prejudice. It means letting your coworkers know that you are aware of the prejudice and are uncomfortable with it but are determined to correct it. Unfortunately, not all discrimination can be eliminated with positive resistance. The next section deals with the strongest means of dealing with discrimination.

Fighting for Your Rights

If you feel your rights are being violated, you have remedies under the law for dealing with this discrimination. However, if you are a victim, your first impulse may be to get even with the offender. This alternative usually does more harm than good. Often it simply increases the prejudice and, as a result, the discrimination. Revenge can take many forms—from vandalizing to physical assault. Be aware of the consequences. They are far more damaging than any pleasure you may receive from getting even.

The appropriate way to fight is to follow these steps. Your first action should be to attempt to correct the situation from an on-the-job

66 Aggressive fighting for the right is the greatest sport in the world. 99
—Theodore Roosevelt

The law is intended to help you fight discrimination.

H. Armstrong Roberts

perspective. Contact a member of your personnel department or union. An investigation will be conducted. If just cause is found, grievance procedures can be initiated. This may be as far as you need to go to correct the discrimination. If you receive no satisfaction from these sources, your next step will be to contact either an attorney or a governmental agency dealing with discrimination.

On a local level, you may contact a human rights agency. On the federal level, you should contact the Equal Employment Opportunity Commission (EEOC). Be aware that if you have a legal case against your employer for discrimination, you must be prepared to face a not-always-sympathetic public that may include your coworkers. If you decide to proceed with court remedies, do not make it a halfhearted attempt. Backing away after you have taken the initiative can be worse than losing. Always keep in mind your right to be judged for yourself—free of stereotypes and prejudices. You have the right to fight discrimination.

Summary

Discrimination is unfair treatment due to attitudes about race, gender, religion, and a variety of other personal characteristics. Prejudice and stereotyping are underlying causes of discrimination in the workplace.

The Equal Employment Opportunity Commission (EEOC) is a government agency that helps with implementation and enforcement of Title VII of the 1972 amendment to the Civil Rights Act of 1964. It also helps private and public agencies and business enterprises to develop and implement affirmative action programs. Affirmative action plans are designed to correct the effects of past discrimination against women and minorities.

Employers are not allowed to use discriminatory practices in hiring. Some of the unlawful practices include asking questions or using selection criteria that would permit the employer to give preference to or reject job applicants because of

- race, color, and national origin

- religious affiliations or practices

- gender and family status

- age

- personal character that does not meet society's standards

The Americans with Disabilities Act (ADA) was passed in 1990. It includes a number of regulations that ensure fair access by persons with disabilities to many jobs that were formerly unavailable to them. Employers are required to disregard the disability and make selections on the basis of job performance capability. They are also required to make reasonable accommodations so the worker will be able to work effectively.

Sexual harassment should not be tolerated. The most important step in eliminating sexual harassment is to confront the perpetrator. Next, if necessary, make the situation known to persons with higher authority. If the harassment is a criminal act, help should be obtained from law enforcement authorities. Human resource departments, human rights officers or commissions, and the EEOC may also provide assistance.

Obvious and subtle discrimination among coworkers can be a problem in the workplace. Examples of subtle discrimination are a person's appearance, values, and family status.

Prejudice and discrimination often can be offset by developing tolerance and understanding for others. When that fails, it may be appropriate to avoid, resist, or fight discrimination in the workplace.

End of Chapter Activities

Questions and Projects

1. Finish the following sentences with your first thoughts. Share your answers with a classmate. As you review the answers, examine them for prejudicial ideas.

a. Overweight people are_____

b. Bosses are _____

c. Alcoholics are _____

d. Foreigners are _____

e. Farmers are _____

f. Old people are_____

g. Blondes are _____

h. Hairdressers are _____

i. Cats are _____

j. Welfare recipients are _____

2. Can you think of any instances in which you were prejudiced against someone because the person did not fit the "right image" in your peer group? Write a short paragraph describing the experience.

3. Search out a documented case of discrimination in the workplace. Newspapers, magazines, or records of court cases may be helpful to you. Study the case and write a report on it. Present the case in class.

4. Create a list of questions that you feel would be discriminatory in an employment interview. Check with a legal authority to find out which of your questions would be illegal.

5. Discuss in a small group how you would respond to an employer who asked you questions during an employment interview that you knew were discriminatory and illegal.

6. Interview or invite as a guest speaker a personnel director of a public agency to explain the agency's affirmative action plan. Perhaps the personnel director will be willing to share a copy of the plan. Be prepared to ask specific questions about the plan and its impact on the workplace. For example: Who wrote the plan? Who sees the plan? What changes have been made in the agency since the plan was adopted?

7. Write an essay on how understanding and tolerance can alleviate prejudice.

Case Problems

1. **Confronting Discrimination in Hiring and Promoting**

The Human Relations Commission of Millville was appointed by the city council to help resolve problems of discrimination in the community. In a public forum, the Commission heard several complaints about the hiring and promotion practices of the city. To better understand the situation, a survey was conducted. Following are some of the highlights of the results of the survey:

- Twenty-three percent of the citizens are Hispanic; seven percent of the city employees are Hispanic.

- Two percent of supervisory-level city employees are Hispanic.

- Fifty-nine percent of the city employees are female.

- Eleven percent of supervisory-level city employees are female.

- The city council consists of six white males and two white females. No ethnic minorities are represented on the city council.

a. What do the survey findings suggest about past hiring and promotion practices?

b. As a member of the Human Relations Commission, what suggestions would you make to help the city council develop plans for correcting the effects of past discrimination?

c. What specific policies and procedures should be included in an affirmative action plan for the city of Millville?

d. As an employee of the city, what are some actions you might take to help eliminate discrimination in your workplace?

2. Age Discrimination

After receiving an outstanding application for the position of teller at Security First Bank, the personnel director decided to call Charles Nelson in for an interview. Charles is 57 years old. He is an accountant who was required by his former employer to "retire early" because of a management reorganization. When the personnel director entered the outer office and saw Charles waiting for his interview, he said, "Sir, these are the managerial offices. The tellers are located in the front section of the bank." Charles replied, "I'm here for an interview with the personnel director." The director looked at Charles' job application, then at the floor. After a short pause he said, "Quite truthfully, we have a problem. Our job application does not include information about a person's age. I'm sorry."

  a. What would be the ethically and legally correct actions for the personnel director to take in this situation?

  b. What actions might Charles take to ensure that he is not subjected to discrimination because of his age?

3. Modeling?

Alice graduated from a two-year fashion merchandising program and obtained a good position as an executive trainee for a large department store. Her main job was salesperson in the camera department. The store advertising manager, George Smith, asked Alice to model in some of the store's newspaper advertisements. During one of the photo sessions, George appeared and stayed for the entire session. After the session he walked over to Alice and said, "I'm working on a swimsuit promotion and doing the photography myself. It's not really for the store. How would you like to pick up a few extra dollars by working overtime on this project?" There was a pause.

  a. Are there any clues in this case to indicate something about George Smith's motives?

  b. What are the important questions that Alice must answer as she considers how to respond to George Smith?

Diversity

Olga grew up in Montana—"big sky country." Her grandparents were immigrants from Norway, and she remembers that in her community there was occasionally a little good-natured teasing about her blonde complexion. She also remembers hearing her relatives tell ethnic jokes. Norwegian farmers were stereotyped as stubborn and not particularly intellectual. But underneath it all was a kind of pride and appreciation of Scandinavian culture. After completing a two-year degree in accounting, Olga went to work in a Minneapolis bank and moved quickly into a management position. Yesterday she was told that the corporation was offering her an exciting challenge if she wanted it. They were sending her to El Paso, Texas, to set up the accounting system in a new branch bank. In addition, Olga would be assigned to train the Hispanic personnel. While she was well qualified for the assignment, she was a little nervous about this career opportunity. In discussing it with George, a trusted friend and coworker, she commented, "I've never worked in a place where the culture is so different from mine. What do I know about the El Paso area—the people and their customs? Will they accept *me*? How will I adjust and feel at home in a culture that's so different from what we have in Montana and Minnesota?"

Objectives

After completing this chapter, you should be able to:

*1.
Explain how the ethnic and minority composition of the work force is different from what it was in the past.*

*2.
Describe how the adjustment to diversity in the workplace has been difficult due to stereotyping, discrimination, and conflict.*

*3.
Describe how employers are coping with diversity, and how they expect workers to adapt to diversity in the workplace.*

*4.
Explain how cultural conflict, misunderstanding, and failure to communicate can be avoided or resolved.*

*5.
Describe how you can help others adjust to the diversity in the world of work.*

Diversity In The Workplace

SCANS
Focus

A competent worker...

■ works well with men and women

■ works well with people having different ethnic backgrounds

■ works well with people having different social or educational backgrounds

■understands and takes pride in his or her own culture

■ understands, appreciates, and respects other cultures

■ helps coworkers with cultural and social adjustments

■ bases personal impressions on performance, not on stereotypes

■ understands the concerns and problems of others in a diverse workplace

Significant changes have made today's workplace far different from what it was 20 years ago. The generation gap continues to widen between older and younger workers. Increasing numbers of women continue to enter the labor market. By the year 2000, more than six in ten workers will be female. Organizations are revamping their physical environment to accommodate persons with disabilities.

Ethnic groups representing a diversity of cultures are being absorbed into the workplace in record numbers. In 1990 Congress passed a law that increased legal immigration levels. Minorities and immigrants are about one-quarter of the work force. Hiring highly skilled immigrants is encouraged, and stiffer penalties are imposed on employers who are reluctant to do so.

While the traditional work force in this country was made up mainly of native-born white males, only one in six of the new workers are in that category. Now as employers compete in the labor market for skilled workers, they are more accepting of **diversity**.

Employer Expectations

Diversity in the workplace sets the stage for many of the problems discussed in Chapter 16—prejudice, stereotyping, sexual harassment, and subtle discrimination. To help avoid and overcome these problems, many employers are voluntarily using affirmative action programs. They are working to accommodate persons with disabilities. They are working to avoid and eliminate sexual harassment. They are making changes that will help workers who are somehow different to fit in, get along, and feel accepted and appreciated.

Past Intolerance of Diversity

It is natural in our society to take pride in ourselves—in our families, our communities, and our culture. The down side of this is that as we elevate ourselves in our own eyes, we tend to look down on others who are different. In this country we have cause for regret in the practice of human slavery, in the exploitation and oppression of Native Americans, and in the reluctance of men to allow women the right to vote. There are many examples.

The founders of our nation realized that where people are justifiably proud, they can also have unjustified feelings of superiority—feelings that can lead to oppression of those who are different. The statement seen on the Statue of Liberty is "Send me your tired, your poor, your troubled masses yearning to breathe free." But when immigrants from Europe, from China, and from neighboring Hispanic

The Statue of Liberty has welcomed immigrants, but they have not been so welcome in the world of work.

R. Krubner/H. Armstrong Roberts

countries arrived in the workplace, they were treated as second-class noncitizens. The predominantly white male work force has been less than cordial in welcoming women, older workers, persons with disabilities, Native Americans, and African-American citizens—anyone who is different.

Typically, those who were different had less access to the better jobs. They had less opportunity for promotion, and they were paid less than the predominant white males when they did the same work. They were subjected to exploitation and abuse. Slowly this intolerance for diversity is being eroded, and people are making an effort to learn about other people's cultures and backgrounds.

66 The resource of bigotry and intolerance, when convicted of error, is always the same; silenced by argument, it endeavors to silence by persecution, in old times by fire and sword, in modern days by the tongue. 99
—G. Simmons

Appreciating Diversity

If you are to develop your appreciation of anything—classical music, western dancing, drag racing, or Japanese food—you must get involved and expose yourself to it. If you are to fit in and get along in a diverse working environment, you need to develop your appreciation for diversity, and that means exposure and involvement. Self-appreciation is a good place to start.

Take Pride in Who You Are

If you are a member of a group that has been subjected to unfair treatment in the world of work, you realize the need for appreciating diversity. You also probably realize that although you may be different, you certainly have no cause to feel inferior.

- As a female worker in a predominantly male workplace, you should see yourself as equal and deserving of fair treatment.

- As a person with a disability, you need not accept second-class status.

- Your ethnic and cultural heritage may be different, but it is not inferior.

- If you are an older worker, you need not accept the stereotypes associated with age discrimination.

- If your religious beliefs and practices place you in a minority in your community, you should not have to endure discrimination.

Critical Thinking

Think about...

who you are. What is there about your background and status in society that might give you reasons to be proud?

If you are African-American, Hispanic, Asian, or Native American, you are probably aware of efforts in your community to foster pride and appreciation of your cultural heritage. In the past it seems that people of a different culture were encouraged to abandon their traditional ways—to change and lose their identity. Now we are seeing more of an effort to preserve the culture and encourage pride. Notions of the superiority of one culture over another are being rejected. No matter what your background or status in society, the fact that you are different should translate into an appreciation of yourself. Take pride in who you are!

Take pride in your cultural and ethnic heritage.

B. Taylor/H. Armstrong Roberts

Widen Your Perspective

Having suggested that you take pride in who you are, the next step is to learn to appreciate other cultures. There are some popular buzzwords for our tendency to let self-pride dampen our appreciation of others. One of these terms is **egocentric myopia**. It simply means that we see and appreciate only what is close (our immediate environment), which gives us a distorted impression of being more important than we really are. Another term is **ethnocentrism**, the assumption that one's own world view is the *only* view.

It is important for you to realize that your ethnocentric view of the world can influence how you feel about people from other cultures. The people around you can misunderstand you as well because they have a distorted image of you and your cultural heritage. You should take pride in who you are without feeling that yours is the only way to view the world—or that your view of the world is necessarily *better* than the view of someone else. As you expose yourself to the diversity of perspectives among your coworkers, your own perspective will widen.

The more you learn about different minority groups and cultures, the more you will come to appreciate them. Here are some suggestions:

- Attend cultural events, festivals, parades, and other activities sponsored by specific ethnic or minority groups.

- Patronize neighborhood restaurants or shop in ethnic grocery stores.

- Take the initiative to socialize with people of different cultures. Strike up a conversation at lunch, on the bus, at a sports event. (Use your imagination.)

- Participate in diversity workshops or other training activities sponsored by your employer or your school.

- Volunteer to help with fund-raising events involving persons with disabilities.

- Pay attention to political and social activists by attending their public appearances, reading their books, and listening to them on radio and TV.

Avoiding Cultural Conflict

Yoko and Alan were at lunch together. Alan had just returned from a meeting with two Japanese purchasing agents who were negotiating to purchase a large quantity of lumber. Alan looked at his tray of food and shook his head slowly. Yoko said, "Alan, are you okay? How are you doing in negotiating for the lumber deal?" Alan looked up and said, "Yoko, you should be doing this. I just can't figure out how to relate to these guys. I have no idea why, but several times they acted embarrassed or insulted. The situation was tense. We just couldn't communicate!" "Well, to be honest, Alan, I'm not too surprised," Yoko said. "Let me tell you about differences in communicating with Asian executives."

"Japanese prefer to spend more time on small talk that has nothing to do with the task at hand. Americans think 10 minutes is sufficient; Japanese might spend 40 minutes in polite social conversation before getting down to business."

"Eye contact is another communication conflict. I was watching you. You would try to make eye contact; they would try to avoid it. They would lower their eyes, and you would look right at them. When you looked down at your notes, they would look up. Japanese children are taught to lower their eyes when being scolded. American parents may say, 'Look at me.'"

You noticed that they had a tendency to remain silent during the negotiations. You thought this meant that they were dissatisfied. They were just being polite and courteous."

"Facial expressions also enter into it. If things are not going well, Americans expect to see frowns. A respectful, tolerant smile may be misread as approval or agreement."

"The word that got you into the most trouble is *you*. One should not address a Japanese businessperson directly, as in 'What do you think?' It's more appropriate to ask, 'What does the company think?'"

Conflict that occurs because of cultural differences is called **cultural conflict**. Egocentric myopia and ethnocentrism reinforce it. Nevertheless, cultural conflict can be avoided if you are alert and sensitive—if you make an effort to learn about other cultures.

Be Sensitive and Respectful of Cultural Differences

You should develop sensitivity to other people's values, dress, eating habits, and leisure-time activities that may reflect a particular culture. For example, what does setting the table mean to someone from Ethiopia, India, or another country where the native food is eaten with the hands? What relevance does "dress for success" have in a job interview for Muslim women who "cover"? How do you react when

Laimute E. Druskis/Stock, Boston

you learn that some Asian families treat colds and flu by rubbing parts of the body with a coin or spoon to balance yin and yang? How do you respond when you see coworkers giggling together while talking in their native language? When coworkers are inscrutably silent (leaving you wondering whether they have heard what you said), how do you feel?

S herman met Rose at a local hospital where they both volunteered their time. Rose grew up in a Mexican border town and had recently moved to the United States. After several weeks of working together at the hospital, Sherman invited Rose to dinner with him and his mother, who had immigrated to the U.S. from Israel.

Sherman was very clear and specific in his invitation to Rose. Appetizers were to be served at 5:30 p.m., and dinner would be at 6 p.m. At 6:15 on the appointed day when Rose had not yet arrived, Sherman's mother felt very insulted.

Rose arrived at 6:30. She cheerfully greeted Sherman with a hug, and when introductions were made, she put her arm around his mother and greeted her warmly. Sherman's mother looked away, brushed Rose's arm off her shoulder, and walked briskly away without saying a word.

The conflict in the scenario above could have been avoided if Sherman and his mother had recognized and understood that punctuality is not as important to people in Mexico as it is to people in Israel. They should also have understood that Mexicans tend to show affection more freely. Rose might have created a better first impression if she had understood that Sherman's mother would interpret her late arrival as an insult and that a physical gesture of friendliness would be considered disrespectful.

Following are some suggestions about how to be sensitive and show respect for cultural differences.

- Study other cultures. You can do this by reading books and articles such as those found in *National Geographic*. Also, be on the alert for newspaper articles, television programs, and movies that can help you learn about other cultures.

- Make friends with people from different cultural backgrounds. Ask them to explain some of the differences.

- Observe people from other cultures in their natural interactions with one another. Notice their gestures, facial expressions, and posture while they are in conversation. Notice how they relate to children and to elderly people.

- Notice the customs and actions of people from other cultures while they are eating and drinking. Watch what they do while shopping, while working, and while playing.

All this information can provide clues that will help you be sensitive and respectful in your relationships with people of different cultural backgrounds.

Manage Language Barriers

Perhaps the most obvious source of cultural barriers is language. What can you do when you find yourself unable to understand or make yourself understood?

First, you can avoid making incorrect assumptions. Assuming that a person is poor or illiterate because he or she speaks broken English is unfair and unrealistic. In fact, that limited English-speaking ability may be greater than your ability to speak another language. Would you want to have someone judge your intellect by your ability to speak another language? Second, you can make an effort to learn another language. When U.S. military forces were guests of another country, someone put up a sign that read, "Remember. . .here, *you* are the foreigner." Americans, it seems, expect everyone else to learn English rather than making the effort to learn another language themselves.

Some suggestions on how to manage language barriers are

- Study the language. You can take courses in high school, in college, and through adult and community education programs. Also, most bookstores and libraries can provide audiotapes and books for you to use.

- Use an interpreter. This includes language interpretation—literally to translate so you can talk freely with someone whose native language is different. It also means interpretation of what you see and hear. Ask,"What does this language or behavior mean? What's the message that this person is sending?"

- Sharpen your foreign language skills by speaking the language instead of English when you are talking with friends or coworkers who are fluent. Ask them to correct your mistakes and coach you in pronouncing and speaking correctly.

Help Others Make Cultural Adjustments

As part of your effort to adapt and feel comfortable in a workplace where there is so much diversity, you should take advantage of opportunities to help others make cultural adjustments. Some ways of doing this are to

- read credible newspapers and magazines so that you will be well informed.

- become aware of the problems and issues that create misunderstanding and cause division rather than unity.

- explain your own culture to those of another culture. Compare the two cultures by finding similarities as well as differences.

- take a stand on issues that promote respect for and appreciation of diversity.

- challenge the way things are and suggest improvements. Be a risk-taker.

Do not be afraid to reach out to your coworkers. Form supportive interpersonal relationships with those whose cultural orientation is different from your own. The same applies to other minorities who may find themselves isolated or subjected to subtle discrimination—older workers, younger inexperienced workers, men or women who may be a minority in your workplace, persons with disabilities, members of minority religious groups, and those whose educational and social backgrounds are different.

Summary

The workplace of today and tomorrow is much more diverse than in the past. There are more women, more persons with disabilities, more older workers, more ethnic minorities and immigrants. Native-born white males are no longer a majority in the work force.

The diversity in the world of work can create problems of prejudice and cultural conflict, but employers are working to avoid them. They expect workers to be able to fit in and get along, and to help others to do so. This includes taking pride in who you are, learning to understand and accept the values and views of others who are different, and making an effort to learn about different minority groups and cultures. Cultural conflict can be avoided when workers are sensitive and respectful of differences among minorities and cultures.

Helping others to adjust and fit in can be rewarding. Getting and giving help with language barriers is an important step. Taking a stand on important issues of promoting acceptance of others, challenging the way things are, and suggesting improvements can lead to unity and overcome divisiveness. Most important, reach out to your coworkers and form supportive interpersonal relationships with those who are different from yourself.

End of Chapter Activities

Questions and Projects

1. Interview a worker who has been employed for 20 years or more in the same workplace, preferably one that employs more than 100 people. Or invite several such people to participate in a panel discussion for your class. Ask for responses to the following questions:

   a. What are some changes that have occurred in the past 20 years in terms of the makeup of the work force—numbers of native-born white males, women, age of the workers, education and training requirements, numbers of and accommodation for persons with disabilities, ethnic minorities, and foreign workers?

   b. Describe any instances of past discrimination. Were women paid less than men for the same work? Were some workers held back for promotion in favor of native-born white males? Were there instances of subtle discrimination? For example, were ethnic jokes more commonplace?

c. What are the attitudes and expectations of management now with respect to diversity? What, specifically, are they doing to help workers who are different to fit in and get along?

2. Prepare a short essay or an oral presentation that begins with "I'm (*your name*) and I'm proud to be (*who you are in terms of minority status or ethnic background*)." Include specific information about what has influenced the development of your character and personality and your cultural values, beliefs, and social behavior.

3. Assume you are going to work (or are already at work) in a situation where you are different from most of your coworkers. Or use the workplace scenario about Olga at the beginning of this chapter.

a. What are some of the problems or barriers that might make it difficult for you to fit in, get along, and reach out to provide support for others?

b. Make a list of five things you would plan to do to overcome or avoid the problems or barriers listed above.

4. Select a culture or minority group with which you would like to become better acquainted. Interview several members of that group to determine interesting, unusual customs, values and beliefs, and behaviors that are characteristic of members of that group. Use the information in the workplace scenario about Japanese executives as an example of the kind of material you should include in a report.

Case Problems

1. **From Another World**
A week had passed in Accounting 101. The 30 students had become acquainted with one another. Study groups were emerging. Small groups were having lunch together. But two students, Laura and Jim, sat in the back of the room and were not included in anything. During the introductions on the first day of class, Laura and Jim said that they were from the Four Corners area—the Indian reservation. They did not say much to each other, and they said absolutely nothing when called upon to answer questions in class. Usually they were a little late arriving, and they were always the first ones out the door. No one, it seemed, took an interest in getting them to join in and become active members of the class.

a. Assume you have decided to help Laura and Jim to fit in and get along with other students in the class and to help them survive the rigorous demands of the course. Develop goals and a plan for accomplishing them.

b. What might you learn from Laura and Jim? In what ways might you and other class members benefit from reaching out to these two who seem to be from another world?

2. Reasonable Accommodation?

Charles had a difficult time finding a job, but finally he was hired to work in the equipment room of a health and fitness club. When he was nine years old, Charles was stricken with an illness that left him with damage to his central nervous system. He is unable to walk and has difficulty with eye and hand coordination. In addition, his speech is slightly impaired. His coworkers were friendly and helpful, and Charles liked the work. But he was a bit slow because of the extra effort required to move around the facility in his wheelchair. There was a step at the doorway of the weight room. Charles was assigned to work behind a counter that he could barely see over. But the most difficult problem was communicating with coworkers and customers. Charles had to speak very slowly to be understood. Often he was misunderstood. On one occasion after asking him to repeat something a second time, a coworker said, "Oh, just forget it!" and walked away.

a. Assume you are the manager of the health and fitness club and part of your job is hiring and supervision. You are having second thoughts about whether or not Charles will fit in and get along in his new job. What are you going to do? Explain how and why.

b. Assume you are a coworker assigned to work with Charles doing the same work. You are concerned that he is apparently not able to do the job as well as you, and you find yourself doing some of his work. You like Charles. He seems to get along with people and has a pleasant personality. But it is sometimes frustrating for you because he is so slow—both in his actions and his speech. What are you going to do? Explain how and why

Unit 6

Developing Your Career

The final unit of *Personality Development for Work* takes you through the steps of getting a job, keeping the job, and moving ahead in your career.

Finding enjoyable and satisfying work is a tough job. You will need to do some planning and preparation. Chapter 18 leads you through the planning stages of (1) preparing for the job search, (2) preparing the employment documents, (3) interviewing for the position(s) you select, and (4) following up after the interviews.

Chapter 19 includes information about the habits you will need to establish in order to keep your position. The closing chapter reviews the importance of the goal-setting process. As you move along the career path, decisions will need to be made about how to ask for a raise, when to accept a promotion, when to change positions, and how to change positions. Helpful hints in making these decisions are provided in this final chapter.

Contents

Chapter 18
Getting The Job

Chapter 19
Keeping The Job

Chapter 20
Moving Ahead In Your Career

Getting The Job

Keiko completed high school and planned to go to college someday. Her financial situation would not permit her to further her education immediately, so she began looking for a job. She scanned the daily newspaper and circled two positions: night desk clerk and nursing assistant. She followed up on both ads and was granted interviews. At the interview for the nursing assistant, she found that she would have to take a 12-week training course at her own expense to prepare for the position. She wanted to begin earning immediately, so she scratched that job off her list. Her second interview was for the night desk clerk position at a hotel. Keiko was impressed by the beautiful lobby of the hotel; the human resources staff was pleasant to her; and she thought it looked like a nice place to work. She was offered and accepted the position. Within a couple of weeks, Keiko realized this was not the job for her. She was an outgoing person and enjoyed being with people. Because her shift began at 11 p.m., many nights she would serve only one or two customers. She also had difficulty adjusting to working the night shift. She had computer skills, but in this position with minimal night traffic, she did not get to use them. She found the job boring and dull. Keiko was in the wrong job.

Objectives

After completing this chapter, you should be able to:

1.
Plan a successful job campaign.

2.
Prepare a quality resume.

3.
Complete a job application form.

4.
Write a quality letter of application.

5.
Conduct yourself in a positive manner during a job interview.

6.
Prepare a thank-you letter as a follow-up to the job interview.

Job Campaign

The formula you will want to use in choosing the best job for you is

$$Q \text{ (qualifications)} + I \text{ (interests)} = JP \text{ (job possibilities)}$$

First, list your qualifications; second, list your interests; then look for job possibilities that fit your qualifications and interests. This formula can be a valuable job tool in finding a satisfying job.

QUALIFICATIONS	+	INTERESTS	=	JOB POSSIBILITIES
Education		Photography		
Personality Traits		Reading		
Special Training		Travel		
Unique Skills		Animal Rights		

Illustration 18-1
Job-seeking formula.

Making Your Inventory List

The first step in preparing for the job campaign is to take a good look at yourself. Make a list of everything that you can think of that might have a bearing on your success. You are actually listing your qualifications. At this point, do not try to organize or prioritize the information. Just get it down on paper.

SAMPLE LISTING OF PERSONAL QUALIFICATIONS

Attended Southwest High School	Graduated with Honors
Experience as a babysitter	Experience as a grocery clerk
Had a role in the school play	Theater Club member
Science Club member	Participated in Science Olympiad
Worked on yearbook staff	Participated in Save the Wetlands projects
Have computer skills	Worked with word processing and database programs

The second step in preparing your campaign is to list your interests and likes. Do not try to organize or prioritize.

SAMPLE LISTING OF PERSONAL INTERESTS

Golfing	Working with people
Reading	Watching football and baseball
Being outdoors	Photography
Fishing	Waterskiing

Organizing Your Inventory List

When you have written down all the items you can think of, you should organize them into separate classifications. Some of the headings you might consider are the following:

- Education

- Work Experience

- Special Talents or Abilities

- Organizational Membership

- Hobbies and Interests

As you organize this list, select items from your qualifications and interests lists. Drop those items that are perhaps not as important to you. Take a large sheet of paper and turn it the long way. Enter your headings across the top of the sheet. Below the headings, list the items from your inventories that belong in each category. (See the example in Illustration 18-2.) Check your inventory to see if the items match some of the requirements of jobs you are considering.

ME				
Education	**Experience**	**Abilities**	**Memberships**	**Interests**
High School Diploma	Grocery Clerk Babysitting	Computer Theatrical	Science Olympiad Science Club	Golfing Reading
Southwest HS		Word Processing	Theater Club	Fishing
Honor Student		Database Programs		Photography

Illustration 18-2
Display the information about yourself in any easy-to-read style.

Checking Your Aptitudes

An **aptitude** is a natural talent, an ability, or a capacity to learn. Having an aptitude makes learning how to do something much easier. For example, you may have an aptitude for working with figures, percentages, and other types of math. In other words, math comes easy for you. Consider occupations where your aptitude is strong.

You may already know a lot about your own aptitudes. One way you learn about your aptitudes is by listening to others. Your friends or neighbors may say, "You'd be a great accountant since you're so good at math," or "A job in public relations would be good because you're so likable." In these comments your friends or neighbors are talking about what they perceive to be your aptitudes.

You probably will discover that you are interested in doing the things for which you show an aptitude. If you have an aptitude for writing, there is a good chance you will enjoy a job in which you will have the opportunity to write. However, you may not always enjoy doing the things you do well. Just because you can do a good job washing windows does not mean that the activity brings you great satisfaction.

Aptitude tests measure your ability to learn something. Aptitude tests help people discover which occupations match the skills they can develop easily. These tests may be given by career or school counselors or employers to determine your aptitudes. One well-known aptitude test is called the General Aptitude Test Battery (GATB). It is used by many state employment agencies. You may want to try to arrange to take this or another aptitude test. These tests measure your ability

- to work with numbers and words

- to work with your hands

- to distinguish between shapes and forms and see relationships between objects

- to perform mechanical and clerical tests

After you have considered your qualifications, interests, and aptitudes, list some jobs you think you would like to try. Each job you consider must match your qualifications, interests, and aptitudes.

Job Resources

Once you have determined your qualifications, interests, and aptitudes, you are ready to begin looking at job resources and job leads. A **job lead** is information about a possible job opening.

People

People you know will be of special help to you because they care about you and your future. Let everyone know that you are interested in employment. Tell everyone you meet that you are in the job market. The more people you talk to about your job search, the more leads and information you will discover. Also, encourage others to tell you about their job experiences—the high points and the low points. You can consider this information when it is time to make a decision. This process of sharing and exchanging job information is called **networking.**

Do not be too proud to ask those who know you for personal assistance in getting a job. The old saying, "It's not what you know, but who you know" holds some truth. There is nothing wrong with having a friend or family member help you get a job for which you are qualified.

Encourage those who know you to help you decide what kind of employment is best suited to you. You may not always hear what you expect to hear.

Newspaper Help-Wanted Ads

Take advantage of the help-wanted ads in your daily newspaper(s). These are not only a source of job openings, but also show trends in the type of openings that are most common. Do not just skim these ads. Read each ad carefully before you respond to it. The help-wanted ads are written and paid for by employers. If an advertised job is not exactly what you are looking for but is related, you may want to follow up on the ad if you think it has potential. *Do not* waste the employer's time and yours by calling about jobs for which you do not qualify. Be sure to follow up on an advertised job opening immediately. A delay may lose the job for you.

Be sure to check the Sunday paper. Sunday news editions usually have the largest job ad section. In fact, some employers only advertise jobs in the Sunday paper.

The newspaper can be a great resource when you are job hunting.

Employment Agencies

An **employment agency** is a business that brings together a potential worker and an employer to fill a job opening. You may find help through state supported and private agencies.

State Employment Agencies. Every state has a job service agency that helps people find employment. The name of the agency varies from state to state. Look for the agency in the local telephone directory, or call the general state government office number. Your state agency will have many job listings in a wide variety of occupations. The staffs in these agencies have knowledge of the business, industry, and government jobs within the state.

There is no fee charged for the services of the state employment agency. The goal of the agency is to make as many placements as possible so that few people are unemployed and the economy of the state is healthy. State agency employment services may include career counseling, vocational assessment, resume preparation, interviewing skills, and job-search workshops.

Private Employment Agencies. Private employment agencies can also be useful in helping you find a job. If you contact a private agency, remember that this agency is in business to make a profit. When you complete the private agency application form, you will be asked to sign a contract. *Read the contract before you sign it.* Many private agencies charge fees to employers to find competent, qualified workers. If you decide to use a private agency, make sure you understand who will be paying the fees.

Civil Service Positions

Civil service jobs are positions working for the United States Government. The United States Government is the largest employer in the country. The government hires thousands of new employees each year for many different jobs. The pay and working conditions for government jobs are usually good. Find out where the federal government offices are that accept applications for civil service positions or provide information about these jobs. You will find the number under U.S. Government Offices in the telephone book.

Other Job Resources

Do not overlook the school placement services that are often available in high schools and postsecondary institutions. Employers often check with school placement services to obtain the names of people with qualifications they need.

If there are large companies in the area where you choose to work, you may want to do some **cold canvassing**. This means stopping by the personnel offices of these large businesses and completing an application. Let them know you are looking for a job and what skills you have to offer.

Local bulletin boards in stores and government buildings can be a good source for job leads.

©Ulrike Welsch/Photo Researchers

Make it a point to read bulletin boards with job postings. These are often found in supermarkets, drugs stores, discount stores, government buildings, and community centers. Watch for help-wanted signs in local businesses where you would like to work.

You should also look into the services of temporary work agencies. Trying out a variety of jobs on a temporary basis is a common first step for entry-level workers in many areas. Always keep in mind that you are looking for a job that matches your aptitudes, abilities, and interests.

Job Search Documents

As you work on your job campaign, you will need to prepare a resume. A **resume** is a written summary of your education, work experience, and other qualifications for a job. You will also need to know how to put together a letter of application and some knowledge of how to "look good" on the application forms you will be completing.

Resume

The resume is sometimes referred to as a *personal data sheet* or a *vita*. As you begin to prepare the resume, use the sheet that you prepared earlier that lists your qualifications and interests. Think of the resume as an advertisement for you. This resume should sell you and your skills. The resume can be left with employers to attach to your application form, attached to letters of application, and shared with those with whom you are networking. Share your resume with everyone interested in helping you find a job.

There are many acceptable formats for resumes. One will be presented in this chapter. You may want to experiment with other formats. The resume must always be typed or word processed. Errors on a resume are totally unacceptable. The resume should be one or two pages and produced on quality paper. Remember, this resume is a "snapshot" of you and should be designed to sell you.

Resumes are typically divided into the following information categories: Personal Information (presented as a heading), Career Objective, Education, Work Experience, Personal Interests, and References.

Personal Information. This section of the resume should include your full name (nicknames are not appropriate), your complete address, and your telephone number. It is not appropriate to list your height, weight, age, or marital status. These topics have nothing to do with your ability to perform a job. You may choose to eliminate the word *RESUME* at the top of the page. Illustration 18-3 shows the first part of the resume (using the optional heading of RESUME.)

RESUME

Twila Louise McDonald
2455 Winding Way
Lincoln, NE 68506-4324
(402) 555-5432

Illustration 18-3
Resume—personal information.

Career Objective. State simply and briefly the type of work you want to do. The employer will want to match your interests with the company's needs. Your objective may be general or specific. For example, a general objective might state: "Full-time position as a laborer in a large manufacturing company." A more specific objective might say: "Full-time position desired as a house framer for a home builder." Illustration 18-4 shows how this statement will look combined with the personal information. This part of the resume is optional. If you are applying for temporary work or if you wish to use the resume for several applications, you may want to eliminate the career objective.

RESUME

Twila Louise McDonald
2455 Winding Way
Lincoln, NE 68506-4324
(402) 555-5432

Objective: To be employed by a large grocery store and
work with inventory.

Illustration 18-4
Resume—career objective.

Education. The education section of your resume should support your objective. An employer will look for schooling or training that will be essential for doing a job. List the highest level of education you have successfully completed. List the name of the school, the address, the dates you attended, and your area(s) of study. If you graduated and earned a certificate, include those accomplishments. If you have earned a GED or are working on it, put that in this section. Employers will be impressed with your initiative.

Any special course, on-the-job training, or military service should be listed in this section. Sample education information is added to the resume for Twila McDonald shown in Illustration 18-5.

RESUME

Twila Louise McDonald
2455 Winding Way
Lincoln, NE 68506-4324
(402) 555-5432

Objective: To be employed by a large grocery store and
work with inventory.
Education: Southwest High School, Lincoln, Nebraska
College Preparatory Program of Study
Graduated: May 19--
JTPA Data Entry Training Program
Earned Certificate
September 19--

Illustration 18-5
Resume—education.

Work Experience. Prospective employers like to see what work experiences you have had. This is a very important section of the resume. You should list your previous jobs in reverse chronological order. That is, list the present or most recent job first, then the next most recent, and so on, until you have all your jobs listed. Include the following information about your previous employment: name of your employer, employer's address, employment dates, job title, duties, and special skills used (if any). Yes, you do list jobs from which you have been fired. There is no need to indicate that you were fired, but be prepared to explain the circumstances in the interview. It is not uncommon to have a less-than-perfect work history. Illustration 18-6 shows the resume with the work experience added.

RESUME

Twila Louise McDonald
2455 Winding Way
Lincoln, NE 68506-4324
(402) 555-5432

Objective:	To be employed by a large grocery store and work with inventory.
Education:	Southwest High School, Lincoln, Nebraska College Preparatory Program of Study Graduated: May 19-- JTPA Data Entry Training Program Earned Certificate September 19--
Work Experience:	Sumner's Grocery Store 56th and Highway 77, Lincoln, NE 68506 June 1993 to Present Grocery Clerk: Assigned to Customer Service Booth
	J. L. Lewis 1432 Apple Road Cortland, NE 68335 June to August 1992 Babysitter of two small children. Position included light housekeeping.

Illustration 18-6
Resume—work experience.

Personal Interests. This section is optional, but it gives the employer a chance to look at the total person. Keep your list of interests short and to the point. Be sure to list those interests that may support your qualifications for the position. You may include such information as your hobbies, sports you enjoy watching or participating in, any community service work, or other things you enjoy. Consult the inventory that you prepared as you were beginning the job search process. Illustration 18-7 summarizes that Twila likes to garden, enjoys playing tennis, likes to read biographies, and volunteers at a hospital.

RESUME

Twila Louise McDonald
2455 Winding Way
Lincoln, NE 68506-4324
(402) 555-5432

Objective: To be employed by a large grocery store and work with inventory.

Education: Southwest High School, Lincoln, Nebraska
College Preparatory Program of Study
Graduated: May 19--
JTPA Data Entry Training Program
Earned Certificate
September 19--

Work Experience: Sumner's Grocery Store
56th and Highway 77, Lincoln, NE 68506
June 1993 to Present
Grocery Clerk: Assigned to Customer Service Booth

J. L. Lewis
1432 Apple Road
Cortland, NE 68335
June to August 1992
Babysitter of two small children. Position included light housekeeping.

Personal Interests: I relax by gardening, playing tennis, and reading biographies.
I enjoy volunteering eight hours per week at Lincoln General Hospital in the children's ward.

Illustration 18-7
Resume—personal interests.

References. The last section of your resume should contain the names, titles, addresses, and phone numbers of three or four individuals who can recommend your work habits, skills, or character. Your references should be over the age of 18 and should not be related to you. Be sure you get permission from the person before you list his or her name as a reference. You may want to ask for references from a coworker, a neighbor, a current or former teacher, a former employer, or possibly a career counselor. Always list at least one former employer. References can be listed on your resume or you can simply use the phrase *References: Available upon request.* You may also prepare a separate reference sheet if you choose not to list specific references on your resume. When the number of job applicants has been narrowed to a few, the employer may ask for this list of references. Illustration 18-8 shows the two ways references can be listed and how your completed resume will look.

RESUME

Twila Louise McDonald
2455 Winding Way
Lincoln, NE 68506-4324
(402) 555-5432

Objective:	To be employed by a large grocery store and work with inventory.
Education:	Southwest High School, Lincoln, Nebraska College Preparatory Program of Study Graduated: May 19-- JTPA Data Entry Training Program Earned Certificate September 19--
Work Experience:	Sumner's Grocery Store 56th and Highway 77, Lincoln, NE 68506 June 1993 to Present Grocery Clerk: Assigned to Customer Service Booth
	J. L. Lewis 1432 Apple Road Cortland, NE 68335 June to August 1992 Babysitter of two small children. Position included light housekeeping.
Personal Interests:	I relax by gardening, playing tennis, and reading biographies. I enjoy volunteering eight hours per week at Lincoln General Hospital in the children's ward.

(continued)

References:	Available upon request.	
	or	
References:	Oliver Upton, Supervisor	Martha Overton (Neighbor)
	Sumner's Grocery Store	2432 Winding Way
	56th and Highway 77	Lincoln, NE 68506
	Lincoln, NE 68506	(402) 555-4321
	(402) 555-1234	
	Rinji Mori (School Counselor)	
	Southwest High School	
	2930 South 37	
	Lincoln, NE 68506	
	(402) 555-5678	

Illustration 18-8
Resume—references; completed resume.

Application

When you decide to apply for a position or visit the employment office of a business, go to the personnel department. (Some businesses call it the human resources department.) Go alone. Do not take a friend or relative. The employer is interested only in you.

Before you leave home, be sure that you have the necessary tools to apply for the job. Take your social security card, two black pens, and any information you have put together about former jobs, your educational background, and your military service (if any). If spelling is a problem for you, take a small pocket dictionary to help you, and *use* it.

Any job for which you apply will require that you complete a job **application form**. This form is used by employers to get the basic information about people who apply for positions in their place of business. Illustration 18-9 shows you what a typical application form looks like. You may want to complete the application form in Illustration 18-9 at home for practice and take it with you as a guide in completing the employer's application form. However, remember that each company has its own application form and each form is a little different.

Completing the Application Form. The completion of the form should be taken seriously as it will provide the employer with

- basic information about you

- how well you follow directions

- what you have achieved in your education

- how neat you are

- a summary of your work experience

If you do not understand a particular question on the form, ask the person who gave you the form for assistance. If there is a word on the form that you do not understand, check your pocket dictionary for help.

The Civil Rights Act of 1964 prohibits discrimination in employment because of race, color, religion, sex, or national origin. Public Law 90-202 prohibits discrimination because of age. The only legal question about your age is, "Are you 18 years or older?" An employer's application form can ask only job-related questions. For example, the employer cannot legally ask if you are married, divorced, or single because marital status does not affect your ability to do the job.

Tips for Completing the Application Form. The following tips will help you successfully complete job applications.

Follow directions. Read each question with care and put down only the information that is requested. If the form says please print, then *print*. If the form says circle your answer, *circle* it. If there is a space to write the position you desire, write in the position(s) in which you would have an interest. Never just put in *anything or anything available*. Be as specific as you can about the job you want.

Be neat. Print or write clearly so that your answers can be read easily. Use a black ink pen unless instructed otherwise. A black pen is usually preferred because the employer may want to photocopy the application, and black ink will photocopy best. Avoid crossing out your answers, writing too large or too small, or making smudges on the paper. You will avoid these errors if you plan ahead. Think about your answer and the space you have for the answer before you write it down.

Be honest in all of your answers. You will be asked to sign the application. Your signature means that you have answered each question truthfully and to the best of your ability. If a question does not apply to you, draw a straight line or write NA for *not applicable*. This lets the employer know that you *did* read the question.

If the application asks for a desired salary and you have little or no experience, write *starting wage*. If you are experienced and have extensive education, write *negotiable*. **Negotiable** means that you want to discuss the salary.

APPLICATION FOR EMPLOYMENT
(PRE-EMPLOYMENT QUESTIONNAIRE) (AN EQUAL OPPORTUNITY EMPLOYER)

PERSONAL INFORMATION

DATE _____

SOCIAL SECURITY
NUMBER

NAME
_____ LAST _____ FIRST _____ MIDDLE

PRESENT ADDRESS
_____ STREET _____ CITY _____ STATE _____ ZIP

PERMANENT ADDRESS
_____ STREET _____ CITY _____ STATE _____ ZIP

PHONE NO. _____ ARE YOU 18 YEARS OR OLDER? YES ☐ NO ☐

EMPLOYMENT DESIRED

POSITION

DATE YOU
CAN START

SALARY
DESIRED

ARE YOU EMPLOYED NOW?

IF SO, MAY WE INQUIRE
OF YOUR PRESENT EMPLOYER?

EVER APPLIED TO THIS COMPANY BEFORE?   WHERE?   WHEN?

EDUCATION	NAME AND LOCATION OF SCHOOL	NO. OF YEARS ATTENDED	DID YOU GRADUATE?	SUBJECTS STUDIED
COLLEGE				
HIGH SCHOOL				
GRAMMAR SCHOOL				
TRADE, BUSINESS, OR CORRESPONDENCE SCHOOL				

The Age Discrimination in Employment Act of 1967 prohibits discrimination on the basis of age with respect to individuals who are at least 40 years of age.

GENERAL

SUBJECTS OF SPECIAL STUDY OR RESEARCH WORK

U.S. MILITARY SERVICE
NAVAL SERVICE   RANK

PRESENT MEMBERSHIP IN
NATIONAL GUARD OR RESERVES

FORMER EMPLOYERS (LIST BELOW LAST FOUR EMPLOYERS, STARTING WITH LAST ONE FIRST).

DATE MONTH AND YEAR	NAME AND ADDRESS OF EMPLOYER	SALARY	POSITION	REASON FOR LEAVING
TO				
FROM				
TO				
FROM				
TO				
FROM				
TO				
FROM				

(CONTINUED ON OTHER SIDE)

REFERENCES: GIVE THE NAMES OF THREE PERSONS NOT RELATED TO YOU WHOM YOU HAVE KNOWN AT LEAST ONE YEAR.

	NAME	ADDRESS	BUSINESS	YEARS ACQUAINTED
1				
2				
3				

PHYSICAL RECORD: DO YOU HAVE ANY PHYSICAL LIMITATIONS THAT PRECLUDE YOU FROM PERFORMING ANY WORK FOR WHICH YOU ARE BEING CONSIDERED? ☐ YES ☐ NO

PLEASE DESCRIBE:

IN CASE OF
EMERGENCY NOTIFY

NAME	ADDRESS	PHONE NO.

I CERTIFY THAT THE FACTS CONTAINED IN THIS APPLICATION ARE TRUE AND COMPLETE TO THE BEST OF MY KNOWLEDGE AND UNDERSTAND THAT, IF EMPLOYED, FALSIFIED STATEMENTS ON THIS APPLICATION SHALL BE GROUNDS FOR DISMISSAL.

I AUTHORIZE INVESTIGATION OF ALL STATEMENTS CONTAINED HEREIN AND THE REFERENCES LISTED ABOVE TO GIVE YOU ANY AND ALL INFORMATION CONCERNING MY PREVIOUS EMPLOYMENT AND ANY PERTINENT INFORMATION THEY MAY HAVE, PERSONAL OR OTHERWISE, AND RELEASE ALL PARTIES FROM ALL LIABILITY FOR ANY DAMAGE THAT MAY RESULT FROM FURNISHING SAME TO YOU.

DATE   SIGNATURE

DO NOT WRITE BELOW THIS LINE

INTERVIEWED BY   DATE

HIRED: YES   NO   POSITION   DEPT.

SALARY/WAGE   DATE REPORTING TO WORK

APPROVED   1.   2.   3.

| EMPLOYMENT MANAGER | DEPT. HEAD | GENERAL MANAGER |

Illustration 18-9

To avoid errors when filling out a job application, consider your answer and the space available before writing the information requested.

Letter of Application

If you apply for a job through the mail, it is appropriate to send a letter of introduction with your resume. This letter is called a **letter of application.** It is easy to write and is important. The application letter will create the first impression of you by the employer. The letter must be

- keyed and formatted so that it is easy to read

- organized logically and look clean and neat

- keyed accurately on 8 1/2" x 11" quality paper

There are seven steps to writing a successful letter of application. Refer to Illustration 18-10 to see how the letter is set up.

Step 1:   **Your Address.** Include your street address, name of city, state, and ZIP Code.

Step 2:   **Date:** The month, day, and year of the writing of the letter.

Step 3:   **Inside Address and Salutation.** Include where the letter is going and to whom. A greeting to the person receiving the letter is called the **salutation.** If you do not know who will receive the letter, use a general salutation, such as Dear Personnel Director. If you know the name of the personnel director, use it.

Step 4:   **First Paragraph of the Letter.** Explain why you are writing the letter. Keep your statements simple. You are writing the letter to apply for a job. Tell the reader where you learned of the job opening.

2455 Winding Way **(STEP #1)**
Lincoln, NE 68506-4324
(Current Date) **(STEP #2)**

Personnel Office
Extra Value Supermarket **(STEP #3)**
P.O. Box 832
Lincoln, NE 68506

Dear Personnel Director:

The position you advertised for an inventory clerk in the Sunday edition of the *Lincoln Star* is of interest to me. Please consider me an applicant. **(STEP #4)**

I have had experience in the grocery store business. I am presently working the customer service desk at Sumner's Grocery Store. My duties include cashing checks, selling postage stamps, helping customers find products, and ordering special products requested by customers. I have had formal training in data entry. **(STEP #5)**

If you are interested in interviewing me, I would be happy to come in and discuss the inventory clerk position at your convenience. My telephone number is 555-5432. Plesae call me any day before 1 p.m. **(STEP #6)**

Sincerely, **(STEP #7)**

(Sign the letter in this space.)

Twila McDonald

Illustration 18-10
Sample letter of application.

Step 5:   **Second Paragraph of the Letter.** Write two or three sentences about yourself that you think will be important to the employer. Give only information about yourself that is related to the job for which you are applying.

Step 6:   **Final Paragraph of the Letter.** Ask for an interview. Tell the reader where, when, and how to reach you.

Step 7:   **Closing.** Use a business closing to the letter. A good closing would be *Sincerely*. Sign the letter.

Be sure to proofread your letter of application. Mistakes are not acceptable!

Job Interview

This is your big chance. You have submitted your letter of application and a resume and have completed an application form. The employer is interested in you or he or she would not have taken the time to schedule an interview.

Preparing for the Interview

Learn all you can about the company before you go for the interview. If you have had any contact with the company or ever used one of its products, be prepared to say something positive about it. Be truthful.

Have the things you may need at the interview ready to take with you. These include your social security card, a pen and pencil, an extra copy of your resume, and a list of your references. Place your resume and references in a file folder or envelope to keep them fresh.

Critical Thinking

Think about...
the image you want to present at your next job interview.

Appearance is an important aspect of your interview presentation.

Photo by Jim Whitmer

Critical Thinking

Think about...

what you would do if an interviewer stopped asking you questions and began to fidget with papers on the desk.

Consider your personal appearance as you prepare for the interview. The clothes you select should be based on the type of job for which you are interviewing. If you are applying for a construction job or factory work, you may want to wear neat, clean work clothes. If you are applying for an office or sales job, wear business attire. Men should wear a dress shirt, slacks, and a tie. Women should wear a dress, suit, or skirt and blouse. If you are in doubt as to what to wear, walk by the business and see what is being worn by employees as they leave work or go to lunch. Dress as the employees dress and you cannot go wrong.

If the qualifications of two people are equal, the employer will be inclined to hire the applicant who best presented himself or herself.

Interview Questions

Be prepared to answer the standard interview questions. (S-6 ee Illustration 18-11.) Your answers should be complete and honest and consistent with the information you have provided in your letter of application, resume, and application. Remember, these questions may or may not be asked. Each employer has his or her own set of questions.

STANDARD INTERVIEW QUESTIONS

Are you looking for temporary or permanent work?

What do you want to be doing in five years?

Why do you want to work for this company?

How did you become interested in this company?

What jobs have you held? Why did you leave those jobs?

Do you prefer working alone or with others?

What are your strengths? What are your weaknesses?

What do you like to do in your spare time?

What makes you think you can do this job?

Illustration 18-11
Interview questions.

You may want to have a friend ask you the standard interview questions as practice for the real interview.

The Interview Process

The interview is a chance for the interviewer to meet you. You have prepared yourself, and you will interview well. Be on time. You

Get comfortable, get organized, and talk honestly and freely to the interviewer.

should arrive at least five minutes before your scheduled interview. Go to the interview alone!

Introducing Yourself. Introduce yourself to whomever is in the reception area of the hiring office. Speak loudly enough to be heard, and do not forget to *smile*! The person in the reception area will take you to meet the interviewer. Introduce yourself to the interviewer and speak confidently. Use the interviewer's name if possible. For example, say, "Good morning, Mr. Jones. I'm Twila McDonald." Do not offer to shake hands unless the interviewer offers first. However, be ready to shake hands. When shaking hands, grasp the interviewer's hand firmly. Limp handshakes are not impressive.

Don't sit until you are offered a seat. When you sit, be relaxed but sit straight in the chair. No slouching allowed. Do not place any of your belongings on the employer's desk. Put your things beside you, in your lap, or on the floor.

Responding to Questions. As the interviewer begins asking questions, talk freely. Give more than just one-word or yes/no answers. For example, if you are asked what subject you enjoyed most in school, do not say, "English," and then stop. Say, "I enjoyed English because it provided me the opportunity to learn more about literature. I also enjoyed the opportunity to put my thoughts on paper." It is never appropriate to try and be cute by saying something like, "I enjoyed recess."

If you do not know an answer, say you do not know. Do not try to fake it. Be honest and sincere in answering all questions.

Listening during the interview is key for success. Listen so you understand each question. If you do not listen carefully and misinterpret a question, you may jump ahead and answer a question you have not heard.

> " Nobody ever listened himself out of a job. "
> —Calvin Coolidge

During the questions, keep your eyes on the interviewer and try to meet his or her eyes often. The following are absolutes in the interview setting:

- Keep your hands still.

- Never chew gum or smoke during an interview.

- Do not lean over the interviewer's desk.

- Never read or give the impression you are reading items on the interviewer's desk.

- Keep a pleasant smile.

Asking Questions. The interviewer will probably give you a chance to ask questions toward the end of the interview. Be prepared. If you are not, you will appear disinterested in the job. All of your questions should be related to the job. Some sample questions might include

What are the working hours?

Is there an opportunity to work overtime?

What training does the company provide?

If nothing has been said about salary, it is appropriate to ask what the salary is for the position. However, this should not be the *first* question you ask.

Be sure that the questions you ask have not been answered previously at another point in the interview.

Closing the Interview. Your cue to depart from the interview is when the questions stop and you have no more questions. If you have not been offered the job, ask when you will be notified of the interviewer's decision. Thank the interviewer for his or her time and leave. You may offer to shake hands.

Follow-Up

After the interview, there is one more opportunity for you to impress the interviewer. Write him or her a thank-you letter. The letter will bring your name to the mind of the interviewer again. The letter should be brief, neat, well-written, and keyed or handwritten. Simply thank the interviewer for his or her time. Mention that you are interested in the position (if you are). If you forgot to say something in the interview about one of your qualifications, you can mention it in the follow-up letter.

The thank-you letter should be sent even if you do not want the position. You want to stay on good terms with all employers. Send

Do not be afraid to walk into a business and ask for an application.

Prepare a resume to advertise yourself to others. The resume should include the following:

1. Personal information

2. An objective (optional)

3. Work experience

4. Personal interests

5. References (or references available upon request)

Special care should be taken when you complete an application form for any position. Be sure that you are prepared to complete the form, that you answer all questions truthfully, and that you take special care to do neat work. The employer can tell a lot about you by how you complete the form.

A letter of application should be sent when you are applying for a position by mail. The letter must be keyed and well prepared. Be sure you proofread your application letter. Mistakes are not acceptable.

The job interview is your chance to shine. Prepare for the interview by:

1. Finding out all you can about the company.

2. Planning what you are going to wear.

3. Reviewing standard interview questions.

4. Preparing questions that you wish to ask.

5. Being on time.

After the interview, follow up with a thank-you letter to the person who interviewed you. Thank-you letters may be keyed or handwritten and should be sent the day after the interview.

your letter the day after the interview. Illustration 18-12 shows a[ple thank-you letter.

2455 Winding Way
Lincoln, NE 68506-4324
(Current Date)

Mr. Don R. Wilcoxson
Personnel Department
Extra Value Supermarket
P.O. Box 832
Lincoln, NE 68506

Dear Mr. Wilcoxson:

Thank you for the time you spent with me yesterday discussing the inventory clerk job at Extra Value. I appreciated your making the extra effort to show me around the store. The store is beautiful and looks like a very pleasant place to work. I am very much interested in the position.

I look forward to hearing from you about the hiring decision soon.

Sincerely,

Twila McDonald

Illustration 18-12
Sample thank-you letter.

Summary

Finding enjoyable and satisfying work is a tough job. Prepare f[the job campaign by listing your qualifications and interests. Focus your search based on these lists. Also, consider your natural talent and abilities known as aptitudes. You can examine your aptitudes completing an aptitude test and listening to others tell you about y strengths.

Once you have determined your qualifications, interests, and ap tudes, you need to begin looking at resources that will help you fi employment. Let everyone you know or meet that you are looking a job. People can be a valuable job resource. Read the help-wante ads in the newspaper. Visit your state employment agency or a pri employment agency. Keep in mind that a private agency is a for-p business and fees may be charged.

Check with government offices, school placement services, temp rary work agencies, and bulletin boards that post job opportunities

End of Chapter Activities

Questions and Projects

1. Prepare an inventory list of your qualifications and interests. Put them in a format similar to the one shown in Illustration 18-2.

2. Prepare a well-organized resume. The resume should be printed on quality paper. Be sure the resume is accurate and complete. This resume should be one that you could use in applying for any job.

3. Prepare a letter of application for the following ad you read in the *Los Angeles Times*. Assume that the position meets your qualifications, aptitude, and interests

> **Well-groomed person** desiring to work F/T as host or hostess in upscale restaurant. Exp nec. Perm with flexible hrs. No wkend work. Available immed. Write the mgr at Bon Appetite, 28 Longacre Road, Carlsbad, CA 92008

4. What is the advantage of using a state employment agency? What services may be provided by them? Call your state employment agency and see what services it provides.

5. Schedule an interview with a private employment agency and find out what services and advantages they offer. Report your findings to the class.

6. If you were applying for the position in Project 3, who would you list as references?

7. Prepare a list of questions you would ask at the interview at the Bon Appetite restaurant. (Project 3).

8. List three to five things you will want to do as you prepare for an interview.

9. What information and items will you need to take with you to an interview?

Case Problems

1. In the Wrong Place

Sue Ellen graduated from high school and was eager to go to work. She took an aptitude test before leaving high school, and she completed an inventory of her qualifications and interests. After a good look at herself, she decided that she would like to work in a health occupation. She applied for a position at a hospital. The only work available was a job in the diet kitchen. Sue Ellen accepted the job without applying anywhere else. After two months on the job, she was miserable. The job required that she work a split shift 5 a.m. to 9 a.m. and 4 p.m. to 8 p.m. She had no contact with patients. She found little job satisfaction in filling trays and placing them on carts to be sent to patients.

   a. What mistake(s) did Sue Ellen make in selecting the job?

   b. Should Sue Ellen stay with the job?

   c. Should Sue Ellen try to find other work within the hospital?

   d. What additional information would you like to have available to you in order to further assist Sue Ellen?

2. Finding a Future

Gregg graduated from high school and spent a year in a community college studying drafting, but he did not complete the program. He was a waiter at a restaurant for a few months but quit the job because he did not like the work. Gregg was fired from a job at a recreation center for being continuously late to work. Now he is working for a temporary job service but not earning enough money to be on his own.

   a. What suggestions would you make to Gregg about his future in the work world?

   b. Do you think Gregg's situation is unusual? Why or why not?

   c. Should Gregg list the recreation center on his resume?

3. First Impressions

Audra applied for a position in an advertising firm. She read the ad in the local paper, and she met the qualifications. She called and set an interview time. She selected from her wardrobe a short, red spandex dress and sandals. She decided to forget about printing a resume; they probably would not look at it anyway. Audra arrived a few minutes late for the interview. Her boyfriend came in with her as he did not want to wait in the car. She knew that the firm was looking for maturity, so she decided to smoke during the interview. She forgot to prepare any questions for the interviewer. At the close of the interview, she was told that her qualifications were acceptable and that she would be informed of her status as a candidate within a few days.

    a. Do you think Audra got the job? Why or why not?

    b. What suggestions would you have for Audra for the next interview?

    c. What do you think about her decision to "forget about" the resume?

    d. What other information would you like to know about Audra in order to assist her in getting employment?

Keeping The Job

Y olanda was very excited. She had conducted a good job campaign, interviewed for a position at St. Elizabeth Hospital, and landed a job in the accounting office. Yolanda felt sure that this was the job she wanted. She arrived at work a few minutes ahead of time on her first day. Her coworkers greeted her warmly and promised to help her get accustomed to the routine of the accounting office. Her supervisor began giving her directions immediately. She answered her telephone, took notes about the messages, and promised to get back to the callers when she could locate the information. She dropped a box of files and had to spend about 30 minutes re-alphabetizing them and making sure that everything went back into the right file. By 5 p.m. she was near tears. It seemed as if there was so much to learn, and everything was taking place faster than she could absorb what was to be done. One of her coworkers, Jorge, walked out to the parking lot with her and said, "I'm sure this was a confusing day for you. I remember my first day. I thought I would never catch on to everything. Each day got a little easier, and now I find myself looking forward to the new challenges of each day. See you tomorrow." Yolanda took a deep breath and said, "Thanks. I'll look forward to it." Yolanda recognized that her earlier concerns were normal for the first day on a new job. Things would get better and she would succeed on this job!

Objectives

After completing this chapter, you should be able to:

1.
Prepare for the first day on the job.

2.
Identify the elements essential for keeping a job.

3.
Describe the importance of understanding the rules of a company.

4.
Describe the work habits essential for keeping a job.

5.
Discuss the importance of valuing and accepting the differences of others.

First-Day Events

Your first day on the job is an important one. You will never get a second chance to make a first impression, so make it a good one. Everyone is nervous on his or her first day. You are eager to get started and show you have the knowledge and skills to do the job. However, you will probably spend most of your first day with personnel department staff. You will fill out employment forms and get information about the company and your benefit options.

Employment Forms

You should be prepared to show your social security card. Every month a portion of your paycheck will be put into a federal Social Security account called FICA, an abbreviation for Federal Insurance Contributions Act. Your employer matches this sum by putting in an equal amount in your account.

You will also complete a Form W-4 Employee's Withholding Allowance Certificate. This form authorizes the company to withhold money from your paycheck to pay your federal and state income taxes. The amount withheld from your check depends on your income level, your marital status, and the number of allowances (dependents) you claim.

You will also complete insurance forms and learn about the benefit package provided by your company.

Shelley was anxious about her first day at her new job. She was eager to get to work. When she arrived at her new workplace, she reported to the personnel department. She completed her Form W-4 and insurance forms and listened to the personnel director explain the fringe benefit package of the company. She was then taken to her workstation and introduced to her supervisor, who walked her through the entire facility so that she could get a picture of the full operation. The supervisor showed her where to clock in and the location of the restrooms and cafeteria. He talked about the company rules as he took Shelley around the company. They then went to his office where Shelley was given a company handbook and a briefing on company rules, policies, and safety procedures. They went back to Shelley's workstation, and her supervisor introduced two of her coworkers. Shelley glanced at her watch and realized she had been on the job for four hours and had not yet begun to work. This could be a typical first few hours on the job.

Introductions

You will meet your supervisor and some of your coworkers during your first day on the job. Make sure you appear competent and professional. Suggestions for the first day:

- Make sure your appearance is neat and clean. People notice your hair, teeth, complexion, eyes, and most of all your smile.

- Walk with confidence.

- If meeting someone for the first time, offer a *firm*, dry handshake.

- When you meet someone, you might say, "I'm very happy to meet you" or "I look forward to working with you." Do not hesitate to introduce yourself to others. You can simply say, "Hi, I'm Yolanda Doe. I just started working in the accounting department." The others will then automatically introduce themselves.

Job Description

A **job description** is a written explanation of the tasks to be performed on a specific job. This is your guide to knowing what is expected of you. Your supervisor will probably review the job description with you on your first day on the job. Read through the description, making sure you understand each task to be performed. If you have questions, ask your supervisor. You may want to take the job description home and read it more thoroughly.

Rules Of The Job

Rules for employees are a little different in every company. A new employee learns these rules and makes every effort to comply with them. The rules of the company are most often found in an employee handbook. If you do not understand a rule, ask your supervisor about it. If you choose to work for a small company, such a handbook may not be available to you. This, however, does not mean there are no rules. You will need to ask about them.

The excuse "I didn't know about the rule" is never acceptable. Learn the rules of your workplace and follow them.

General Policies and Rules

Some of the rule topics you will want to inquire about immediately are

- Expected working hours

- Breaks and meal arrangements

- Personal use of company equipment—telephones, fax machines, copiers

- Family, vacation, sick, and other leave policies

- Smoking policy on company property

- Who to call if you are ill

Some of these basic policies and rules may have been explained to you at the interview. If not, be sure you ask about the policies before the end of your first work day.

Safety Rules

In addition to the general rules, a company may also have safety rules that are published and posted for all employees. You may be required to wear safety shoes and glasses or a helmet. Your company must enforce the rules to meet government safety standards and insurance requirements. Also, they want to take care of *you*.

Observe all safety rules. These rules are for your protection.

Bohdan Hrynewych/Stock, Boston

"Understood" Rules

Some rules are not written, but rather they are "understood." It is wise to learn these rules quickly and follow them. For example, a company may prefer that no one wear jeans to work. This is not a written policy or rule. It is simply not done in the company. You will learn these unwritten rules by observing and listening. Other rules are ones that you instinctively know. For example, *be on time*. This rule is not written; it is expected. Your employer and your coworkers depend on you being at work on time. Return to work on time after breaks and lunch. You are expected to give an honest day's work for a day's pay.

Work Environment

Once you begin working, you will need to be aware of the environment around you. This work environment includes physical aspects, such as your work area as well as other aspects, such as work habits and workplace politics.

Work Area

Your employer is required to provide a safe place for you to work. You are responsible for keeping your work area in good condition. If there is a problem with your area, you will need to tell the supervisor so the problem can be corrected. If you share your work area with coworkers, you must respect their rights and feelings in order to help maintain a good work environment for everyone.

Good Work Habits

Establish good work habits from the beginning of your new employment. This list of habits will start you off on the right foot with your employer.

- Do not waste supplies.

- Take orders and follow directions willingly.

- Follow the "understood rules."

- Dress appropriately for the type of work you are doing.

- Be pleasant and friendly.

Workplace Politics

You will need to keep on top of and understand workplace politics if you want to keep your position. **Workplace politics** is an undefined force in an organization that develops because people want to protect themselves or gain power. The "politicking" that goes on is usually done to benefit an individual rather than to benefit the organization.

Think about a regular political campaign. What do the candidates usually talk about? They talk about their good characteristics or record. Candidates also talk about their opponents' bad characteristics. Workplace politics is very similar to what goes on in political campaigns. People talk about their good personal qualities and talk disrespectfully about their supervisors, coworkers, and company officials. You cannot ignore these aspects of your work environment.

Some parts of workplace politics can be helpful. For example, as an employee, you are expected to be part of a team. Through your teammates you can learn about the unwritten rules and sensitive topics.

Unfortunately people tend to get involved in workplace politics that are unproductive and even destructive to the work environment. Gossip is a part of workplace politics. You may want to refer to Chapter 8, page 123, and reread the section relating to gossip and the rumor mill.

The best way to handle workplace politics is to stay neutral. That means you do not take sides. Be courteous and concerned about all of your coworkers, and concentrate on doing your job well.

Employment Insurance

There are several characteristics that you will want to exhibit to ensure that you keep your job. These characteristics are discussed in the following paragraphs.

Do Your Best

Your employer and coworkers expect you to do the job you were hired to do. Doing your job to the best of your ability has another benefit. It allows you to feel good about yourself and build your self-esteem. Self-esteem is necessary for job success.

Do not do just what you are told. Employees who truly do their best notice other jobs that need to be done. They do the little *extras* without being told. Put effort and energy into whatever you do on the job. The process of starting a task or project without being told to do so is called showing **initiative**.

❝ Knowledge of human nature is the beginning and end of political education. **❞**
—Henry Brooks Adams

Critical
Thinking

Think about...

how workplace politics is similar to a political campaign. Have you experienced this at work or school? How did you respond?

❝ Have confidence that if you have done a *little* thing well, you can do a *bigger* thing well, too. **❞**
—Moorfield Storey

| DOING YOUR BEST = |
| Approval by Your Coworkers |
| Approval by Your Supervisor |
| Employment Insurance |
| Improved Level of Self-Esteem |

Illustration 19-1
The benefits of doing your best.

Quantity of Work

The amount of work you produce in some positions is very important. In fact, in some positions you may be paid by the amount of work you produce. Your employer is looking for quality work done in an efficient manner.

Look for Ways to Improve

After you are comfortable and feel competent doing your job, look for new knowledge or skills that you can master. Watch the experienced workers do their jobs. Ask them to show you how to do some advanced tasks. Do not be afraid to ask for new, challenging assignments and opportunities.

Let your supervisor know when you are willing to take on additional responsibilities. However, before you do this, be *sure* you are doing an excellent job on your present duties. If opportunities for extra training are made available, sign up. The more you learn and do on the job, the more valuable you are to your employer.

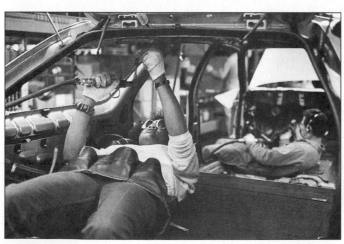

Strive for quality work, even when performing jobs paid based on the amount you produce.

Photo by Richard Younker

Accept Responsibility for Your Job

You will make mistakes because you are human. Do not be afraid to admit your mistakes, but be sure that you learn from your mistakes. Whatever you do, do not try to hide your mistakes or blame them on someone else. Accept responsibility for your work and your errors. You will gain respect from your coworkers and your supervisor when you do.

Dale had been on his new job for two weeks. His job was to check all invoices against the merchandise received at the Arnold Manufacturing Company. He was enjoying his work and meeting all expectations of his supervisor. One morning the receiving dock was extremely busy, and Dale did not take the time to check the invoice of materials received from Twin Rivers Electronics. He signed the invoice for the driver and just put the merchandise aside. When things quieted down later in the day, Dale took a look at the invoice. He realized that four items had not been a part of the shipment, but he had signed a sheet saying that the order was complete. Dale immediately went to his supervisor, explained his error, and asked what steps should be taken to correct the error. The supervisor said, "Thanks for catching the error. We only want to pay for what we receive. No matter how busy you are always take time to check the invoices. I'll call Twin Rivers Electronics and inform them of the shortage. Thanks for bringing the mistake to my attention."

Have a Good Attitude

The "can do" attitude shows you believe in your own ability to succeed. This type of attitude will help you accomplish your assigned job tasks to the best of your ability.

Employers can teach you the skills you need. Good attitudes, on the other hand, must be developed by *you*. Illustration 19-2 lists some signs of a good attitude. This would be a good checklist to review every week that you are on the job.

Accept Criticism Positively

You must be prepared to accept suggestions and criticism on the job. Criticism is suggestive remarks about your job performance. In Chapter 6 you read that criticism is a form of self-improvement. If no one points out what you are doing wrong, you cannot improve. Respond to criticism in a positive way. Do not overreact and assume that you are a failure. Tell yourself you can and will continue to improve.

Critical
Thinking

Think about...
how many signs of a
good attitude you pos-
sess. What areas can
you strengthen and
how?

SIGNS OF A GOOD ATTITUDE

_____ +Listens to suggestions.

_____ +Desires to please.

_____ +Gives a day's work for a day's pay.

_____ +Does not make excuses for errors.

_____ +Respects the opinions of others.

_____ +Tries to see things from the point of view of others.

_____ +Is willing to change.

_____ +Seldom complains.

_____ +Helps others.

_____ +Smiles often.

Illustration 19-2
Checklist for signs of a good attitude.

66 Criticism should be
a plow that plows a
furrow only to sow in
it seeds that will
grow. 99
—Jerome P. Fleishman

Keep a Good Sense of Humor

You have read in earlier chapters about the importance of a sense of humor for fitting in and getting along in the workplace. Having a sense of humor includes being able to laugh at yourself. Know how and *when* to use humor in the workplace. Do not take yourself so seriously that you forget how to laugh. Showing a sense of humor does not include telling jokes that hurt or degrade others or telling jokes that are crude. A person who tells these kinds of jokes is not held in high regard by coworkers or supervisors. Demonstrating a sense of humor does not mean continually telling jokes, acting silly, or attempting to be the "company clown." You could get a few laughs from coworkers, but they may begin to see you only as a clown. Worse yet, your supervisors might see you as a goof-off.

Getting Along with Others

Chapters 4, 5, and 6 were devoted to fitting in and getting along with coworkers and supervisors. You may want to reread these chapters as you think about the topic of "keeping the job." Getting along with all types of people can be tough. It takes patience and under-standing. Accept people and their differences. When you accept someone, you create a beginning point for building a good relation-ship with that person. For example, if you and a coworker belong to different races, simply accept that as fact and value that difference.

To work well together, employees need to appreciate each other's differences.

Valuing individual differences means accepting people who are different, taking a positive attitude toward their differences, learning from others who are different, and recognizing that *similarities* are more important than *differences*. You will have coworkers different from you in gender, race, mental ability, physical condition, age, religion, geographic origin, education, ethnic heritage, culture, and lifestyle.

It is important to value differences on the job because it creates a good work environment. It benefits the business and the employees because satisfied workers are productive and happy workers, and it is the law.

Businesses are required by law to provide equal employment opportunities to all employees without regard to race, color, religion, gender, national origin, age, disability, or veteran status. In addition to such legal requirements, company values usually dictate that employees treat each other fairly and with respect.

Summary

Once you have a job that matches your qualifications, aptitudes, and interests, you need to take special care to see that you succeed on that job and keep it. Good jobs can be hard to find.

Your first day on the job is an important one as you will be making a first impression on your supervisor and coworkers. The first day you will complete employment forms and be introduced to your supervisor and coworkers. Also, the first day will be your opportunity to be introduced to the rules, including the understood rules and the safety rules of your company. Be sure that you understand the rules and clarify any questions you may have.

To keep your position, you will need to establish good work habits that include not wasting supplies, taking orders and following directions willingly, being punctual, dressing appropriately, and being pleasant and friendly. Pay attention to workplace politics and take a neutral position. Other characteristics that you will want to exhibit include the following:

1. Do your best.

2. Produce an acceptable amount of work.

3. Look for ways to improve.

4. Accept responsibility for your job.

5. Realize that you will make mistakes. Admit them.

6. Keep a good attitude.

7. Accept criticism positively.

8. Keep a good sense of humor.

9. Accept your coworkers and value their differences.

Welcome to the world of work!

End of Chapter Activities

Questions and Projects

1. Obtain a current copy of a Form W-4 and review the contents of the form. Determine how you would complete the form.

2. Visit a manufacturing organization in your area and ask to see copies of the safety rules of the company. Also, ask to see the safety warnings, lines, and precautions that are in place in the company.

3. Describe a situation in a workplace or in your daily routine where you have demonstrated initiative.

4. Write down three greetings that you could use as you are introduced to coworkers on your first day at work.

5. What would you do if you were satisfied with the work you were doing and wanted to learn some additional knowledge or skills to enhance your work or to do additional work?

6. Determine whether the following statements are true or false:

a. Coworkers should not take a positive attitude about their differences.

b. Sharing your traditions and customs with coworkers means that both of you will better understand each other.

c. To value differences in the workplace, coworkers need to accept people who are different.

d. Coworkers' differences are more important than their similarities.

Case Problems

1. **Discrimination?**

Sandra, an employee at General Stores, Inc., works as an inventory clerk. Her coworkers are Cindy, Ray, and Josefina. Their responsibilities are equal. They are expected to work well together and keep an accurate inventory of all products stocked by General Stores. Sandra is the newest clerk. Sandra feels that she is a quality employee and that the quantity of work she does is exceptional. Cindy is an older employee who has 18 years of experience. Sandra gets very frustrated with Cindy because she does not move as quickly as Sandra, and Sandra feels that Cindy is often in her way. Sandra frequently gives looks of disgust at Cindy, and her body language toward Cindy is very negative. Sandra has told Ray and Josefina on several occasions that she thinks Cindy is too old to be in her position. She also makes remarks about Cindy's weight as being a deterrent to her ability to move swiftly and climb up ladders to check on merchandise.

a. In your opinion is Sandra guilty of discriminating against a coworker?

b. If you were Sandra's supervisor and you became aware of her feelings, what would you do? What problems could you experience if you ignore the situation?

c. What qualification does Cindy have that Sandra may be overlooking?

d. If you were Ray or Josefina, what might you say to Sandra when she makes negative remarks about Cindy?

2. Dilemma

Salvador arrives at his first day of work for Heritage Home Builders, Inc. He reports to the office of Heritage. The only person at the site is the secretary. She gives Salvador a Form W-4 and then asks him if he wants to sign up for the insurance program. Salvador signs the Form W-4. However, because he does not understand the insurance program, he does not sign those forms. The secretary tells him that he is to report to a job site at 434 Lyncrest Avenue. Salvador drives to Lyncrest Avenue and finds one other employee who is roofing the house. Salvador introduces himself to the employee. The employees says, "Hello. I guess you're supposed to help me." Salvador applied for the position of a house framer, but with a little direction from his coworker, he begins roofing. Salvador's boss arrives at the site at about 11:30 a.m. He introduces himself to Salvador and says, "Glad to have you with us," and leaves the work site.

a. What information does Salvador not have at the end of his first day?

b. What questions would you have at the end of the day if you were Salvador?

c. How should Salvador go about finding the information he needs to know?

Moving Ahead In Your Career

Monica graduated from high school with honors. She did not want to go on for advanced education right away. She wanted to go to work and do some career exploration. Monica took a job as flagperson on a road crew. She did not like it and quit. She tried working at a day-care center and did not like it. She worked in an office for a few weeks as a temporary and became very bored with the job. After a couple of years and many unsatisfying job experiences, Monica decided it was time to put some focus on her future. She worked with an employment counselor, established her qualifications and goals, and through testing determined her aptitudes. Monica soon had developed a strategy to reach her new career goal—a physical therapist. Monica volunteered in a local hospital while she worked on the educational requirements for this position. She worked part time as an aide in a physical therapy office. Monica felt good about herself as she was finally on a career path.

A Vision For Your Future

This chapter encourages you to develop a vision of a career. The vision can become reality if you plan and prepare to be successful in your present position and in the various jobs that will become part of your career path. A **career path** is a plan that you can follow that will lead to a position with more responsibility

Objectives

After completing this chapter, you should be able to:

1.
Define a career path.

2.
Plan a career strategy.

3.
Implement your career plans.

4.
Conduct yourself professionally in a performance appraisal.

5.
Prepare for a job raise or promotion.

6.
Determine if and when you should change jobs.

or satisfaction. Success in a career consists of discovering your potential and developing it. It includes making the most of what you have to offer an employer, of sharpening your skills and remaining abreast of what is new in your chosen career. Your on-the-job hours should be satisfying—adding to your self-fulfillment and contributing to your professional growth and personal happiness. If you are happy during your hours at work, your overall mental and emotional health will be enriched.

Visualize Success In Your Career

There are no shortcuts to success. There are no substitutes for planning if you want a satisfying career. Having a plan does not guarantee success, but planning by setting goals greatly improves your chances. Visualize where you want to be in your career in 10 years, in 20 years, and at retirement. One of your life goals should be moving ahead in your career to reach your full potential.

You read in Chapter 2 about the importance of goal setting. Goals are the steps you must take to get from where you are to where you want to be. Now it is time to visualize the success you want to enjoy and develop a strategy to reach success. Remember, a strategy is a plan of action to reach your goals.

Career Goals

The most common reason that people do not reach their goals is because they never set them. Having your goals in mind is not enough. Your goals need to be in writing. If your goals are in writing, you can refer to them, you can review them, and you can stay on track because of them. Put your goals in a place where you can see them every day.

Be Specific. To be meaningful your career goals must be specific. For example, perhaps you think you would like a career driving a truck. The goal "I want to drive a truck" is not specific enough. The goal might be "I want a steady job driving a semitrailer truck across the country for a large, well-established trucking company." Having specific goals makes it easier for you to plan your strategy for success.

Be Realistic. Your goals must be realistic. Not everyone can be a brain surgeon, a criminal lawyer, a professional football player, or the owner of a Fortune 500 company. If you are 5'2" and weigh 103 pounds, you will probably never play football for the Dallas Cowboys. You need to look closely at your interests, abilities, and aptitudes as you set realistic career goals.

66 Life is too short to be unhappy in business. If business were not a part of the joy of living, we might almost say that we have no right to live, because it is a pretty poor man who cannot get into the line for which he is fitted. 99
—George L. Brown

66 Vision is always a long view into the future as well as a fresh insight into the facts of the present. 99

66 Aim at your career as the archer aims at the target. 99

Be Honest. Your goals should be what you really want to do. Do not put down on paper things you think you should do or list careers that others think you should work toward. If you put down a goal just because you think it will impress or please others, you will have trouble meeting that goal. Be sure your career goal is one you want to meet.

Goal Planning

Your goal will be specific, realistic, and honestly stated. Recognize that this career goal will be a long-range goal. The career goal will not be attainable tomorrow, next week, or even next year. Think big; think long term! You are planning a lifetime career.

Short- and Medium-Range Goals

You will need to set and write down short- and medium-range goals as stepping stones to meeting your long-range goals. Setting short- and medium-range goals is the second step in your strategy to make your career plan happen. These goals keep you on track.

For example, if your long-term goal is to be a head nurse in a large community hospital in the pediatrics ward, your short-term goal might be to arrange for some volunteer work with sick children in a local

Volunteering is another learning process.

©Spencer Grant/Photo Researchers

Critical
Thinking

Think about...

your long-term goals. Develop short- and medium-range goals to help you reach your future.

hospital. A medium-range goal might be to find a good paying job in the health field as you work toward acquiring the education you will need to be a nurse.

Can Goals Change?

You may need to change your goals because of life circumstances. You may need to change a goal because of poor health or a family situation. Changes in the workplace may also take place. Career fields can shift in this rapidly changing technological world. You may move far beyond your expectations and exceed your goal earlier than planned. If changes occur, you need to set a new long-term career goal. You may want to develop a Plan A and a Plan B to be sure that you have well-established goals. Also, as you grow older, your priorities may change. Yes, your goals may change!

Energize Yourself

Once your goals are written, your job is *not* done. You have only just begun. As you plan for your future career, never neglect your present job. Your present job is important, you are building a reputation as a worker. You are gaining knowledge and skills, and you are making contacts that may be important to you as you move toward your goals.

" People have a way of becoming what you encourage them to be . . . "
—Johann Wolfgang von Goethe

Make Others Aware of Your Goals

Share your career goals with others. Share the goals with people who are supportive of you and who will encourage, push, and help you along the way. Sharing your goals with others will also increase your sense of responsibility, and you will have someone to help motivate you.

Use Self-Talk

Use positive self-talk to keep yourself on track toward accomplishing your career goal. You must believe in yourself. Believe you can accomplish your goals, and you *will* achieve your goals. If you prepared your goals realistically, specifically, and honestly, you know they are achievable. Look at yourself in the mirror as you check your progress toward your goals and say, "I can complete this short-range or medium-range goal, and I'll be a (state your long-range career goal)."

Whenever you are talking to yourself or others, use positive phrases when communicating your goals. Use phrases and words such as I can, I will, I will do, I look forward to.

Illustration 20-1
Phrases for positive career goal self-talk.

Avoid negative words and phrases such as I'll try, I can't, someday, maybe, impossible, I should do, or I have to. Positive words help communicate to others how important your career goal is to you.

Performance Appraisal

You will know how well you are doing on the job as a result of your performance appraisal. A **performance appraisal** is an official evaluation of your work. The evaluation is done by your supervisor. He or she may use a special form that is used for all employee performance evaluations. An appraisal is usually a chance for your supervisor to tell you your strengths and weaknesses on the job.

Discussing your weaknesses is meant to help you become a better worker. It is not meant as a way to pick on you or to reduce your level of self-esteem.

Both you and your supervisor can learn from the performance appraisal conference. This conference gives your supervisor a formal opportunity to talk about your job, its responsibilities, and its potential

Critical
Thinking

Think about...

the performance appraisal process. What value could this experience have for you personally and professionally?

A performance appraisal conference has benefits for both the employee and her supervisor.

for growth. Your supervisor can tell you how you fit in at the company, if you need extra training, and if you are making the best use of your skills. The evaluation session also gives you a chance to speak openly about your view of your job. Your supervisor will probably encourage you to talk about any problems you see with your job, to ask questions, to share changes you would like to see made, and to offer suggestions for the betterment of the company.

When your evaluation session is over, both you and your supervisor will sign the appraisal form. The original copy will become part of your permanent personnel file. You will get a copy for your records. As the appraisal form goes into your permanent file, it is important for you to make a good impression during the appraisal conference. The appraisal conference may determine future promotional opportunities for you. Workers who make an effort to improve their work are often rewarded with raises and promotions.

Raises And Promotions

Your short- and medium-range goals will include efforts to secure raises and promotions.

Requesting a Raise

In most companies your performance appraisal is directly related to any increase in pay you may receive. A good appraisal may result in a pay raise. If your company has no pattern set for salary increases, it may be appropriate for you to request a raise based upon a satisfactory performance evaluation. When you ask for a raise, the request should be based on your work and accomplishments. Do not talk about your financial need or obligations. Before you ask for a raise, think about your accomplishments of the past year. Be prepared to tell your supervisor

- what new responsibilities you have accepted since you were hired,
- what new skills you have acquired and are now using on the job, and
- how your work has made a special contribution to the company.

In other words, you need to justify why you feel you are worthy of a salary raise.

Consideration for a Promotion

Part of getting ahead on the job is going up the career path in your company. You can move up the career path by getting a promotion from one level to the next. Promotions usually come from getting a positive rating on your performance appraisal. The positive or glowing appraisal says you have proven your ability to accept more responsibility and to do more challenging work. In addition to doing well on the performance appraisal, the following steps will assist you in obtaining a promotion.

- Be the best at what you do.

- Set goals.

- Get to know the company and the promotion policies.

Do You Really Want the Promotion?

In most situations a promotion means that you will need to accept more responsibility. You do not have to accept a promotion just because it is offered to you. Be sure that you weigh the advantages and disadvantages of accepting a promotion. The promotion should be one that is in line with your set career goals. If the promotion is not in your plan, you have a decision to make. You will need to change your career goals or turn down the promotion.

66 Real leaders are ordinary people with extraordinary determination. *99*
—John Seaman Garns

Leadership

If you want to advance in your career, you must develop leadership qualities. Supervisors are leaders. **Leadership** is the ability to lead or direct others on a positive course. Effective leaders have traits that give them the ability to lead others. Do you have the traits listed in Illustration 20-2?

LEADERSHIP TRAITS

Leaders respect and support the rights of others.

Leaders communicate in a clear and understandable manner.

Leaders are competent, confident, and honest.

Leaders are open-minded.

Leaders are positive about the group's work.

Illustration 20-2
Leadership traits.

Regardless of your position with a company, you should work to exemplify the traits of a leader.

Changing Jobs

There may come a time when you consider changing your employment. This is a part of the career path climb. Changing jobs can be difficult because of the relationships you have developed and the security you feel within the job. Changing jobs is an important decision. Be sure you change jobs for the *right* reasons. The acceptable *right* reasons are listed in Illustration 20-3.

THE RIGHT REASONS FOR CHANGING JOBS

- Your current employer can offer no advancement for you.

- Your current job does not further your career goal.

- The economy causes layoffs.

- Your department or job is eliminated.

- You do not agree with the policies and goals of your company.

- You wish to move to a new geographic location.

- You have a changed career goal. This job does not fit into your plan.

Illustration 20-3
Reasons for changing jobs.

Do not quit your present job until you find a new one. Prepare a written list of reasons to either stay or leave your present position. Avoid rushing into a job change without doing some planning. Look at all aspects of any new job you consider. Another job or company may look good on the surface. Be careful. If you do not do your research, you could end up working with a difficult supervisor; you could be given a heavy, unpleasant workload; or you could find yourself in a position with no growth potential. A job change should not be taken lightly.

Choose Your Job Carefully

As you seek to build a satisfying career, do not sell yourself short just to obtain immediate employment. Your goal is to market your services for the best possible measure of job stimulation and challenge, security, appreciation, and other rewards. The most important question to ask yourself before accepting a new job is, "Does this position move me toward reaching my long-term career goal?" Other questions to consider before taking a new job include those listed in Illustration 20-4.

SHOULD I TAKE THE JOB

- How stable is the company?

- What is the reputation of the company?

- What opportunities are there for advancement?

- What are the policies for promotion in the company?

- Will I need more education if I remain with this company?

- What security does the position offer?

- Will the work be interesting and challenging enough for me?

- Do I have the interests, qualifications, and aptitudes for this position?

- Are there any negative characteristics about the job?

Illustration 20-4
Questions to ask before taking a job.

obuko has been offered a promotion that carries a $50 per week salary raise. Nobuko's new duties will require her to supervise ten people who are currently her coworkers. Her supervisory duties will include attending plant meetings two evenings per week on her own time. As a supervisor, she will not be eligible for overtime. Nobuko now holds a 40-hour per week job and is paid $9 per hour. She gets time and a half for overtime and typically puts in 44 to 48 hours per week. She carefully weighs the pros and cons of the promotion. The salary increase is insignificant, but she decides to take the supervisory position because it is in line with her career goal.

The best time to plan for advancement is before you take a job. One of the considerations to weigh is the job's possibilities for promotion. For example, a well-established firm may offer more security than advancement. A new firm, on the other hand, may provide rapid advancement to those employees who are promotion material; yet the position may be less stable than with the established firm. You will need to weigh your options; weigh one against the other.

If you are serious about advancement and reaching your established career goal, you should study the possible jobs to which you might be promoted. What other skills, abilities, and traits, in addition to those you now possess, are needed in the new job? Be willing to prepare yourself in these areas before asking for advancement.

Upgrading Your Skills

In this changing world, keeping up with the technical preparation in most jobs is a challenge. Your skills can become obsolete in short order. For example, you may have become proficient on a certain piece of equipment only to discover that your employer has installed an upgrade of the equipment you have been using. Or you may find that the methods, systems, and routines of a new position are entirely different from those you learned. What should you do?

Keep a Learning Attitude. A learning attitude means that you pay extra attention and ask questions about new tasks. Ask for demonstrations of new equipment or procedures. Pledge to yourself that you will remain flexible and accepting of change. You may want to make this pledge an ongoing part of your career goal.

Take Advantage of Training. On-the-job training may be offered to current employees needing to learn new skills, to new employees, or to employees who have been transferred into new positions. If such training is available, welcome the opportunity to learn something new. This will set you apart from the other employees. Learning

Take advantage of the opportunity to learn new skills by enrolling in classes.

something new is a guaranteed way of improving your vigor, effectiveness, and security.

If after you have been working in a firm for several years and there are promotional opportunities available, you may want to be considered for advancement. If that is the case, you might be asked to take some sort of advanced training. Special training is usually needed before a worker is promoted to a supervisory post. If such an honor should come to you, be aware of the benefits such training will bring. For example, you may be given help in developing your leadership qualities, in planning your work, or in evaluating your work and the work of others. This type of training is sure to be helpful to you through all your working life.

Self-Training

You have a responsibility to your employer and to yourself to upgrade your skills and knowledge whenever possible.

Reading. Reading has been an educational tool for thousands of self-made business leaders. If you have not developed the regular reading habit, decide to become knowledgeable in some area of interest that is job related. Get a book or two on the subject from the public library; then start reading. It will help if you set aside a special time for reading of this type. Reading will increase your vocabulary as well as your knowledge.

❝A mind expanded never returns to its original boundaries. ❞

Reading and studying about your chosen field of interest can be a boost to your promotion possibilities.

A. Teufen/H. Armstrong Roberts

Do not overlook professional magazines and periodicals. There are magazines devoted to hundreds of career topics; choose one that relates to your work, subscribe to it, and faithfully read it. Serious reading is a positive, addictive habit that is good for you. Educational videos may also be available at your local library.

Educational Courses. Special courses related to your employment may be offered at a community college, at a university, or at your place of employment. College credit may be earned if it is desired. These courses provide an outstanding opportunity for the ambitious worker to improve and expand his or her knowledge.

In addition to prescribed courses, adult education classes are offered by many high schools and community organizations as well as community colleges and universities. Many colleges have an extended-day enrollment equal to that of their regular programs. The community college in your area may even provide special classes related to your place of employment. These classes are developed in a partnership arrangement between local industries and the community colleges.

66 Fear of change is always a brake on progress. 99

Advantages to Changing Employers

While it is sometimes more comfortable to stay with your present employer, there may also be some advantages to making a change. Consider the advantages of job changes in Illustration 20-5.

ADVANTAGES TO CHANGING EMPLOYERS

- A job change may result in a better salary or fringe benefits.

- You may increase your job interest by becoming involved with a new job challenge.

- You may gain knowledge, broaden your experience, and perhaps expand your career growth opportunities.

Illustration 20-5
Advantages to changing employers.

How to Resign

Make every effort to leave your present job with good feelings. Throughout your working life, references from past employers will be requested. For this reason you must leave your job on a pleasant note. Do not leave angry or in a huff no matter how dissatisfied you are with the position. Give your employer at least two weeks' notice that you are resigning. Be sure to be on the job right up to your last working day. Say good-bye to your coworkers and supervisors. If the job experience has been valuable, tell them so.

Summary

Your desire for success in a career takes work. It takes a plan and some goal setting. Having a plan does not guarantee success, but planning by setting goals greatly improves your chances. Once your goals are established you will need to make others aware of your goals, talk to yourself, and energize yourself to work toward those goals.

As you move up the career path, you must do a good job on each position you hold. Your performance will be evaluated by your supervisor in performance appraisal sessions. These sessions provide your supervisor with a chance to report your strengths and weaknesses. The session also provides you with an opportunity to ask questions and share your ideas and opinions. Raises and promotions generally result from outstanding performance appraisals. If you are offered a promotion, be sure that the promotion fits with your overall career goal. If it does not, turn it down or adjust your career goal.

There may come a time when you consider changing employment. Be sure you are changing jobs for the right reasons. Carefully choose each job you take. Evaluate the company and the opportunities that lie within that company for you. Do not take a new job until you have properly resigned from your old one.

End of Chapter Activities

Questions and Projects

1. List five career goals that you have considered for yourself. Indicate how you might reach these goals.

2. Practice writing short-, medium-, and long-term goals by preparing the goals for someone who wants to be an electrician, a secretary, or an accounting clerk. Be sure your goals are specific, realistic, and honest. (Use your imagination.)

3. List some of the things that could cause a change in your career goal.

4. How would you prepare yourself for a performance appraisal?

5. How would you prepare yourself to ask for a raise?

6. List the leadership traits that you feel you currently possess.

7. Visit several businesses in your community, and ask them for a copy of the form they use in employee performance appraisals. Compare these forms. Present them to class members.

Case Problems

1. **Decision Time**

Lucille has been a candy wrapping machine operator for five years. Lucille enjoys her work, likes her coworkers, and finds the salary and fringe benefit package offered by the company to be a fair one. She is happy doing repetitive work and likes the fact that when she leaves the company at night, she does not need to think about the job on her own time. Her performance appraisals are excellent. Mary Elton, her supervisor, calls her in and asks if she would like to be the supervisor of the 15 wrapping machine operators. The promotion offers her an additional $150 dollars per month; her work hours will remain the same. Lucille asks for time to think about the offer.

a. What questions should Lucille ask herself?

b. What advantages and disadvantages does the role of a supervisor include?

c. Based on what you know about Lucille, would you suggest that she accept the position? Why or why not?

2. **Promotion**

Manuel has been working at the Millard Lumber Company as a salesperson for several years. He knows the company products and has proven himself to be a dependable worker; his work area is always neat and tidy. The position of buyer becomes available. Manuel wants this position because it involves travel and a pay increase and is a step toward his career goal to be the general manager of Millard Lumber Company. The buyer would negotiate with major suppliers across the country for the best prices.

Manuel is very opinionated. He enjoys working with only a few of the other sales staff members. He feels that some of the sales staff are incompetent because they have not worked in construction and he has. Manuel's performance appraisals have been satisfactory, but at each session the supervisor has reminded him that he needs to work on his people skills.

    a. Will Manuel get the promotion? Why or why not?

    b. What leadership skills does Manuel possess?

    c. What leadership skills does Manuel need to acquire?

    d. Would you hire Manuel as the buyer for Millard Lumber Company?

    e. As his present supervisor, what advice would you have for Manuel?

Glossary

A

Active Listening
The process of paraphrasing and interpreting what is being said.

Affirmative Action
Plans made by employers to help reverse the effects of past discrimination in the workplace.

Ageism
A form of discrimination against older workers or younger workers.

Aggression
An emotional response to conflict.

Aggressive Communication
Communicating your feelings without regard to the feelings or rights of others.

Americans with Disabilities Act
Legislation designed to prevent discrimination and provide equal access in employment for Americans with disabilities.

Analytical Problem Solving
A procedure for solving problems using critical thinking and logical analysis.

Application Form
A form used by employers to get information about people who apply for jobs with their company.

Aptitude

A natural talent, ability, or capacity to learn.

Aptitude Tests

Tests that measure your ability to learn something.

Assertive Communication

Communicating your feelings and standing up for your rights without stepping on the rights of others.

Attitude

How a person feels about something.

Autocratic Supervisor

One who dictates procedures, policy, and tasks to employees.

B

Behavior Modification

A method of using reward or punishment to motivate a person to change.

Brainstorming

A technique used in creative problem solving to produce many ideas.

C

Career Path

A plan you can follow that will lead to a job with more responsibility or satisfaction.

Channel

The route that a message takes to get to the receiver in the communication process.

Cognition

A thinking ability that is not higher-order; to recognize.

Cold Canvassing

Stopping by personnel offices and completing applications.

Communication
The effective transfer of a message from a sender to a receiver; the message is shared and understood.

Complementary Transaction
A communication event where there is no apparent reason for conflict.

Conflict
The clash of opposing attitudes, behaviors, ideas, goals, or needs.

Conscientious
Following the dictates of one's conscience.

Convergent Thinking
A higher-order thinking ability used in analysis, logical problem solving, and decision making.

Cooperation
The ability to work smoothly with others.

Creative Problem Solving
A procedure for solving problems using divergent thinking.

Creativity
Thinking that uses divergent thinking and a variety of skills such as brainstorming, imagination, originality, etc.

Critical Listening
The act of separating facts from opinions as you listen.

Critical Thinking
Thinking that uses convergent thinking ability or analysis; also known as reasoning.

Criticism
A form of self-improvement; suggestions from others about the quality of your work.

Crossed Transaction
A communication event where the participants speak from conflicting ego states.

Cultural Conflict
Conflict and failure to communicate that occurs when people of different cultures interact negatively in the workplace.

Curiosity
The ability to ask revealing questions about causes, consequences, etc.

D

Delegate Authority
To entrust activities, decisions, and responsibilities to an employee.

Democratic Supervisor
One who likes to involve employees in the management process.

Dependable
Doing what you say you will do.

Depression
An emotional disorder that is marked by sadness, inactivity, and a feeling of emptiness.

Dilemma
A situation where one way or another you are bound to create a problem for yourself.

Diligent Worker
One who does his or her work carefully and completely.

Discovering Structure
Creating order out of what appears confusing.

Discrimination
Unfair treatment because of race, gender, religious affiliation, sexual orientation, or physical disability.

Divergent Thinking
A higher-order thinking ability otherwise known as creativity.

Diversity
A term used to represent the variety of different ethnic and minority groups that are represented in today's work force.

E

EEOC
Equal Employment Opportunity Commission, the agency responsible for enforcement of Title VII of the Civil Rights Act of 1964.

Efficiency
A characteristic of being able to make economical use of time or resources.

Ego
Feeling of self worth.

Ego Conflict
Conflict involving feelings of self-worth.

Ego State
The way a person feels about something that causes certain behavior.

Egocentric Myopia
Overemphasizing the importance of what and who you are; seeing only what is part of or close to you as being important.

Elaboration
The ability to add interesting detail to ideas.

Emotion
A powerful feeling from within that creates either pleasure or distress.

Empathy
The ability to understand and feel another person's emotions or feelings.

Employment Agency
An organization that brings together a worker and an employer to fill a job opening.

Enthusiasm
To inject energy into your work.

Enunciation
Pronouncing each part of each word clearly.

Envy
Wanting what someone else has.

Ethics
A moral duty or obligation to conform to accepted professional standards of conduct.

Ethnocentrism
The assumption that one's own world view is the only view.

Evaluation
A higher-order mental ability used in exercising judgment.

Evaluation Criteria
Features or characteristics that indicate quality when judgments are made.

External Motivation
Motivation that comes from people or things outside yourself.

F

Facts
That which can be proven.

False Conflict
Conflict that appears to be real but does not really exist.

Feedback
Information you can use to evaluate yourself; a response from the receiver in the communication process.

Flexibility
The ability to produce a variety of ideas; not getting in a mental rut when brainstorming.

Fluency
The ability to produce many ideas quickly, as in a brainstorming session.

G

Goal
A broad, general statement of what you want to become or achieve.

Grand Larceny
A legal term for theft of something of great value.

H

Higher-order Thinking
Evaluation, convergent thinking, divergent thinking, critical thinking, and creative thinking.

Hysterical Conversion
When a person is unable to cope with a highly stressful situation and changes the stress to a physical symptom.

I

Imagination
The ability to come up with ideas and to visualize.

Imaging
Searching your mind for images of your renewed and improved personality.

Incubation
A period of rest from thinking that can result in insight.

Inflection
The rising and falling of your voice.

Initiative
The process of starting a task or project without being told to do so; the energy or aptitude displayed in the initiation of action.

Intangibles
Items that are sold but you cannot actually touch or possess.

Integrity
Adherence to a code of moral values.

Internal Motivation
Motivation that comes from within.

J

Jargon
Simplified language used by people in the workplace to communicate in an abbreviated style.

Jealousy
Feeling of rivalry toward one whom you believe has an advantage over you.

Job Breakdown
A procedure of job analysis that results in identification of the specific tasks that make up the job.

Job Description
A written explanation of the tasks to be performed on a specific job.

Job Lead
Information about a possible job opening.

L

Laissez-faire Supervisor
One who avoids giving specific direction to employees and permits them to work independently, giving only general guidance.

Larceny
Theft.

Leadership
The ability to lead or direct others on a positive course.

Letter of Application
A letter of introduction.

Listening
The process by which we make sense out of what we hear.

Logical Inference
The process of inferring or drawing conclusions using logic.

Loyalty
Believing in your place of employment and having a commitment to it.

M

Management Style
The manner in which the supervisor directs workers in order to accomplish the goals and objectives of the organization.

Mask
Any behavior that we use to present a false image or create a false impression.

Memory
A thinking ability that is not higher-order; to remember factual information.

Mentor
A person, usually a coworker or supervisor, who takes a personal interest in helping you learn and improve on the job.

Message
The thought or idea that is transferred from the sender to the receiver involved in the communication process.

Meticulous
Being careful and concerned about details.

Monotone
A voice with no expression.

Monotony
Doing a task repeatedly.

N

Negotiable
An indication that you are open to discussion.

Networking
The process of sharing and exchanging job information.

Nondirective Approach
A technique used by counselors that recommends that you reflect back what a person has said as you respond to him or her; this technique works particularly well with the complainer and the arguer.

Nuanced Judgment
Being sensitive to slight variation in meaning.

O

Objective
A specific, observable or measurable statement that describes evidence of the achievement of a goal.

Opinions
Information that is based on the speaker's personal beliefs or feelings.

Orderliness
Logical, systematic, efficient behavior of an organized person.

Organized
If you are an organized person, your behavior is methodical, logical, and directed toward goals or outcomes that you have clearly in mind; you are motivated to be orderly, systematic, and efficient.

Originality
The ability to produce ideas that are clever, interesting, and unusual.

P

Parkinson's Law
Work expands to fill the available time for its completion.

Passive Communication
Giving into others without expressing your feelings or rights.

Performance Appraisal
An official evaluation of your work.

Persuasion
Attempting to get others to adopt or agree with an idea that you have.

Petty Larceny
A legal term for theft of something of little value.

Pitch
The highness or lowness of your voice.

Politeness
Comments or actions which are acknowledgments that you care about and appreciate others.

Positive Resistance
Clearly recognizing and confronting prejudice.

Prejudice
To prejudge or form an opinion without taking the time or effort to judge in a fair manner.

Problem-solving Technique
Basic method of solving a problem by answering a series of five questions.

Pronunciation
Saying a word correctly.

R

Receiver
The participant in the communication process who is to receive the message.

Reinforcement
A term psychologists use to describe the reward or punishment in behavior modification.

Reliability
The ability to supply what was promised, dependably and accurately, to a customer.

Resentment
A feeling of displeasure over something that you consider wrong.

Responsible
Answerable or accountable for something within one's power to control; it includes being dependable and reliable.

Resume
A written summary of your education, work experience, and other qualifications for a job.

Reverse Discrimination
Discrimination toward an individual or a group that is in a majority.

Rhetoric
The art of using words effectively to communicate the results of thinking.

S

Salutation
A greeting to a person receiving a letter.

Selective Communication
Hearing and reading only what you want to hear and read.

Self-actualization
A process of growing to reach your greatest potential.

Self-control
The ability to direct the course of your behavior; the capacity to manage your own thoughts, feelings, and actions.

Self-esteem
A high level of self-respect.

Self-motivation
Energy and drive that comes from within.

Self-pity
Feeling sorry for yourself and your situation without regard for the positive things in your life.

Sender
The participant in the communication process who is to send the message.

Sexual Harassment
Conduct by one employee that focuses on another employee's sexuality in a way that interferes with an individual's ability to work effectively.

Shaping
Changing a group or an individual so that the group works better together.

Simple Conflict
Conflict over facts.

Standards
Tell how much or the level of quality that is required.

Stereotyping
Judging others based on widely held beliefs rather than considering people as individuals.

Strategy
A plan of action or a procedure that is used as a means of accomplishing an objective.

Stress
The feeling one gets from prolonged, pent-up emotions.

Subtle Discrimination
Discrimination based on appearance, values, or character.

Supervisor
An individual in charge of a group of workers.

Sympathy
Involves identifying with, and even taking on, another person's emotions.

T

Tact
A sense of what to do or say in an effort to maintain good relations with others without offending them.

Tactic
A specific action designed to implement a strategy.

Time Management
A process by which a person identifies time-consuming activities, considers their importance, and allocates time to them—typically by preparing and following schedules.

Title VII of the Civil Rights Act of 1964
A law that makes it illegal to discriminate in employment.

Transaction
A communication event in conversation between two people.

Transactional Analysis
A theory of personality developed by Eric Berne.

Try-out Experience
Using a regular job, a class, or some other "hands-on" activity to test your interest and aptitude for a job or career.

Type A Personality
A person who is hard-driving.

Type B Personality
A person who is easygoing.

V

Value-added Qualities
Personality traits that add value to your technical skills, expertise, and work experience.

Values or Beliefs Conflict
Conflict that occurs when the values or beliefs you have placed on certain aspects of your life may not be the same as those of others.

Visualization
Seeing things in the mind's eye.

Volume
The loudness or softness of your voice.

W

Wellness Programs
Actions or programs designed to help a person maintain and improve his or her physical health and well-being.

Workplace Politics
An undefined force in an organization that develops because people want to protect themselves and gain power

A

Absenteeism at work, 185–186
Abuse
  drug and alcohol, 240–242
  expense account, 236–239
  fringe benefits and privileges, 239–240
Action
  affirmative, 250–253
  plans for improving self, 23–24
  responsibility for, 8
Active listening, 130–131
Adult ego, 4–5
Affirmative action, 250–253
Ageism, 253
Agencies, employment, 283–284
Aggressive
  behavior, 162
  communication, 124–125
Alcohol abuse, 240–242
Americans with Disabilities Act, 254–255
Analysis, transactional, 3
Analytical versus creative problem solving, 208
Application
  form for employment, 291–294
  letter, 295–297
Appraisal, performance, 325–326
Approach, nondirective, 72–73
Aptitude, 281–282
  tests, 26–27
Arguments with coworkers, 74–75
Assertive communication, 125–126
Attitude
  affecting behavior, 36–40
  coping with negative, 40–41
  development of, 35–36
  positive, 121–122
  reflecting image, 33–34
  work, 177–178, 314–316
Authority, delegation of, 82–87
Autocratic management style, 85–86

B

Barriers
  communication, 118–120
  listening, 127–129
Behavior
  affected by attitudes, 36–38
  modification, 24–25
Beliefs conflict, 158–159
Body language, 126
Brainstorming, 208

Index

C

Campaign, job, 280–282
Career
  goals, 322–325
  path, 321–322
Channel
  communication, 117
  openers, 120–124
Character types of work group, 73–75
Characteristics, of getting along, 48–52
Child ego, 5
Civil
  Rights Act, 250–253, 292
  Service positions, 284
Coaching, 25–26
Cold canvassing, 284
Communication
  barriers, 118–120
  body language, 126
  channel, 117
  with customer, 107–110
  listening skills, 126–131
  model, 117
  positive versus negative, 139
  rules for sending message, 138–139
  styles, 124–126
  with supervisor, 89–91
  transactions, 3–6
Complementary transactions, 5
Concientiousness shown at work,
  186–187
Conflict
  adjustments, 160–165
  defined, 155–156
  with inner self, 12
  with self-image, 8–9
  stages, 159–160
  types, 156–159
Confrontation with supervisor, 92–95
Convergent thinking, 201
Conversation skills, 139–146
Cooperation with coworkers, 62–66
Cooperative education, 29
Counseling, 27–28
Coworkers
  character types, 73–75
  loyalty to, 66
  problems with, 71–75
Creative
  versus analytical problem solving, 208
  thinking, 204–205
Crisis handling, 175–176
Critical
  listening, 131
  thinking, 202–203

Criticism
  accepting, 92–95, 314
  by coworker, 74
  learning from, 13–15, 20–21
Crossed transactions, 5
Cultural conflict, 270–273
Customer
  communication, 107–110
  empathy for, 104–105
  expectations, 102–106
  recognition, 106
  reliability to, 102–104

D

Decision-making
  employee participation, 84
  strategies, 208–209
Delegation of authority, 82–87
Democratic management style, 84–85
Dependability at work, 184–186
Depression caused by stress, 216, 219
Disabilities, rights of persons with,
  254–255
Discrimination, 247–250
  how to stop, 258–260
  subtle, 257–258
Divergent thinking, 202
Diversity, tolerance of in workplace,
  266–269
Drug abuse, 240–242

E

Education
  cooperative, 29
  for further training, 330–332
Ego
  conflict, 157
  states affecting communication, 3–6
Egocentric myopia, 268–269
Emotion used to develop attitudes,
  35–36
Empathy
  for customer, 104–105
  versus sympathy, 51–52
Employment
  agencies, 283–284
  Equal Employment Opportunity,
  250–253
  forms, 308
  insurance, 312–316
Envy and jealousy, 55–56
Equal Employment Opportunity,
  250–253
Ethics in the workplace, 231–232

Ethnocentrism, 268–269
Evaluation strategies, 205–206
Expectations
   of customer, 102–106
   of employer, 232
Expense account abuse, 236–239
Experiences, try-out, 28–29
External motivation, 175

F

Failure leading to success, 11–12
False conflict, 157–158
Favoritism by supervisor, 74
Feedback, 117, 145–146
   being sensitive to, 13–15
Flirting, 256

G

Goals
   career, 322–325
   for improving self, 21–22
Gossip, 116, 123–124
   by coworker, 74
Grapevine, 116
Group
   character types, 73–75
   psychology, 70–75

H

Habits
   irritating, 54–55
   work, 311
"Hands-off" management policy, 82–83
Harrassment, sexual, 255–256
Higher-order thinking, 200–202
   strategies, 205–210
Honesty in the workplace, 234–239
Hysterical conversion, 217

I

Ideas, how to express in group, 69–70
Identity, success, 1, 29
Image
   portrayed to others, 9–11
   reflected by attitudes, 33–34
Imaging, 21
Improvement, process of, 19–20
Initiative at work, 175–178
Inner self, conflict, 12
Insight from criticism, 13–15
Insurance, employment, 312–316
Integrity in the workplace, 231–232

Interest tests, 26–27
Internal motivation, 173–174
Interview, job, 297–300
   follow-up, 300–301
   standard questions, 298

J

Jargon, 120
Job
   campaign, 280–282
   first-day events, 308–309
   resources, 282–285
   rules, 309–311
Job
   changing, 328–330
      advantages of, 332
   description, 309
   interview, 297–300
      follow-up, 300–301
      standard questions, 298
Judgment at work, 176–177

L

Laissez-faire management style, 82–84
Language barriers, 272–273
Larceny in the workplace, 235
Leadership traits, 327
Listening skills, 126–131, 142–143
Logical inference, 208
Loyalty
   to coworkers, 66
   in the workplace, 233–234

M

Management
   participatory, 84
   resource, 194–195
   self, 187–189
   stress, 221–224
   styles, 82–87
   time, 191–194
Masks of self-image, 9–11, 15, 20–21
Mentoring, 25–26
Message
   receiving, 127–131
   verbal versus nonverbal, 116–118
Mistakes at work, 177–178
Monotony, causing stress, 218
Motivation
   external, 175
   internal, 173–174
   self, 173–175

N

Networking, 282
Nondirective approach, 72–73
Nonvalue-added qualities, 53–57

O

Objectives for improving self, 22–23
Organization, maintaining, 189–195

P

Parent ego, 4
Parkinson's law, 193
Participatory management, 84
Passive communication, 124
Path, career, 321–322
Performance appraisal, 325–326
Personal data sheet, 285–291
Personality
  image of, 20–21
  profile, 21–22
  theory of, 3–6
Plan for self-improvement, 19–20
Politics, workplace, 311–312
Praise, learning from, 13–15, 20–21
Prejudice, 247–250
Problem
  with coworkers, 71–75
  presenting to supervisor, 90-92
  solving
    five-step, 163–165
    strategies, 207–208
Profile, personality, 21–22
Promotion, 326–327
Psychology, group, 70–75

Q

Qualities
  nonvalue-added, 53–57
  value-added, 48–52
Questioning technique, 122, 144

R

Raise, 326–327
Receiver of communication message, 116–118
Relationship with supervisor, 81–95
Relaxation techniques, 189
Reliability to customers, 102–104
Resign, how to, 332
Resource management, 194–195
Resources, job hunting, 282–285
Responsibility

for actions, 8
shown at work, 183–187
Resume, 285–290
Reverse discrimination, 251
Role-playing, 9–11, 20–21
Rumor mill, 116, 123–124

S

Schedule, work, 193–194
Search, job, 280–282
Self
  -actualization, 21
  conflict with, 12
  -control, 187–189
  -esteem, 9–15
    affecting communication, 3–7
    building others', 66–67
  -image, conflicts with, 8–9
  -improvement
    process, 19–20
    strategies, 29–30
  -management, 187–189
  -motivation, 173–175
  -pity, 56–57
Sender of communication message, 116–118
Sexual harassment, 255–256
Shaping formula, 71
Shoplifting, 235
Signals of stress, 219–220
Skills
  conversation, 139–146
  upgrading, 330–332
Solution to conflict, 162–165
Speech
  in conversation, 139–146
  before groups, 146–150
Stages of conflict, 159–160
Standards of ethics in workplace, 231–232
Stealing, 235
Stereotyping, 247–250
Strategies for self-improvement, 24–25, 29–30
Stress
  effects, 216–217
  management of, 221–224
  self-evaluation, 221
  signals, 219–220
Styles of management, 82–87
Success
  identity, 1, 29
  resulting from failure, 11–12
Supervisor
  autocratic style, 85–86

criticism from, 92–95
democratic style, 84–85
expectations, 87–89
laissez-faire style, 82–84
Sympathy versus empathy, 51–52
Symptoms of stress, 220

T

Tardiness at work, 184–185
Team
effort, 61–62
player, 75–76
your position on, 67–68
Tests, aptitude and interest, 26–27
Theft in the workplace, 235
Theory of personality, 3–6
Thinking
critical, 202–203
higher-order, 200–202
skills, how to develop, 210–211
strategies, 205–210
Time management, 191–194

Title VII of Civil Rights Act of 1964,
250–253
Training, 330–332
Transactional analysis, 3
Transactions of communication, 3–6
Try-out experiences, 28–29

V

Value-added qualities, 48–52
Values conflict, 158–159
Visualization, 204
Vita, 285–290
Voice qualities, 140–141

W

Work
attitude, 314–316
group, character types, 73–75
habits, 311
quantity versus quality, 313
showing initiative, 312–313
team, 61–62